W9-BYC-230

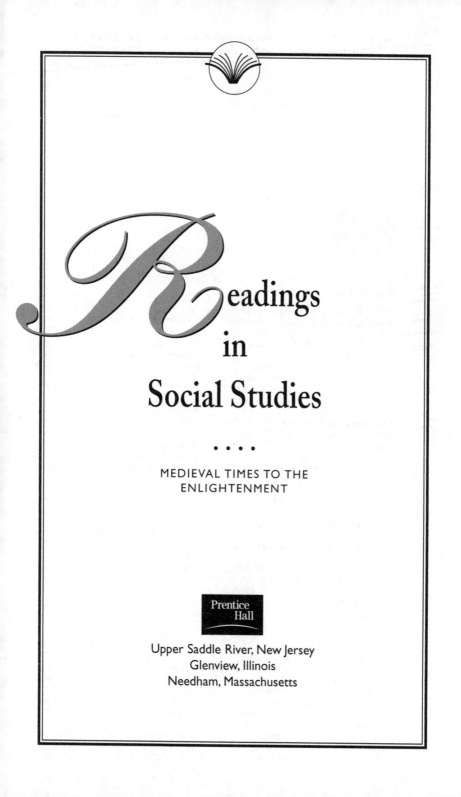

Readings in Social Studies

MEDIEVAL TIMES TO THE ENLIGHTENMENT

Prentice Hall

Upper Saddle River, New Jersey
Glenview, Illinois
Needham, Massachusetts

ISBN: 0-13-068389-2

7 8 9 10   06

Acknowledgments

Grateful acknowledgment is made to the following for permission to reprint copyrighted material:

Peter Bedrick Books "Spain and the Power of Gold" from *The Renaissance and the New World* by Giovanni Caselli. © Macdonald & Company (Publishers) Ltd. 1985.

Canongate Publishing Limited, Edinburgh "Children of Wax" from *Children of Wax: African Folk Tales* by Alexander McCall Smith. Copyright © 1989 by Canongate.

Children's Press "Prologue" from *The Merry Adventures of Robin Hood* by Howard Pyle. Copyright © 1968 by Classic Press, Inc.

Michael Courlander. *"The Judgment of the Wind"* from *The Fire on the Mountain* by Harold Courlander and Wolf Leslau. Copyright © 1978 by Harold Courlander and Wolf Leslau. Reprinted by permission of The Emma Courlander Trust.

Coward, McCann & Geoghegan, Inc. "The Trial: Florence and Rome, 1632–1633" from *Truth on Trial: The Story of Galileo Galilei* by Vicki Cobb. Text copyright © 1979 by Vicki Cobb.

Curtis Brown Ltd. "The Boy Who Drew Sheep" by Anne Rockwell first appeared in *The Boy Who Drew Sheep* published by Atheneum. Copyright © 1973 by Anne Rockwell.

Doubleday, a division of Random House, Inc. "The Sun's Way. . ." from *An Introduction to Haiku* by Harold G. Henderson, copyright © 1958 by Harold G. Henderson. Used by permission of Doubleday, a division of Random House, Inc.

Farrar, Straus & Giroux, Inc. "In Which I Confess" (Chapter 10) from *I, Juan de Pareja* by Elizabeth Borton

de Treviño. Copyright © 1965, 1993 by Elizabeth Borton de Treviño. Reprinted by permission of Farrar, Straus & Giroux, Inc., LLC.

Franklin Watts, a division of Scholastic, Inc. "Crete: The Island of Bulls" from *Lost Cities* by Roy A. Gallant. Copyright © 1985 by Roy A. Gallant.

Harcourt, Inc. "Art & Science" from *Italian Renaissance* by John D. Clare, editor. Text copyright © 1995, 1994 by John D. Clare. Used with permission of Harcourt, Inc.

HarperCollins Publishers "A Strange, Funny-Looking Vegetable" from *The Amazing Potato* by Milton Meltzer. Copyright © 1992 by Milton Meltzer. "Our History" by Mbella Sonne Dipoko from *Poems from Africa.*

HarperCollins Publishers Ltd., UK "Introduction" from *The Bayeux Tapestry, The Story of the Norman Conquest: 1066* by Norman Denny and Josephine Filmer-Sankey. Copyright © 1966 by Norman Denny and Josephine Filmer-Sankey.

Houghton Mifflin Company "The Battle of Gainsborough" from *Cromwell's Boy* by Erik Christian Haugaard. Copyright © 1978 by Erik Christian Haugaard.

Hyperion Books for Children, an imprint of Disney Book Publishing, Inc. From *Morning Girl* by Michael Dorris. Copyright © 1992 by Michael Dorris. Reprinted by permission of Hyperion Books for Children.

Japan Publications Haiku ("Falling upon earth . . .") by Bashō from *One Hundred Famous Haiku,* translated by

Acknowledgments continued on page 257

Contents

V. Civilizations of China and Japan

VI. Europe and Japan in the Middle Ages

VII. The Renaissance and the Reformation in Europe

Acknowledgments continued from copyright page

Barbara S. Kouts for Joseph Bruchac "Loo-Wit, the Fire-Keeper," a Nisqually myth retold by Joseph Bruchac, from *Keepers of the Earth: Native American Stories and Environmental Activities for Children* by Michael J. Caduto and Joseph Bruchac. Copyright © 1988 by Joseph Bruchac.

The Millbrook Press and Editions Nathan, Paris "Sharing Knowledge" from *The Arabs in the Golden Age* by Mokhtar Moktefi. Originally published in French as *Les Arabes au temps de l'âge d'or* (*Peuples du passé* series), Editions Nathan, Paris. Translation copyright © 1992 by The Millbrook Press. Copyright © 1991 by Editions Nathan, Paris.

William Morrow & Company, a division of HarperCollins Publishers, Inc. From *Leonardo da Vinci* by Diane Stanley. Copyright © 1996 by Diane Stanley.

New World Press, Beijing, China "Hailibu the Hunter" from *Favourite Folktales of China*, translated by John Minford.

Oxford University Press UK "In Spring It Is the Dawn" and "The Cat Who Lived in the Palace" from *The Pillow Book* of Sei Shōnagon by Sei Shōnagon, translated and edited by Ivan Morris.

Penguin Books Ltd. "One cannot ask loneliness" by Priest Jakuren and "When I went to visit" by Ki no Tsurayuki from *The Penguin Book of Japanese Verse*, edited and translated by Geoffrey Bownas and Anthony Thwaite (Penguin Books, 1964). Translation copyright © Geoffrey Bowans and Anthony Thwaite, 1964. "The Fisherman and the Jinnee" from *Tales from The Thousand and One Nights* (pp. 79–92) translated by N.J. Dawood (Penguin Classics 1954, Revised edition 1973). Translation copyright © N.J. Dawood, 1954, 1973.

Prentice-Hall, Inc. "African Musical Instruments" from *The Music of Africa* by Dr. Fred Warren with Lee Warren. Copyright © 1970 by Dr. Fred Warren and Lee Warren.

G.P. Putnam's Sons, a division of Penguin Putnam, Inc. "Vasco Núñez de Balboa" from *Around the World in a Hundred Years: From Henry the Navigator to Magellan* by Jean Fritz. Text copyright © 1994 by Jean Fritz.

"The Historical Background" from *Everyday Life of the Maya* by Ralph Whitlock. Text © Ralph Whitlock, 1976.

Random House, Inc. and Methuen Publishing Ltd. From *A Man for All Seasons* by Robert Bolt. Copyright © 1960, 1962 by Robert Bolt. Copyright renewed 1988, 1990 by Robert Bolt.

Ian Serraillier "Grendel" from *Beowulf, the Warrior*, retold by Ian Serraillier. Copyright Ian Serraillier.

Silver Burdett Company "Who Are the Muslims?" from *The Muslim World* by Richard Tames. © Macdonald & Co. 1982.

La Société Nouvelle Présence Africaine "Childhood" and "The Lion's Awakening" from *Sundiata: An Epic of Old Mali* by D.T. Niane, translated by G.D. Pickett. Copyright © Présence Africaine, 1960 (original French version: *Soundjata, ou L'Epopée Mandingue*). © Longman Group Ltd. (English).

Time, Inc. From "The Pax Romana" from *Imperial Rome* by Moses Hadas. Copyright © 1965 by Time Inc.

Lawrence Starr Untermeyer for the Estate of Louis Untermeyer "The Dog of Pompeii" from *Donkey of God* by Louis Untermeyer. Copyright 1932 by Harcourt, Inc. renewed 1960 by Louis Untermeyer.

Watson, Little Limited, Authors' Agents "How Coyote Stole Fire" by Gail Robinson and Douglas Hill from *Coyote the Trickster: Legends of North American Indians*. Copyright © Gail Robinson and Douglas Hill 1975.

Henry Z. Walck, Inc. "The Old Man Who Made the Trees Bloom" from *Japanese Tales and Legends*, retold by Helen and William McAlpine. Copyright © Helen and William McAlpine.

Wayland (Publishers) Ltd. "What Was the Renaissance?" from *Leonardo and the Renaissance* by Nathaniel Harris. Copyright © 1986 by Wayland (Publishers) Ltd.

Note: Every effort has been made to locate the copyright owner of material reprinted in this book. Omissions brought to our attention will be corrected in subsequent printings.

Introduction

Literature creates its own vivid pictures of historical events. This anthology of fiction, nonfiction, poetry, and drama offers you a window into the thoughts, feelings, and dreams of people who lived from the medieval times to the Enlightenment. You'll read literature from a variety of countries, cultures, and civilizations. As you read the literature in this collection, let it bring history to life for you and help you connect historical events to your own unique experiences.

The history of the world includes stories that inspire, inform, and sometimes amaze. From the remote past to the seventeenth century, this anthology provides literature that gives voice to the lives and dreams of people around the world whose lives were so different from, and yet so similar to, your own.

The Remote Past to the Fall of Rome

You'll begin your journey from medieval times to the Enlightenment with the distant past of lost cities and the remarkable legend of King Minos. Then, Moses Hadas's account of the establishment of the Roman Empire will give you a context for Louis Untermeyer's moving story of a young blind boy and his dog caught in the last moments of Pompeii. Tragedy is timeless and so is triumph—and a dog's devotion to his master was as real in Pompeii as it is today.

The Growth of Islam

For many people, both in the past and today, religion is central to their experience of the world. As one of the world's major religions, Islam has a unique place in the development of civilizations. Richard Tames's account will help you understand the basic beliefs of Islam, while Mokhtar Moktefi presents an enlightening look at the origin in the Arab world of many things that we take for granted today. A fascinating tale from the world-famous story collection *The Thousand and One Nights*, also known as *The Arabian Nights*, challenges your imagination with its vivid characters and amazing events.

Civilizations of Africa

A traditional poem introduces your journey through the ancient civilizations of Africa, while two intriguing folk tales—one from Eritrea and Ethiopia and the other from Zimbabwe—present different aspects of this diverse continent. A section from an epic of old Mali provides a vivid reminder of the difference between appearance and reality. Then, Dr. Fred Warren presents a musical view of African culture that includes a history of three major musical instruments.

The Ancient Americas

Ancient cultures, far from being primitive and simple, often developed highly sophisticated civilizations. Ralph Whitlock gives a brief history of the brilliant Mayan culture, while the adventures of Cabeza de Vaca assert the fascination of explorers with the cultures of the early American peoples. Like many myths, the Native American myth featuring Coyote the trickster explains several aspects of the natural world, such as why the tip of a coyote's tail is white and why there are three stripes down a chipmunk's back. Then, the account of Loo-Wit the Fire-Keeper offers the Nisqually Indian explanation of the earth's formations, characteristics, and weather, while Michael Dorris's moving story of a young girl's questions about her identity uses the ancient art of mythic storytelling to help you identify with a young person from the distant past.

Civilizations of China and Japan

Poems and legends anchor your visit to the ancient civilizations of China and Japan. The haunting legend of "The Old Man Who Made the Trees Bloom" provides a remarkable view of the potential for good in all human beings, and the magical powers of Hailibu help him understand the language of animals. Sei Shōnagon's stories from the tenth-century imperial court of Japan describe pets that will probably remind you of your pets, while the selection from John Roberson's history of China from Manchu to Mao gives you a chance to see Westerners from China's point of view—as barbarians.

Europe and Japan in the Middle Ages

The legendary King Arthur introduces your journey through the Middle Ages with Mary MacLeod's version of Arthur as a teenager. Other legendary heroes like Lochinvar, Beowulf, and Robin Hood provide insights into life in these perilous and exciting times, while a description of the Bayeux Tapestry shows history preserved in a unique way. A fictionalized biography of the famous painter Giotto takes you deep into the daily life of the Middle Ages, while the simplicity of haiku intrigues you and challenges you to stretch your mind and heart.

The Renaissance and the Reformation in Europe

As you move into the Renaissance, Nathaniel Harris gives you essential information about this vibrant and important time, while Diane Stanley and John D. Clare help bring to life one of the most striking figures of the Renaissance, Leonardo da Vinci. You learn of the crucial role Spain played during this period, and you see the challenges of leadership in Robert Bolt's play about Thomas More and Henry VIII, as well as in Elizabeth I's speech to her troops. Vicki Cobb's account of the trial of Galileo will motivate you to think carefully about the importance of truth and the challenges of scientific investigation.

Exploration to the Enlightenment in the Western World

The adventures of the famous explorer Balboa show you the realities of life in a new world, and Milton Meltzer tells you more than you've ever imagined about the humble potato. In his commitment to his art, Juan de Pareja may remind you of Giotto, and "The Battle of Gainsborough" will show you a boy caught up in tumultuous times and thrown into battle without preparation.

From medieval times to the Enlightenment, literature has reflected and revealed the history of the world. Without the dimension of literature, history loses some of its richness and immediacy. The visions and inspirations of writers will always have the power to move and to inform.

The literature in this anthology will enrich your reading in your social studies textbook and in your literature textbook with additional information, images, stories, and dramatic renditions from nonfiction, fiction, poetry, and drama.

The Remote Past
to the Fall of Rome

Crete: The Island of Bulls

from Lost Cities

Roy A. Gallant

In this selection, one professor's fascination with the legend of King Minos and the Minotaur leads him to a remarkable discovery: the Minoan remains at Knossos.

THESEUS AND THE MINOTAUR

According to a Greek myth going back more than 2,500 years, there once was a young man named Theseus, son of the king of the great city of Athens, the capital of Greece. At this time there also lived on the nearby island of Crete a king named Minos. Minos was so powerful and so greatly feared that he was able to demand and get whatever he wished, not only from the people of his island-state but also from the people of nearby Athens on the Greek mainland.

Now it happened, according to the myth, that Minos kept on Crete a fierce monster called the Minotaur, a beast that was half bull and half man and ate human flesh. The word "minotaur" is built out of two words—King Minos's name and the Greek word *tauros*, meaning "bull." The Minotaur was supposedly kept in a labyrinth, a great maze or place of numerous winding corridors that was so complex that it was impossible to find the way out without help.

From time to time, Minos demanded that the king of Athens send him the seven handsomest young men and the seven most beautiful maidens of the land. These fourteen youths were then led into the labyrinth, where one by one they were found and devoured by the Minotaur.

When Theseus came of age he told his father that he wanted to be one of the youths sent to King Minos so that he might slay the Minotaur and once and for all end this terrible sacrifice the people of Athens were forced to make. Although he feared that his son would never return, Theseus's father granted the young man his wish.

On the appointed day the fourteen youths boarded the ship to Crete, a ship that always flew black sails, a sign of the certain death awaiting its passengers. When they arrived the youths were paraded before King Minos, for him to judge whether all were fair enough for the Minotaur. When the king's daughter, Ariadne, saw Theseus, she fell in love with him. She then managed to see him alone before the youths were led off to the labyrinth. Ariadne told Theseus of her love and gave him a small sword and a ball of thread.

As Theseus led the way into the maze he carefully unwound the ball of thread. On hearing the ferocious roars of the Minotaur as it came charging around a corner of the labyrinth to attack him, Theseus dropped the ball of thread and began slashing at the beast with the sword given to him by Ariadne. He managed to weaken the Minotaur and finally cut off its head. He then picked up the thread and followed it out of the labyrinth, leading his thirteen companions to safety and home.

Before he had departed from Athens, Theseus had agreed to change the black sails to white if all had gone well and he had slain the Minotaur. He forgot to do so. When his father, waiting for the ship's return, saw the black sails, he presumed that his son had been killed. He was so stricken with grief that he killed himself before the ship docked. Theseus then became king.

SIR ARTHUR EVANS
AND THE MINOTAUR LEGEND

Was there any truth to the account of Minos and his kingdom on the island of Crete? The Greek poet Homer, who lived about 850 B.C., gave us the first known account of the Cretan king Minos and his palace. Later, in 455 B.C., the Greek scholar Thucydides, who lived in Athens, wrote an account of King Minos and his powerful fleet of ships that ruled the Aegean Sea. Still later, the philosopher Aristotle, born in 384 B.C., also wrote of King Minos dominating the whole Aegean area. And there were some who thought that Crete might have been the legendary kingdom of Atlantis, mentioned by the philosopher Plato about 400 B.C.

So Crete must have had a long history, one that stretched back even before Greek scholars wrote about the land. Crete itself did not have a written history until about 2,500 years ago. Even then the Minoans left very little in writing, unlike the neighboring civilizations of Egypt and Babylonia. The Cretans were called Minoans after King Minos. The legend of King Minos and his Minotaur had existed for centuries before the Minoans used writing. It had been handed down orally in story form from one generation to the next. But because it was only a legend, no one could be certain that there had actually ever been such a kingdom.

Fascinated by the Minotaur legend and poetic accounts of a highly developed civilization much older than any other known European civilization, an English scholar from Oxford University named Sir Arthur Evans decided to find out if there was any truth to the Minotaur legend and other accounts of an ancient Cretan civilization. The Minoans had ruled supreme from about 3000 to 1450 B.C., although as a civilization they were still older. The Minoan population at its peak was about 80,000, slightly less than the present population of Portland, Maine.

Evans's interest in Crete began during a visit to Athens where he bought a few moonstones from a Greek merchant. The stones, worn by his wife as lucky charms, had strange writing scratched on them. It was the writing that led Evans to Crete in 1894, where he found more of the stones containing the same writing. He first went to the capital of the island, Knossos, where he noted that many of the women were wearing similar round stones of clay around their necks or wrists as lucky charms. Although some of the stones had simple designs carved on them, others had what appeared to be some form of writing. As he traveled around Crete, Evans saw many such stones. They turned out to be very old indeed, and some had been used as personal identity disks by the ancient Cretans. One such stone had the design of a labyrinth. Another had the shape of a creature half human and half bull.

While in Knossos, Evans became curious about several large blocks of carved stone lying about. He decided to dig a few test trenches near the stones to see if anything might lie buried below. Only a few inches beneath the surface one of his thirty workers struck something hard with a spade. Evans's excitement grew as they continued to dig around the hard object. After only a few hours of digging Evans was almost certain that he had stumbled onto the walls of a large and ancient building, possibly the palace of the mighty Minos. In all, he spent more than twenty-five years working in Crete reconstructing the Minoan remains at Knossos. The hard object just beneath the surface indeed turned out to be the palace of King Minos, built some 3,500 years earlier, even earlier than the time of the great rulers of ancient Egypt just across the sea to the south.

Month after month, year after year, the work continued. The palace of Minos turned out to be enormous, sprawling over an area larger than ten city blocks. It was shaped like a large rectangle, in the center of which was a huge courtyard of red cement. Some sections of the building were five stories high. There were twisting corridors and stairways. There were dead-end passageways and a bewildering number of rooms. Indeed, it was a labyrinth. Evans had no doubt that here was the building described in legend as both the home of Minos and of the dreaded Minotaur.

There was great excitement when the workers uncovered the first fresco. Frescoes are paintings done on walls when the walls are being plastered. In this way the plaster and the colors of the painting dry together, a process that preserves the paintings for a long time. One such fresco was a life-size painting of a young man holding a large cone-shaped cup. His skin was a deep reddish color from exposure to the sun. Other frescoes showed Minoan women, who spent most of the time indoors, as white-skinned. Throughout the palace were images of a two-bladed axe, a symbol associated with the Cretan mother-goddess, whom the Greeks called Rhea. At will she was able to enter the double-axe and vanish. An ancient word for this axe was *labrys*, from which the word labyrinth comes.

As the digging continued, Evans realized that the enormous palace had not all been built at the same time. Hallways, rooms, and storage areas were added on century after century. Minos seems to have been the name of the first Cretan king who constructed the original palace.

In his honor, each of the future kings of Crete took the name of Minos and added to the palace to suit his own taste. Evans discovered large storerooms with great jars for wine and olive oil. Some of the jars stood as tall as a man and can be seen in place today. There were also containers lined with stone and with fragments of gold leaf. These were probably from the rooms where the Minoan kings kept their stores of gold, silver, and other precious metals. Nearby were apartments for the royal guards who kept watch over the king's wealth.

Evans again became excited when his workers uncovered what is probably the oldest known royal throne. As described by Evans, there "was a short bench, like that of the outer chamber, and then, separated from it by a small interval, a separate seat of honour or throne. It had a high back, like the seat, of gypsum, which was partly imbedded in the stucco of the wall. It was raised on a square base and had a curious moulding below . . . probably painted to harmonise with the fresco at its side."

As the weeks and months passed, many more discoveries were made—the paved courtyard mentioned earlier, stairways with frescoes of olive branches in flower, a wall painting of a monkey gathering flowers in baskets, and a large fresco of a bull with young acrobats. Paintings and impressions of bulls on vases and other objects were so common that it caused Evans to remark: "What a part these creatures play here!"

Like the people of Spain today, the ancient Minoans seem to have loved a sport involving acrobats and bulls. One large fresco shows a bull in full charge and three young acrobats, two girls and a boy. If we read these frescoes correctly, some sport like this may have taken place: Three youths entered a sports arena containing a bull. As the bull charged, one of the youths would grab the animal's horns, leap over the bull's head, and do a handspring off the bull's back, landing upright on his feet and in the arms of one of the other two youths. This sounds like an impossible trick, but so many Cretan artifacts suggest that some such event took place that it is hard to doubt. Is it possible that this type of event inspired the myth of the fourteen Athenian youths, King Minos, and the deadly Minotaur?

There are frescoes that also show audiences watching the contests in the bull ring. Although in Spain the object of the cruel contest is to kill the bull by plunging a sword into it, in ancient Crete the purpose seemed to be to demonstrate the athletic skills of the acrobats. But surely, from time to time, some of the youths must have been killed during the contests.

With a navy second to none, the Minoan kings ruled the seas. They were wealthy, as suggested by an elaborate game table Evans found, set with crystal, ivory, and gold and silver pieces. And they were enlightened, as evidenced by the modern system of plumbing unearthed at Knossos. Enormous clay pipes, some large enough for a person to stand up in, carried water and sewage away from the palace. There also was a system of pipes for hot and cold water flowing through the palace. After four thousand years, the drainage system at Knossos is still in working order. Nothing equal to it was built in all of Europe until the mid-1800s. Since Evan's time at least three other palaces have been found in other parts of the island, some with as many as 1,500 rooms.

Who were the Minoans, and what happened to bring their splendid civilization down? What they left behind shows them as a people of uncommon grace and elegance who reached an astonishingly high level of craftsmanship. Their vases and bowls of stone and their finely carved gems were unmatched anywhere. And they were apparently a peace-loving people; they had no defense fortifications and none of their art shows scenes of battle, warriors, or weapons, although finely made real weapons of bronze have been found.

Their wealth most likely came from overseas trade. Elegant pottery made by them, and copied by other people, has been unearthed in Egypt, in the Near East, on the Aegean Islands, and in Greece. For many centuries the Minoans enjoyed the good life, but then their civilization collapsed and quickly disappeared.

About the year 1450 B.C. Knossos and other Minoan centers burned. By about 1400 B.C. these cities were completely destroyed. While some scholars have supposed that invaders swept over the island and conquered it, others doubt that this is what happened. They suspect that the catastrophic explosion of the volcanic island of Thera (also called Santorin), 60 miles (97 km) north of Crete, sent the Minoans and their splendid civilization into oblivion.

The Pax Romana

from Imperial Rome

Moses Hadas

Here is an account of the establishment of the Roman Empire and its continuation for many years, during which it was ruled by both good and bad rulers.

Rome had been torn by civil war for almost a century when Octavian, Julius Caesar's heir, at last emerged as undisputed head of the Government. Having disposed of his co-consul, Mark Antony, and repossessed the Eastern provinces that Antony controlled, Octavian returned to the capital. In 27 B.C., in a carefully staged meeting, he entered the Senate and announced that the Republic had been restored. Then, in a show of humility, he offered to resign. Instead of accepting his offer, the Senate, knowing it could not really oppose him, made him *princeps,* or "first citizen," and bestowed upon him various offices of state. Octavian himself took the title "Augustus," or "revered one."

Thus was the Roman Empire formally established, although Augustus carefully refrained from calling himself emperor. The irony of this performance was not lost on men like Tacitus, who had idealized the old Republic. Augustus, wrote Tacitus, "was wholly unopposed, for the boldest spirits had fallen in battle, or in the proscription, while the remaining nobles . . . preferred the safety of the present to the dangerous past." Yet Augustus was not mocking the ancient institutions; he was merely being pragmatic. The fact was that the Republic had broken down: the provinces were mismanaged, the armies undisciplined, the Senate incompetent and corrupt. Rome had grown into an empire and needed an emperor to manage its affairs. Augustus knew it, but he also knew that Romans would never give up the time-honored traditions of the Republic. He met these conflicting demands by preserving the forms of the old institutions while reserving the real powers of state to himself. He created a new edifice[1] under cover of restoring the old.

---

1. edifice (ed' i fis) *n.* building or organization.

The powers which the Senate granted Augustus gave his regime a basis of constitutionality. For a time he was officially consul, then proconsul, and finally the Senate granted him the additional powers of tribune. Holding the authority of several offices at once, he was able to serve as head of the state and governor of the important provinces, and to exercise veto power over the Senate as well, all under the cloak of legality. The fact is that Augustus did not really rule by virtue of any office. His authority was derived from the prestige that was associated with his title of *princeps*. Under this title three centuries of emperors were to rule Rome—sometimes wisely, as Augustus did, sometimes despotically, as in the cases of Nero and Domitian.

Once the foundations of his government had been established, Augustus turned to the task of administering it. Like several of his predecessors, he found the old offices of the Republic distinguished but inadequate. Julius Caesar had tried to cope with the problems of a burgeoning[2] empire and the need for more public servants by proposing to expand the size of the Senate. The additional members would have come from among Caesar's supporters in the Roman middle class and from high-ranking provincial families. But the Senate had resisted this change in its historic character.

Augustus took a different tack. He left the historic offices of government untouched and continued to appoint Senators to head them. But he turned over the everyday business of government to an imperial "household" that was in embryo a true civil service. For its membership Augustus drew largely upon the lower levels of Roman society.

Under Augustus, talented freedmen and even slaves began to hold routine administrative posts in the imperial household. Although their titles might be insignificant, their functions were often important. The secretary of accounts and finance was really the secretary of the imperial treasury, and the secretaries for correspondence and petitions were in effect secretaries of state. The imperial household also included the palace cook and butler. Thus staff positions had connotations of personal service, and because of this, upper-class Romans would not take

---

2. **burgeoning** (bur′ jən iŋ) *adj.* growing.

household posts; they considered such work beneath their dignity. Not until the reign of the Emperor Vespasian, almost a century after Augustus, did Roman Senators deign to become part of the imperial household. By that time the household had become a vast and very influential bureaucracy.

With a competent civil service to carry out his edicts and programs, Augustus was free to turn his attention to improving the state in other ways. In the epitaph he prepared for himself, called the *res gestae*, or "achievements," he could boast that he had beautified the city with magnificent buildings (Suetonius says Augustus claimed to have found Rome brick and left it marble); encouraged religion by building temples and shrines; strengthened morality by imposing on Rome a variety of strict laws governing personal behavior; and established a peace which endured throughout his long reign.

Augustus' civil service kept him in such close touch with the affairs of the Empire that he was able before his death to give a complete accounting of his stewardship. It summarized, says Suetonius, "the conditions of the whole empire; how many soldiers there were in active service . . . how much money there was in the public treasury . . . and what revenues were in arrears.[3] [Augustus] added, besides, the names of the freedmen and slaves from whom the details could be demanded." In later years, the civil service expanded even more. An inscription recording the death of a slave named Musicus, who served Augustus's successor Tiberius as a minor functionary in a province in Gaul, reveals that Musicus himself had a staff: a businessman, a purchasing agent, three secretaries, a doctor, a man and woman in charge of silver, a valet, two chamberlains, two footmen, two cooks, and one girl named Secunda, whose duties go unrecorded.

This was the retinue of an imperial slave, at the bottom of the bureaucracy. At the top there were freedmen who in time became so powerful they could sneer at the Senate. In one of his letters Pliny notes that during the reign of Claudius the Senate voted to reward the freedman Pallas with a gift of 15 million sesterces for his services as the Emperor's secretary of finance. The arrogant

---

3. in arrears (ərirz') *n.* behind in paying a debt.

freedman refused the gift, saying that this was "the only way he could show more contempt." Later, when the same Pallas was dismissed by the Emperor Nero, he made it a condition of his resigning that he not be questioned for any of his past acts, and that his accounts with the state be considered balanced.

Augustus died in 14 A.D. Although there was no constitutional formula for the choice of his successor—this was a difficulty that would plague the principate to its end—Augustus had solved the problem simply. He had designated his stepson Tiberius to be his successor, conferring upon him in advance the powers which would guarantee his acceptance as the next *princeps.*

It quickly became clear that not all *principes* were the equal of Augustus. Tiberius dissipated much of the prestige which his stepfather had accumulated. Morose, suspicious and unpopular, and almost 55 years old at the time of his succession, he quickly gained a reputation as a depraved and brutal ruler who disposed of anyone he so much as suspected of treachery. "Not a day passed without an execution," Suetonius wrote, "not even days that were sacred and holy, for he put some to death even on New Year's day. Many were accused and condemned with their children and even by their children. The relatives of victims were forbidden to mourn for them. . . . The word of no informer was doubted."

Nevertheless, Tiberius seems to have been an efficient administrator. One writer, Velleius Paterculus, described his reign as one in which "strife has been banished from the Forum, canvassing for office from the Campus Martius, discord from the senate house . . . the magistrates have regained their authority . . . the courts their dignity . . . and all have either been imbued with the wish to do right or have been forced to do so." Tiberius, it seems obvious, respected the accomplishments of Augustus and tried to emulate him; the very idea of *princeps* had begun to take on a life of its own, above and beyond the character of the man who served in the office at any particular moment.

Tiberius spent the last 11 years of his reign at Capri, scandalizing Romans with his debauchery and terrorizing them by leaving the Government in charge of a powerful and unscrupulous lieutenant, Sejanus. "The people were so glad of his death," Suetonius wrote of Tiberius, "that at the first news of it some ran about shouting 'Tiberius to the Tiber' while others prayed to Mother Earth . . . to allow the dead man no abode except among the damned."

Tiberius was succeeded by his grandnephew Caligula. The new Emperor was at first hailed as a popular hero. He pardoned political offenders, banished informers, reduced taxes and sponsored lavish games. But Caligula soon carried the limitless powers of the *princeps* beyond all bounds. He claimed the right to be addressed as a god and proposed that his horse be elected consul; he outfitted the animal for the office by giving it a marble stall and purple blankets. When the treasury was exhausted by his extravagance, he forced rich men to bequeath their wealth to the state, on pain of death and the confiscation of their property. His cruelty and caprice bordered on madness and outraged all of Rome—including, at last, even some members of his own household troops, the Praetorian Guard.

In 41 A.D. a group of officers in the guard assassinated Caligula and hastily buried the body, leaving Rome not only without an emperor, but without even an appointee. Caligula had been only 30 and had not named a successor. While the Senate debated the problem, the Praetorian Guard decided to pick its own emperor. Roaming through the palace, members of the guard found Claudius, the 50-year-old uncle of Caligula, cowering behind a curtain, and promptly made him Emperor. The Senate, still vacillating,[4] was forced to accept him.

Claudius, paralytic and ungainly, was said by some people to be a fool; his grandfather Augustus, while acknowledging that the boy had brains, had been ashamed to have Claudius sit with him in public. Yet in spite of appearances Claudius proved to be a sensible, steady ruler. During his regime the civil service was expanded and made more efficient, and new powers were extended to imperial governors abroad. This seeming paradox between the weakness of the man and the strength of his government has suggested to some modern interpreters that Claudius promoted his doltish reputation as a form of protective coloring, to lull the Praetorians and possible rival claimants.

---

4. **vacillating** (vas′ ə lāt iŋ) v. showing indecision.

The Empire which Claudius governed was a restless one. Provincial cities were becoming industrial centers as important as Rome, and were demanding a larger role in the Roman Government. The pattern was not new, but the pace had stepped up, creating internal stresses which led Claudius to abandon some of the old Augustan policies of geographical and political containment. Augustus had urged that the Empire be kept within the boundaries of the Danube, the Rhine and the Euphrates; Claudius found it expedient to include Britain, which had become a haven for Celtic tribes fleeing from Roman Gaul.

Augustus had seldom extended Roman citizenship to provincials; he had felt that Roman citizens should have Italian ancestry. Claudius returned to Julius Caesar's more liberal policy of permitting some highly placed provincials to be citizens of Rome. In 48 A.D. he went still further: he admitted Gallic chieftains to membership in the Senate.

Once this course was charted, there was no turning back. Roman citizenship was now theoretically available to any qualified person in the Empire. The satirist Petronius invented a convincing tale of an Asian king who became a slave in Rome so that he might, upon gaining his freedom, become a Roman and advance in the world. Pliny notes that one official who supervised Rome's grain supply was "descended on his father's side from a tribe that went about in skins." The great Seneca himself was a Spaniard, and his wife came from southern Gaul.

By the time of Claudius' death in 54 A.D., the word "Latin" no longer had a geographical meaning. More and more provincial cities held the "Latin right," a prerogative which bestowed Roman citizenship on their top officials, although not on the people at large. The Latin right was much sought after, since it gave cities, through their officials, a certain status in dealing with Rome. The Latin right was soon extended to cities in the western Alps; before long it was further extended to all the cities that Rome controlled in Spain.

Claudius was killed by a dose of poison administered by his fourth wife, Agrippina. Before serving him the fatal dish of mushrooms, she had persuaded him to adopt her son by an earlier marriage, a youth named Nero, and to give Nero precedence over Claudius' own son, Britannicus, as heir to the scepter.

Nero became Emperor at the age of 16. He had been in office scarcely a year when he poisoned Britannicus. Later he decided that his mother too should be dispatched. First he tried poison, only to discover that Agrippina, apparently alarmed by the fate of Britannicus, had foresightedly built up an immunity to the poison by taking small amounts at a time. When the poison did not work, Nero arranged for the ceiling over Agrippina's bed to collapse. When this failed, too, he sent her cruising in a ship so constructed that it fell apart at sea. But Agrippina swam ashore. Finally Nero took direct action: he accused her of plotting against the Emperor and had her assassinated.

A great fire swept Rome in 64; Nero was suspected of starting it, especially when he used it later as an excuse to rebuild Rome to his own glory. "Whether [the fire was] the result of accident or of the emperor's guile is uncertain," wrote Tacitus, "as authors have given both versions. . . . It started first in that part of the Circus which adjoins the Palatine . . . where, amid the shops containing inflammable wares, the conflagration broke out, instantly gathered strength, and, driven by the wind, swept down the length of the Circus. . . . The blaze in its fury ran first through the lower portions of the city, rose to the hills, then again devastated the lower portions." The fire continued to spread for more than six days.

Nero, away at Antium at the time, did not return until his own palace was threatened. Then, notes Tacitus, "he threw open the Campus Martius, the public structures . . . and even his own gardens, and put up temporary structures to receive the destitute multitude. The necessities of life were brought up from Ostia and neighboring towns, and the price of grain was reduced. . . . These acts, though popular, were of no effect, because a rumor had spread about that, at the very time when the city was in flames, the Emperor had mounted his private stage and sung of the destruction of Troy, comparing present misfortunes with the calamities of the past."

Nero had always fancied himself an artist and insisted on giving public performances, in which he sang and played the lyre. Roman traditionalists were outraged: it was a scandal for a nobleman to be seen on the stage. Nero, unabashed, made attendance compulsory. "While he was singing," Suetonius wrote, "no one was allowed to leave the theater even for the most urgent reasons. And so it is said that some . . . feigned death and were carried out as if for burial."

Nero's excesses created wide discontent. In 65 A.D. a Senate-inspired conspiracy against him was discovered and crushed; Seneca was among the prominent Romans implicated and forced to take their own lives. At the same time Nero was faced by local disorders in Armenia, Britain and Judaea, and finally, in 68 A.D., by rebellion within the Army itself. Roman commanders in Gaul, Africa and Spain tried to seize power in their respective provinces. Confronted by mounting resistance, Nero at last fled the city. He was thereupon condemned to death *in absentia* by the Senate. At this, he took his own life. His last words were: "What an artist the world is losing!"

The death of Nero touched off a period of virtual anarchy[5] known as the Year of the Four Emperors. As Tacitus noted: "The secret of Empire was out: emperors could be made elsewhere than in Rome." The first of the four new emperors was Galba, one of the military commanders who had rebelled against Nero's rule. He took office with the support of the Praetorian Guard, but the Guard, dissatisfied with his stinginess, soon murdered him and handed the office to Otho, Governor of a province in southwest Spain. Then soldiers stationed outside Rome decided to play the same game. The legions on the Rhine, acclaiming their general Vitellius as Emperor, marched on Rome and defeated the forces of Otho near Cremona. Otho committed suicide, leaving Vitellius in control— whereupon the legions on the Danube, supporting still another general, Vespasian, marched on Rome and killed Vitellius.

The ravages of war once again spread over Italy. In the fighting that brought Vespasian to power, the city of Cremona fell to his forces. "Forty thousand armed men now burst into the city," Tacitus writes, "together with sutlers and camp followers. . . . Old men and women, well stricken in years and of no value for plunder, were maltreated by way of sport. Grown-up maidens and comely youths that came in the way were violently torn to pieces. . . . Men carrying off for themselves money or offerings of

---

5. **anarchy** (an' ər kē) *n.* complete absence of government; political disorder.

solid gold from the temples, were hewn down by others stronger than themselves. . . . In an army so varied in character and tongue . . . every man had his own cupidity . . . nothing was unlawful."

Vespasian, whose cause had provoked these acts, was actually many miles away in the East, completing the campaign to suppress the Judaean insurrection of 66–70. His men proclaimed him Emperor in an apparently spontaneous demonstration. As Tacitus reports it: "One day, as Vespasian emerged from his bedchamber, a few soldiers standing by in the usual formation . . . saluted him as emperor; then others ran up, calling him Caesar and Augustus and heaping on him all the titles of the principate. [Soon] all Syria had sworn the same allegiance. . . . All the provinces washed by the sea as far as Asia . . . and all the territory extending inland to Pontus and Armenia, took the oath." To consolidate his position, Vespasian seized Egypt, thus cutting off the grain supply on which Rome depended. Then, after the death of Vitellius, he proceeded to Rome and asked that his imperial authority be officially confirmed by the Senate.

Vespasian, like Augustus, recognized the value of a constitutional base for his reign. Glad to have an end to the year-long confusion, the Senate decreed "that he shall have the right . . . to conclude treaties with whomever he wishes . . . to convene the Senate . . . to extend and advance the boundaries . . . to transact and do whatever he deems to serve the interests of the state and the dignity of all things divine, human, public and private." Ever since Nero's death, the Army had been openly in control of the Roman Government. Now, with Vespasian's installation under civil law, the Government was—in form, at least—returned to the hands of the Senate and civil authority.

With Vespasian, whose family name was Flavius, began the Flavian dynasty and a new era of peace. Vespasian was a wise ruler, and during his reign Romans became encouraged to think that the Empire was, in the end, more important than the man who ruled it. In 70 A.D., according to Tacitus, a Roman general, Petilius Cerialis, observed in an address before a group of ex-revolutionary Gauls: "From praiseworthy emperors you derive equal advantage though you dwell far away, while the cruel ones are most formidable to those near them.

Endure the extravagance and rapacity of your masters just as you bear barren seasons and excessive rains and other natural disasters. . . . The good fortune and order of eight centuries has consolidated this mighty fabric of empire, and it cannot be pulled asunder without destroying those who sunder it."

Vespasian, pursuing Claudius' policies of extending citizenship to the provinces, gave Latin status to cities throughout Spain. He also carried these policies a step further by granting citizenship to all provincials who served in his armies. To stabilize the spreading Empire, he tightened discipline in the provincial governments and in the Army, strengthened the frontiers in Britain, Germany and the Near East through a system of new roads and forts, and established colonies of veterans in backward areas.

Vespasian also sought to restore the bankrupt treasury by cutting expenses and introducing new taxes. But, according to Suetonius, he took care not to be too severe in enforcing his economies: "To a mechanical engineer who promised to transport some heavy columns to the Capitol at small expense, he gave no mean reward for his invention, but refused to make use of it, saying that he should not be forced to take from the poor . . . the work that fed them."

The imperial household, as before, saw to the details of government, carrying the business of the principate into every province. Through this huge civil service, as much as through his armies, Vespasian's presence was felt everywhere. The inscription on a milestone along a road near Smyrna, in Asia Minor, reads: "The Emperor Caesar Vespasian Augustus, pontifex maximus, holding the tribunician power for the sixth year, acclaimed imperator thirteen times, father of his country, consul six times, designated consul for a seventh time, censor, saw to the repair of the roads."

Using the prestige of his office, Vespasian led Rome out of what Tacitus called "a period rich in disasters." In doing so he performed what was, perhaps, his greatest service: he restored good relations between *princeps* and Senate. On that slender constitutional prop rested the peace begun by Augustus. This peace had at first been taken as no more than another lull in the chronic wars which had plagued the world from the beginning of Greek and Roman times. Slowly, as it stretched out beyond the first Emperor's lifetime, it had come to be recognized as a peace not of Augustus the man, but of his system of government, a *pax Romana* rather than a *pax* of Augustus.

Under Vespasian and his successors, the Senate changed somewhat in character. The high posts of the imperial household, now recognized as too important to be limited to freedmen, were being taken over by equestrians, and the Senate began to function as an upper body of civil servants. Through its members' accumulated experience in posts of authority throughout the Empire, the chamber also became a repository for administrative advice. When the Flavian dynasty foundered, it was this change in the Senate's role which enabled it to take on the task of naming an emperor.

Vespasian was succeeded in 79 A.D. by his son Titus, who reigned for only two years. With Titus' death, Vespasian's second son, Domitian, inherited the mantle of empire at the age of 29. He was a man beset by suspicion and fear, and for 15 years he terrorized Rome. Domitian ferreted out suspected opponents in the Army and Senate and had them executed. His informers were so diligent, it was said, that men forgot the use of their tongues. He was killed at last by a member of his own household. After his death, the Senate ordered Domitian's name removed from all public places and refused to give him a state burial. Then, for the first time in Rome's history, the Senate designated its own choice as Emperor, a respectable old lawyer named Nerva.

With Nerva began the era of the "five good emperors." While his own reign was short, he left as his legacy a rational approach to the problem of imperial succession: he adopted a qualified candidate and trained him for the job. The result was a long period of stability. Indeed, Trajan, Hadrian, Antoninus Pius and Marcus Aurelius, who followed Nerva in succession, were among the greatest men ever to govern Rome. In time, the plan of succession instituted by Nerva would break down; perhaps it was too much to expect that in disposing of the power of the principate men would always be guided by reason. During the reign of the good emperors, however, the Empire reached its height.

Nerva's immediate successor, Trajan, was a comparatively unknown but promising Spanish commander.

Under him the boundaries of the Empire were pushed to their outermost extent. Trajan moved beyond the Danube into Dacia and, at the end of his reign, led an expedition into Armenia and Mesopotamia.

Trajan also made changes in the Government, especially in the internal administration of provincial cities. Heretofore the emperor had administered the provinces through a Roman governor who operated at the provincial level. Local self-development and civic affairs were left to native magistrates and town or city councils. But abuses and extravagances at the local level led Trajan to send out curators to supervise municipal governments, either as advisors or as administrators charged with specific duties. This was the beginning of a bureaucratic expansion which would go on into the Fourth Century.

The Empire under Trajan enjoyed unparalleled prosperity, the provinces flourishing no less than Rome. One index of this prosperity was the increase in public and private philanthropy throughout the Empire. Philanthropy was an old Roman tradition, inherent in the relation of a patron to his freedmen. But it became, in many instances, a matter of civic pride. The Younger Pliny, for example, discovering that children in his native town of Como had to go to school in Milan because Como had no teacher for them, put up a third of the expense of hiring an instructor, stipulating that his fellow townsmen must raise the rest. During his lifetime Pliny also gave 30,000 sesterces a year from rentals on his lands for the support of Como's lower-class children; in addition, he built the city a municipal library and provided for its upkeep. On his death, he left the town a great sum of money for the support of 100 freedmen who had been his slaves, adding that after their death the income should be used to provide an annual banquet for the people. Throughout the Empire, cities were growing rich and foundations were being established to do for other communities what Pliny had done for Como.

Philanthropy was also a Government concern. Grain was given free to the poor: there was no charge for the circuses or the theaters. In one of the most remarkable philanthropies of all, Trajan took the equivalent of the imperial budget for a single year and with it established a system of low-cost farm loans, the interest from which was used to support orphans and the children of the poor. Although girls were granted somewhat less than boys, and illegitimate children received still less, all got some degree of public support. This program, known as the *alimenta*, was expanded by Trajan's successors and continued to operate for almost 200 years.

Following Nerva's precept, Trajan adopted a Spanish kinsman, the brilliant general Hadrian, as his heir. Thus, when Trajan died in 117 A.D., the continuity of the principate was assured. Hadrian departed somewhat from Trajan's policies. He felt that the Empire had been overextended, and he gave up Trajan's foothold in Armenia and Mesopotamia. He also thought it best to withdraw a bit in northern Britain, where Rome had just lost a whole legion in border warfare. It was Hadrian who built the famous wall separating the Roman-held south of Britain from the unconquered north.

Hadrian traveled widely within his Empire, visiting almost all the provinces, taking a personal interest in their far-flung administrations, raising new buildings for them and attempting to ease their heavy tax burden. Perhaps his most noteworthy act on their behalf was the standardization of Roman law, making all legal procedures the same throughout the Empire. The Roman world was becoming a genuine commonwealth, rather than a central Government ruling over scattered overseas dominions.

The changing status of cities reflected this increasing unity. From Republican times and throughout the first part of the Empire, Rome had governed provincial peoples by giving their established towns the status of city, administered on the Roman model. Beyond this, so long as the taxes were collected and public order maintained, the provincials were left to govern themselves. For convenience, in isolated, backward areas Roman administrators sometimes combined several small towns or granted the status of city to a scattered tribe.

Slowly, in province after province, more and more cities appeared, and the older, more developed ones made application for closer association with Rome. Towns were granted the Latin right, making their magistrates Roman citizens, and in time were recognized as *municipia*, or municipalities, all of whose people were accepted as citizens of Rome.

Utica, an old Phoenician colony in Africa, underwent such an evolution. Julius Caesar had granted it the Latin right in 44 B.C., and Augustus later made it a municipium. Under Hadrian, the town applied for a further change of status, requesting the designation of *colonia*, or colony. This would theoretically give it the same status as a town founded by emigrants from Italy. Although there was no legal or financial benefit to this designation, it was rich in prestige: to be a *colonia* was to be as Roman as Rome itself. By Hadrian's time, municipia throughout the Empire were eager to be called colonies, to adopt the Roman heritage as well as the citizenship. Rome had never tried to impose its own culture on the provinces, but the grants were freely made.

The last of the five good emperors, Antoninus Pius and Marcus Aurelius, presided over the most majestic days of the Empire. During Antoninus' reign, Aristides, a visiting professor from Asia Minor, delivered an oration on what he considered to be Rome's greatest accomplishment: "I mean your magnificent citizenship with its grand conception . . . there is nothing like it in the records of all mankind. Dividing into two groups all those in your Empire, [which covers] the entire civilized world, you have everywhere appointed to your citizenship, and even to kinship with you, the better part of the world's talent, courage and leadership. And the rest you have recognized as a league under your hegemony."

Under Marcus Aurelius, whose reign lasted from 161 to 180 A.D., the sense of unity, the reconciliation of peoples, was remarkable. Greek writers could say with sincerity that "an attack on Rome is an attack on us," and Greek scholars studied Roman law at a great law school established by Rome in distant Syria. Provincial families, having risen generation by generation into the higher ranks of Roman society, were sending their members to serve in the Roman Senate.

Yet at the same time there were ominous signs of change. In the last years of Marcus Aurelius' reign, Rome's borders on the Rhine, the Danube and the Euphrates were all endangered at once. Although it would be another 200 years before those borders were breached in any strength, Marcus Aurelius' time was increasingly taken up with military matters. He was often at the frontiers, moving from camp to camp, personally leading his armies (and, between battles, finding time to write down his enduring *Meditations*). The military campaigns eventually put a severe strain on the treasury and on civilian manpower. With so many men called up for military service, provinces along the borders began to turn to barbarian peoples for help on their farm lands—leading, ironically, to the appearance of barbarian settlements within Rome's borders. And, as a final portent of trouble, plague spread through the Empire, demoralizing the people and undermining the economy.

At its very height, Rome faced some of its severest tests. "Our history now plunges," wrote the Roman historian Cassius Dio, "from a kingdom of gold to one of iron and rust."

The Dog of Pompeii

Louis Untermeyer

The ancient Roman city of Pompeii is the setting for this story of a boy and his loyal dog. Though the story is fiction, many of its details are based on discoveries made by scientists who studied the ruins of Pompeii.

Tito and his dog Bimbo lived (if you could call it living) under the wall where it joined the inner gate. They really didn't live there; they just slept there. They lived anywhere. Pompeii was one of the gayest of the old Latin towns, but although Tito was never an unhappy boy, he was not exactly a merry one. The streets were always lively with shining chariots and bright red trappings;[1] the open-air theaters rocked with laughing crowds; sham[2] battles and athletic sports were free for the asking in the great stadium. Once a year the Caesar[3] visited the pleasure city and the fireworks lasted for days; the sacrifices in the Forum were better than a show. But Tito saw none of these things. He was blind—had been blind from birth. He was known to everyone in the poorer quarters. But no one could say how old he was, no one remembered his parents, no one could tell where he came from. Bimbo was another mystery. As long as people could remember seeing Tito—about twelve or thirteen years—they had seen Bimbo. Bimbo had never left his side. He was not only dog, but nurse, pillow, playmate, mother and father to Tito.

Did I say Bimbo never left his master? (Perhaps I had better say comrade, for if anyone was the master, it was Bimbo.) I was wrong. Bimbo did trust Tito alone exactly three times a day. It was a fixed routine, a custom understood between boy and dog since the beginning of their friendship, and the way it worked was this: Early in the morning, shortly after dawn, while Tito was still dreaming, Bimbo would disappear. When Tito woke, Bimbo would be sitting quietly at his side, his ears

---

1. **trappings** (trap′ iŋz) *n.* ornamental coverings.
2. **sham** (sham) *adj.* make believe; pretended.
3. **Caesar** (sē′ zər) the Roman emperor Titus. From the time of Julius Caesar until Hadrian (49 B.C.–A.D. 138), all Roman emperors were called Caesar.

cocked, his stump of a tail tapping the ground, and a fresh-baked bread—more like a large round roll—at his feet. Tito would stretch himself; Bimbo would yawn; then they would breakfast. At noon, no matter where they happened to be, Bimbo would put his paw on Tito's knee and the two of them would return to the inner gate. Tito would curl up in the corner (almost like a dog) and go to sleep, while Bimbo, looking quite important (almost like a boy) would disappear again. In half an hour he'd be back with their lunch. Sometimes it would be a piece of fruit or a scrap of meat, often it was nothing but a dry crust. But sometimes there would be one of those flat rich cakes, sprinkled with raisins and sugar, that Tito liked so much. At supper time the same thing happened, although there was a little less of everything, for things were hard to snatch in the evening with the streets full of people. Besides, Bimbo didn't approve of too much food before going to sleep. A heavy supper made boys too restless and dogs too stodgy—and it was the business of a dog to sleep lightly with one ear open and muscles ready for action.

But, whether there was much or little, hot or cold, fresh or dry, food was always there. Tito never asked where it came from and Bimbo never told him. There was plenty of rainwater in the hollows of soft stones; the old egg-woman at the corner sometimes gave him a cupful of strong goat's milk; in the grape season the fat winemaker let him have drippings of the mild juice. So there was no danger of going hungry or thirsty. There was plenty of everything in Pompeii, if you knew where to find it—and if you had a dog like Bimbo.

As I said before, Tito was not the merriest boy in Pompeii. He could not romp with the other youngsters and play Hare-and-Hounds and I-spy and Follow-your-Master and Ball-against-the-Building and Jackstones and Kings-and-Robbers with them. But that did not make him sorry for himself. If he could not see the sights that delighted the lads of Pompeii he could hear and smell things they never noticed. He could really see more with his ears and nose than they could with their eyes. When he and Bimbo went out walking he knew just where they were going and exactly what was happening.

"Ah," he'd sniff and say, as they passed a handsome villa,[4] "Glaucus Pansa is giving a grand dinner tonight. They're going to have three kinds of bread, and roast pigling, and stuffed goose, and a great stew—I think bear stew—and a fig pie." And Bimbo would note that this would be a good place to visit tomorrow.

Or, "H'm," Tito would murmur, half through his lips, half through his nostrils. "The wife of Marcus Lucretius is expecting her mother. She's shaking out every piece of goods in the house; she's going to use the best clothes— the ones she's been keeping in pine-needles and camphor[5]—and there's an extra girl in the kitchen. Come, Bimbo, let's get out of the dust!"

Or, as they passed a small but elegant dwelling opposite the public baths, "Too bad! The tragic poet is ill again. It must be a bad fever this time, for they're trying smoke fumes instead of medicine. Whew! I'm glad I'm not a tragic poet!"

Or, as they neared the Forum, "Mm-m! What good things they have in the Macellum today!" (It really was a sort of butcher-grocer-marketplace, but Tito didn't know any better. He called it the Macellum.) "Dates from Africa, and salt oysters from sea caves, and cuttlefish, and new honey, and sweet onions, and—ugh!—water-buffalo steaks. Come, let's see what's what in the Forum." And Bimbo, just as curious as his comrade, hurried on. Being a dog, he trusted his ears and nose (like Tito) more than his eyes. And so the two of them entered the center of Pompeii.

The Forum was the part of the town to which everybody came at least once during each day. It was the Central Square and everything happened here. There were no private houses; all was public—the chief temples, the gold and red bazaars,[6] the silk shops, the town hall, the booths belonging to the weavers and jewel merchants, the wealthy woolen market, the Shrine of the Household Gods.[7] Everything glittered here. The buildings looked as if they were new—which, in a sense, they were. The

---

4. villa (vil′ ə) *n.* large estate.
5. camphor (kam′ fər) *n.* hard, clear substance with a strong smell, used as a moth repellent.
6. bazaars (bə zärz′) *n.* streets where people sell things.
7. Household Gods gods that were said to protect the hearth, the crops, the livestock, and so on.

earthquake of twelve years ago had brought down all the old structures and, since the citizens of Pompeii were ambitious to rival Naples and even Rome, they had seized the opportunity to rebuild the whole town. And they had done it all within a dozen years. There was scarcely a building that was older than Tito.

Tito had heard a great deal about the earthquake though, being about a year old at the time, he could scarcely remember it. This particular quake had been a light one—as earthquakes go. The weaker houses had been shaken down, parts of the outworn wall had been wrecked; but there was little loss of life, and the brilliant new Pompeii had taken the place of the old. No one knew what caused these earthquakes. Records showed they had happened in the neighborhood since the beginning of time. Sailors said that it was to teach the lazy city folk a lesson and make them appreciate those who risked the dangers of the sea to bring them luxuries and protect their town from invaders. The priests said that the gods took this way of showing their anger to those who refused to worship properly and who failed to bring enough sacrifices to the altars and (though they didn't say it in so many words) presents to the priests. The tradesmen said that the foreign merchants had corrupted the ground and it was no longer safe to traffic in imported goods that came from strange places and carried a curse with them. Everyone had a different explanation—and everyone's explanation was louder and sillier than his neighbor's.

They were talking about it this afternoon as Tito and Bimbo came out of the side street into the public square. The Forum was the favorite promenade for rich and poor. What with the priests arguing with the politicians, servants doing the day's shopping, tradesmen crying their wares, women displaying the latest fashions from Greece and Egypt, children playing hide-and-seek among the marble columns, knots of soldiers, sailors, peasants from the provinces—to say nothing of those who merely came to lounge and look on—the square was crowded to its last inch. His ears even more than his nose guided Tito to the place where the talk was loudest. It was in front of the Shrine of the Household Gods that, naturally enough, the householders were arguing.

"I tell you," rumbled a voice which Tito recognized as bathmaster Rufus's, "there won't be another earthquake in my lifetime or yours. There may be a tremble or two, but earthquakes, like lightnings, never strike twice in the same place."

"Do they not?" asked a thin voice Tito had never heard. It had a high, sharp ring to it and Tito knew it as the accent of a stranger. "How about the two towns of Sicily[8] that have been ruined three times within fifteen years by the eruptions of Mount Etna?[9] And were they not warned? And does that column of smoke above Vesuvius[10] mean nothing?"

"That?" Tito could hear the grunt with which one question answered another. "That's always there. We use it for our weather guide. When the smoke stands up straight we know we'll have fair weather; when it flattens out it's sure to be foggy; when it drifts to the east—"

"Yes, yes," cut in the edged voice. "I've heard about your mountain barometer.[11] But the column of smoke seems hundreds of feet higher than usual and it's thickening and spreading like a shadowy tree. They say in Naples—"

"Oh, Naples!" Tito knew this voice by the little squeak that went with it. It was Attilio, the cameo-cutter.[12] "*They* talk while we suffer. Little help we got from them last time. Naples commits the crimes and Pompeii pays the price. It's become a proverb with us. Let them mind their own business."

"Yes," grumbled Rufus, "and others, too."

"Very well, my confident friends," responded the thin voice which now sounded curiously flat. "We also have a proverb—and it is this: Those who will not listen to men must be taught by the gods. I say no more. But I leave a last warning. Remember the holy ones. Look to your temples. And when the smoke tree above Vesuvius grows to the shape of an umbrella pine, look to your lives."

Tito could hear the air whistle as the speaker drew his toga[13] about him and the quick shuffle of feet told him the stranger had gone.

---

8. **Sicily** (sis′ əl ē) island off the southern coast of Italy in the Mediterranean Sea.
9. **Mount Etna** (et′ nə): volcano in eastern Sicily.
10. **Vesuvius** (və soo̅′ vē əs) volcano in southern Italy.
11. **barometer** (bə räm ət ər) *n.* instrument used to forecast changes in weather.
12. **cameo-cutter** (kam′ ē ō) *n.* person who makes cameos, carvings on gems or shells that form raised designs, usually of heads in profile.
13. **toga** (tō′ gə) *n.* one-piece outer garment worn by people of ancient Rome.

"Now what," said the cameo-cutter, "did he mean by that?"

"I wonder," grunted Rufus, "I wonder." Tito wondered, too. And Bimbo, his head at a thoughtful angle, looked as if he had been doing a heavy piece of pondering. By nightfall the argument had been forgotten. If the smoke had increased no one saw it in the dark. Besides, it was Caesar's birthday and the town was in holiday mood. Tito and Bimbo were among the merry-makers, dodging the charioteers who shouted at them. A dozen times they almost upset baskets of sweets and jars of Vesuvian wine, said to be as fiery as the streams inside the volcano, and a dozen times they were cursed and cuffed. But Tito never missed his footing. He was thankful for his keen ears and quick instinct—most thankful of all for Bimbo.

They visited the uncovered theater and, though Tito could not see the faces of the actors, he could follow the play better than most of the audience, for their attention wandered—they were distracted by the scenery, the costumes, the byplay, even by themselves—while Tito's whole attention was centered in what he heard. Then to the city walls, where the people of Pompeii watched a mock naval battle in which the city was attacked by the sea and saved after thousands of flaming arrows had been exchanged and countless colored torches had been burned. Though the thrill of flaring ships and lighted skies was lost to Tito, the shouts and cheers excited him as much as any and he cried out with the loudest of them.

The next morning there were *two* of the beloved raisin and sugar cakes for his breakfast. Bimbo was unusually active and thumped his bit of a tail until Tito was afraid he would wear it out. The boy could not imagine whether Bimbo was urging him to some sort of game or was trying to tell him something. After a while, he ceased to notice Bimbo. He felt drowsy. Last night's late hours had tired him. Besides, there was a heavy mist in the air—no, a thick fog rather than a mist—a fog that got into his throat and scraped it and made him cough. He walked as far as the marine gate to get a breath of the sea. But the blanket of haze had spread all over the bay and even the salt air seemed smoky.

He went to bed before dusk and slept. But he did not sleep well. He had too many dreams—dreams of ships lurching in the Forum, of losing his way in a screaming crowd, of armies marching across his chest, of being pulled over every rough pavement of Pompeii.

He woke early. Or, rather, he was pulled awake. Bimbo was doing the pulling. The dog had dragged Tito to his feet and was urging the boy along. Somewhere. Where, Tito did not know. His feet stumbled uncertainly: he was still half asleep. For a while he noticed nothing except the fact that it was hard to breathe. The air was hot. And heavy. So heavy that he could taste it. The air, it seemed, had turned to powder, a warm powder that stung his nostrils and burned his sightless eyes.

Then he began to hear sounds. Peculiar sounds. Like animals under the earth. Hissings and groanings and muffled cries that a dying creature might make dislodging the stones of his underground cave. There was no doubt of it now. The noises came from underneath. He not only heard them—he could feel them. The earth twitched; the twitching changed to an uneven shrugging of the soil. Then, as Bimbo half pulled, half coaxed him across, the ground jerked away from his feet and he was thrown against a stone fountain.

The water—hot water—splashing in his face revived him. He got to his feet, Bimbo steadying him, helping him on again. The noises grew louder; they came closer. The cries were even more animal-like than before, but now they came from human throats. A few people, quicker of foot and more hurried by fear, began to rush by. A family or two—then a section—then, it seemed, an army broken out of bounds. Tito, bewildered though he was, could recognize Rufus as he bellowed past him, like a water buffalo gone mad. Time was lost in a nightmare.

It was then the crashing began. First a sharp crackling, like a monstrous snapping of twigs; then a roar like the fall of a whole forest of trees; then an explosion that tore earth and sky. The heavens, though Tito could not see them, were shot through with continual flickerings of fire. Lightnings above were answered by thunders beneath. A house fell. Then another. By a miracle the two companions had escaped the dangerous side streets and were in a more open space. It was the Forum. They rested here awhile—how long he did not know.

Tito had no idea of the time of day. He could *feel* it was black—an unnatural blackness. Something inside—

perhaps the lack of breakfast and lunch—told him it was past noon. But it didn't matter. Nothing seemed to matter. He was getting drowsy, too drowsy to walk. But walk he must. He knew it. And Bimbo knew it; the sharp tugs told him so. Nor was it a moment too soon. The sacred ground of the Forum was safe no longer. It was beginning to rock, then to pitch, then to split. As they stumbled out of the square, the earth wriggled like a caught snake and all the columns of the temple of Jupiter[14] came down. It was the end of the world—or so it seemed.

To walk was not enough now. They must run. Tito was too frightened to know what to do or where to go. He had lost all sense of direction. He started to go back to the inner gate; but Bimbo, straining his back to the last inch, almost pulled his clothes from him. What did the creature want? Had the dog gone mad?

Then, suddenly, he understood. Bimbo was telling him the way out—urging him there. The sea gate of course. The sea gate—and then the sea. Far from falling buildings, heaving ground. He turned, Bimbo guiding him across open pits and dangerous pools of bubbling mud, away from buildings that had caught fire and were dropping their burning beams. Tito could no longer tell whether the noises were made by the shrieking sky or the agonized people. He and Bimbo ran on—the only silent beings in a howling world.

New dangers threatened. All Pompeii seemed to be thronging toward the marine gate and, squeezing among the crowds, there was the chance of being trampled to death. But the chance had to be taken. It was growing harder and harder to breathe. What air there was choked him. It was all dust now—dust and pebbles, pebbles as large as beans. They fell on his head, his hands— pumice[15] stones from the black heart of Vesuvius. The mountain was turning itself inside out. Tito remembered a phrase that the stranger had said in the Forum two days ago: "Those who will not listen to men must be taught by the gods." The people of Pompeii had refused to heed the warnings; they were being taught now—if it was not too late.

---

14. **Jupiter** (jōō′ pit ər) the chief Roman god, known as Zeus in Greece.
15. **pumice** (pum′ is) n. spongy, light rock formed from the lava of a volcano.

Suddenly it seemed too late for Tito. The red hot ashes blistered his skin, the stinging vapors[16] tore his throat. He could not go on. He staggered toward a small tree at the side of the road and fell. In a moment Bimbo was beside him. He coaxed. But there was no answer. He licked Tito's hands, his feet, his face. The boy did not stir. Then Bimbo did the last thing he could—the last thing he wanted to do. He bit his comrade, bit him deep in the arm. With a cry of pain, Tito jumped to his feet, Bimbo after him. Tito was in despair, but Bimbo was determined. He drove the boy on, snapping at his heels, worrying his way through the crowd; barking, baring his teeth, heedless of kicks or falling stones. Sick with hunger, half dead with fear and sulfur fumes,[17] Tito pounded on, pursued by Bimbo. How long he never knew. At last he staggered through the marine gate and felt soft sand under him. Then Tito fainted. . . .

Someone was dashing sea water over him. Someone was carrying him toward a boat.

"Bimbo," he called. And then louder, "Bimbo!" But Bimbo had disappeared.

Voices jarred against each other. "Hurry—hurry!" "To the boats!" "Can't you see the child's frightened and starving!" "He keeps calling for someone!" "Poor boy, he's out of his mind." "Here, child—take this!"

They tucked him in among them. The oarlocks creaked; the oars splashed; the boat rode over toppling waves. Tito was safe. But he wept continually.

"Bimbo!" he wailed. "Bimbo! Bimbo!"

He could not be comforted.

Eighteen hundred years passed. Scientists were restoring the ancient city; excavators were working their way through the stones and trash that had buried the entire town. Much had already been brought to light— statues, bronze instruments, bright mosaics,[18] household articles; even delicate paintings had been preserved by the fall of ashes that had taken over two thousand lives. Columns were dug up and the Forum was beginning to emerge.

---

16. vapors (vā′ pərz) *n.* fumes.
17. sulfur (sul′ fər) **fumes** choking fumes caused by the volcanic eruption.
18. mosaics (mō zā′ iks) *n.* pictures of designs made by inlaying small bits of colored stone in mortar.

It was at a place where the ruins lay deepest that the Director paused.

"Come here," he called to his assistant. "I think we've discovered the remains of a building in good shape. Here are four huge millstones that were most likely turned by slaves or mules—here is a whole wall standing with shelves inside it. Why! It must have been a bakery. And here's a curious thing. What do you think I found under this heap where the ashes were thickest? The skeleton of a dog!"

"Amazing!" gasped his assistant. "You'd think a dog would have had sense enough to run away at the time. And what is that flat thing he's holding between his teeth? It can't be a stone."

"No. It must have come from this bakery. You know it looks to me like some sort of cake hardened with the years. And, bless me, if those little black pebbles aren't raisins. A raisin cake almost two thousand years old! I wonder what made him want it at such a moment?"

"I wonder," murmured the assistant.

The Growth of Islam

Who Are the Muslims?

from The Muslim World

Richard Tames

Islam, the religion whose followers are known as Muslims, is one of the major religions of the world. Here is a summary of its basic beliefs and its history.

God's will

Islam is an Arabic word which means 'submitting.' Islam is the religion based on the will of God as revealed to humanity by Prophets sent since the beginning of time. A follower of this religion is a Muslim, a person who is submitting to God's will and trying to live in the way that they believe God requires them to.

Worldwide following

There are Muslims in almost every country in the world. In more than fifty countries Muslims form the majority of believers. Most of these Muslims live in the great belt of arid lands stretching from Morocco to Pakistan; others live in West Africa and South East Asia.

Indonesia, followed by Bangladesh and Pakistan have the largest Muslim populations but there are also tens of millions living as minorities in India, China and the [former] USSR. Other minorities are to be found in East Africa, the West Indies, Yugoslavia and Western Europe.

Many of the Muslims living in Western Europe (such as the Turks in West Germany and the North African Arabs in France) have come to work there rather than to settle.

Britain's Muslim population is very mixed, consisting of students from Nigeria and Malaysia, businessmen from the Middle East and East Africa and former farmers from Pakistan, Bangladesh and India. Many of these people now regard Britain as their permanent home where they look for education and a good future for their families.

United by the Qur'an and Five Pillars

Muslims are united by their belief in the Qur'an (Koran: the holy book of Islam) and their wish to follow the example of Muhammad, its Prophet, even though they live in so many countries, speak different languages and follow different customs in daily life. They also accept the same five duties as 'pillars of the faith.' These are:

Shahadah—to confess their belief—'*I witness that there is no god but Allah and that Muhammad is the Prophet of Allah.*' (Allah is an Arabic word meaning 'the God.')

Salat—to pray five times a day.

Zakat—to give alms for the needy.

Saum—to fast in the month of Ramadan.

Hajj—to make the pilgrimage to Mecca.

Islam also means 'peace.' Muslims greet each other by saying '*as-salaamu alaykum*' (peace be upon you). They believe that when all people submit to Allah's will and live by the Qur'an, peace will come to everyone.

THE STORY OF MUHAMMAD

Mecca—Muhammad's birthplace

Muhammad was born in the trading city of Mecca, in about the year 570 of the Christian era. His early life was passed in poverty because both his parents had died by the time he was six years old. Later on while working as a trader Muhammad soon became known as *al-Amin* (the trustworthy). When he was 25 he married his employer, a rich widow of 40 called Khadijah.

He could have had an easy life. But he was troubled by conditions in Mecca. The rich merchants oppressed the poor. There was much gambling, drunkenness and violence. Women and children were often cruelly treated. Although the city had a famous shrine, the Ka'aba, the religion of the day seemed cruel and useless. The people believed in many gods and worshipped idols. Muhammad thought that making sacrifices to idols was senseless. He retired for long periods to the mountains around Mecca to meditate.

God's message

Muhammad was sitting in a cave on Mount Hira, when he sensed the presence of a strange being. This was perceived by him as the angel Gabriel, who commanded

Muhammad in the following words:

'*Recite! In the Name of thy Lord who created, created Man from congealed blood.*' This was Muhammad's first revelation from God, which is the first part of the Qur'an.

Muhammad told the Meccans (people of Mecca) that there was only one God, *Allah*, (*the* God) and that the worship of idols was wicked. He said that God was the Creator of the world and there would be a day of Judgment when every man and woman would be sent to Heaven or Hell. Some of the Meccans became his followers but many of the most powerful people turned against him and said that he was either lying or mad. Many of Muhammad's followers were beaten and insulted.

The departure

At last, in 622, Muhammad accepted an invitation from the people of Medina to go and live among them. He and his followers left Mecca. This event is known as the *hijra* (the departure). It marks the beginning of the Muslim calendar because, at Medina, Muhammad established the first Muslim community.

The return to Mecca

While they were at Medina, raids and battles took place between the Muslims and the people of Mecca. At last, in 630 the Meccans were defeated and Muhammad returned in triumph to Mecca. The people accepted Islam as their religion and the idols were taken from the Ka'aba and destroyed.

In 632 Muhammad died. Abu Bakr, his close friend, told the people 'If there are any among you who worshipped Muhammad, he is dead. But if it is God you worship, He lives forever.'

HOW ISLAM SPREAD

Muslim rule expands

After Muhammad's death some of the tribes who had become Muslims decided to give up Islam because they did not want to pay *zakat*. The Muslims chose Abu Bakr to be Caliph (*Khalifa* means successor).

He went to war against the tribes who had deserted Islam until they submitted. After the Muslims had conquered all Arabia they turned against the non-Muslim empires of Byzantium and Persia. Within a century a vast area was under Muslim rule.

The Muslims allowed the Christians and Jews in these lands to keep their religions but made them pay extra taxes.

Shiites and Sunni

Abu Bakr was followed as Caliph by other close companions of the Prophet—Umar and Uthman. In 656 Ali (Muhammad's cousin and son-in-law) became Caliph but he was murdered in 661 and was succeeded by a member of the Umayyad family. Ali's supporters, the *Shi'at-Ali* (party of Ali) carried on fighting for his son Hussein, who was killed in 680.

The descendants of these people became known as the Shia or Shiites. They are a minority group in Islam and have some beliefs and customs which differ from the majority, called Sunni, who follow the *Sunna* (tradition) of the Prophet. Nowadays the Shia form the majority of the population in Iraq and Iran.

Baghdad—the new capital

The Umayyad dynasty was overthrown in 750 by descendants of the Prophet's uncle, Abbas. The Abbasids moved the capital of the empire from Damascus to the new city of Baghdad. When Baghdad was destroyed by the Mongols in 1258 the Abbasids' rule ended.

By then the empire had for some time ceased to be one territory ruled from a single centre. Local princes and generals tried to make themselves independent wherever they could. At one time there were three rulers claiming to be Caliph. But as a civilization Islam remained united by the Arabic language, by laws based on the Qur'an and by ties of trade and pilgrimage.

ISLAMIC EMPIRES

The Ottoman Empire

Of the three great Muslim empires which had been founded by the mid-16th century the Ottoman Empire was the one which lasted the longest. It began with the

13th-century conquests of Osman, a Turkish nomad chief. Osman's descendants crushed the Byzantine Empire and after 1453 made its capital (Constantinople) their own, but re-named it Istanbul. The court of Suleyman II so dazzled European visitors that they called him 'the Magnificent.'

The Ottomans twice laid siege to Vienna but the climate and great distances involved set limits on their powers of conquest. In 1699 the Ottomans signed a treaty giving up territory for the first time but it was only defeat in the First World War (1914–18) that finally brought the empire to an end.

The Safavid Empire

The Ottomans fought many border wars against the Safavid rulers of Persia, whose main achievement was to make Shiite Islam the official religion of their country. Under Shah Abbas a magnificent new capital was built at Isfahan. In the 18th century the Safavids were followed by the weak Qajar dynasty.

The Mughal Empire

Safavid Persia also fought against its other neighbour, the Mughal Empire. The Mughal Empire was founded by Babur, almost lost by his son Humayun but regained by Akbar (Babur's grandson) who doubled the size of its territory.

Akbar reigned at almost exactly the same time as Queen Elizabeth I of England. Like her he was a great patron of the arts and lavishly praised by courtiers. He built massive palace forts at Delhi and Agra as well as a whole new capital at Fatehpur Sikri which was abandoned almost as soon as it was completed.

In 1739 the Persians sacked Delhi and carried off a fabulous, jewelled Peacock throne. The Mughal Empire never really recovered and its power passed gradually into the hands of the British, who stayed as rulers until 1947.

Common features

These three Islamic empires—Ottoman, Safavid and Mughal—had a number of features in common. The ruling class was not Arab in those empires. The Ottomans relied on Christian converts, recruited as boys, to serve as civil servants and members of the famed Janissary corps of troops. In each empire the power of gunpowder was used to make remote provinces obey the power of central government. Each court was a place of splendour, luxury and intrigue. Each, at its height, was more powerful than any comparable state in Europe.

Sharing Knowledge
from The Arabs in the Golden Age

Mokhtar Moktefi

Many things that we take for granted—paper, books, libraries, numbers, and certain kinds of medicine—originated in the Arab world. Here is an account of some of the ways our knowledge began long ago and far away.

Paper was invented by the Chinese in the beginning of the second century. But it was not until the eighth century that Chinese prisoners of war revealed the secrets of papermaking to the Arabs. The first paper manufactured in the Arab world was probably made at Samarkand in 751. Other paper mills opened shortly thereafter in Baghdad, Yemen, Syria, Egypt, Spain, and Sicily.

To make paper, rags of linen, hemp, or cotton were plunged into tubs filled with water. Mallets powered by a waterwheel ground the rags until they were transformed into a fibrous, milky substance. Sheets of paper were made by placing this gummy paste on a sieve stretched over a wooden frame. Years later, Arabs brought this technique to Europe.

The spread of paper mills throughout the Arab world led to a tremendous increase in administrative record-keeping. Paper was also responsible for the widespread distribution of books, knowledge, and culture.

Bookstores

There was a section in every large city where bookstores were easy to find. People who shopped in bookstores were of varied social backgrounds. Booksellers made lots of money from their trade because most urban residents knew how to read and write. Since reading was popular, there was an impressive number of books to choose from.

Manuscripts sold in bookstores had to be copied by hand. Booksellers often did this slow work themselves, but sometimes they employed male and female scribes to do it for them. Authors often made their living by working as scribes. Their salaries were determined by their intellectual capabilities, the quality of their handwriting, and their motivation. The better the book was copied, the more it cost.

Specialists traveled the world over looking for new titles to "publish." Some of these specialists hunted down rare manuscripts for collectors. Beautiful editions of rare books were sold at public auctions for very high prices.

Libraries

Princes and wealthy individuals owned their own libraries. Each city had at least one, and sometimes several, public libraries. In the old city of Cairo, the great palace library contained 1.6 million volumes. This library, spread over forty different rooms, was open to the general public. Some visitors to the library stayed to read in one of the great rooms, while others borrowed books and took them home to read. Borrowers were required to give only their name and address. Paper and plumes were available for those who wanted to remain at the library and copy interesting passages.

In some libraries, books were kept locked in bolted closets lining the walls of the room. Lists of the books inside were tacked on the door of each closet. In other libraries, volumes were stored in stacked-up compartments. People wishing to view a book had to look up its title in a catalog and ask a librarian to retrieve it. Sometimes there were several copies of the same manuscript.

Beginning in the tenth century, the spirit of liberty and tolerance that had once characterized the Arab world began to disappear. For example, one dictator who had begun to feel the pressure of fanatical religious movements opposed to such a free flow of knowledge "purged," or cleaned out, the palace library in Cordova. He burned and destroyed everything contained in this unique European institution. Civic trouble and unrest also led to arson and the plundering of palaces and residences—and libraries—belonging to prominent people.

Then, in 1258, the Mongols took Baghdad. These tribes came from the northeastern steppes of Central Asia. Under the strong leadership of Genghis Khan the Mongols expanded, spreading into China, Russia, and Arabia. It was Hülegü, one of Khan's successors, who conquered the city of Baghdad. In the longterm, the Mongol invasion spurred the scholarship, arts, and political life of the Islamic world. But at first, their invasion physically destroyed much of the Arab empire. The Mongols murdered thousands of scholars. They threw entire libraries into the river and burned any book that they found.

Education

"Search for knowledge, even if you must go to China to find it." This advice given by the prophet Muhammad shows how greatly the Arabs valued learning.

Primary schools were to be found wherever there was a mosque. There were free schools for poor children, so that almost everyone learned how to read and write. Boys and girls attended separate schools.

Aside from reading and writing, schoolchildren studied history, grammar, mathematics, and the Koran. Seated on mats or carpets, they recited and memorized texts written on tablets. Discipline was strict. When a student learned sixty chapters of the Koran, his or her family prepared a large feast at which cakes were served and gifts were offered to the teacher.

It was also an important part of a child's education to learn how to use a bow and arrow and how to swim. A caliph once told the tutor of his sons, "Teach them to swim and accustom them to little sleep."

Advanced Studies

Up until the eleventh century, advanced courses were given by scholars and masters in mosques. Classes were also given among closed circles of acquaintances and friends. Advanced education could last for as long as ten, fifteen, even twenty years. During the course of this continuous program, students went from one master to another and often traveled to new cities when they reached advanced levels in their studies. Large universities attached to mosques were founded in Cairo, Tunis, and Fez.

The first *madrasah*, or university, was founded in the eleventh century. One hundred years later there were thirty-five such institutions in Baghdad alone. Professors and students from outside the city were given lodging. Scholarships were granted to the top students and to those who could not afford to pay for their studies. A director served as head of the institution while other civil servants worked as professors, tutors, accountants, and librarians. An imam was named to lead the prayers.

Well-known masters attracted large audiences. They delivered their lectures from a pulpit around which students sat on chairs or benches. At the end of the lecture, students could ask questions orally or by writing them down.

When a professor felt that his student was capable of teaching or of practicing his discipline, he granted him an *ijazah*, or diploma. Some students even received several diplomas from different universities. In Baghdad, an ijazah was required of those wishing to practice medicine.

Science

"The ink of the scholar is more sacred than the blood of a martyr," said Muhammad. Muslim missions brought back foreign manuscripts from abroad as early as the eighth century. Ancient Greek, Persian, Indian, and Chinese texts were translated and collected in such places as the House of Wisdom in Baghdad and the Hall of Wisdom in Cairo.

In these institutions, researchers from the far ends of the empire worked to develop new knowledge. Hunain ibn Ishaq, who was in charge of translating works from Greek to Arabic, was also an outstanding physician. He wrote ten books on the eye, creating the earliest known volume of its kind.

These cultural treasures, which were later brought to the West and translated into Latin and other languages, became the basis for philosophical and scientific discovery in the modern world. In fact, the writing of the ancient Greek philosophers Aristotle and Plato first came to Western Europe in Arabic, as did the medical learning of Hippocrates.

Studying the Stars

Ninth-century astronomers had observatories in Baghdad and Damascus. The study of the stars allowed them to determine the direction of Mecca, what times prayers were to be held, and the exact length of the month of Ramadan. The astrolabe, a portable instrument that made it possible to measure the height of the stars in the sky, allowed caravaneers and captains of ships to know exactly where they were. A short while later, the Arab navy brought the concept of the magnetized needle, or compass, back to the Arab empire from China.

Progress in mathematics allowed astronomers to calculate the length of the meridian, the imaginary north-south line on the earth's surface that passes through the poles and determines longitude. In the year 1000 al-Biruni calculated the circumference of the earth and was only 9 miles (15 kilometers) off. This discovery was made several hundred years before Europe admitted that the earth was not flat.

Clever Engineers

A book written in 869 listed no fewer than one hundred inventions, including devices for hot and cold water, mechanical toys, and service elevators. Engineers built countless windmills and watermills on the banks of rivers. They made water clocks, medical devices, and many automatic devices. For example, they developed an amazing sink equipped with a figurine that poured water from a jug before handing the user a hand towel and a comb.

A great Andalusian inventor perfected the manufacture of crystal. He produced a "canopy of heaven" with clouds, lightning and thunder. Because he wanted to fly like a bird, he made a sheath with movable wings out of silk and feathers. One day, he put on this new contraption and jumped off a cliff. He managed to glide for a few minutes before landing safely on the ground.

Arabic Figures

Just try doing a few calculations with Roman figures to see how difficult it is. In Baghdad, during the eighth century, people began using Indian figures. Five centuries later, Europeans began using the same figures and referred to them as "Arabic." This is the ten-digit system of numbers that we use today. It was the Arabs who invented the zero, allowing for representation of very large numbers. Zero was called *sifr*, which means empty.

It was also the Arabs who invented algebra (an Arabic word) and trigonometry. Logarithims were discovered at this time, too.

Arab Medicine

Arab doctors were responsible for developing original and precise medical descriptions. Their knowledge provided the framework upon which European universities would later be modeled.

Arab medical scholars made some very important observations. Abu Bakr al-Razi, known as Rhazes, wrote an enormous medical encyclopedia. He studied infections, such as measles and smallpox, and researched childhood diseases and the influence of psychology on sick patients. He was also the first to use animal gut to stitch wounds and plaster of Paris to set broken bones.

When choosing a site for a new hospital in Spain, Rhazes hung up raw meat in different parts of town. He said that the hospital should be built at the spot where the least putrified meat hung. He had made a connection between bacteria and infection, something that Europeans would not discover for some time to come.

Other Great Doctors

The Muslim Spaniard, Abu al-Qasim, known as Albucasis, summarized everything that was known about surgical methods in the thirtieth volume of his work *The Art of Healing Wounds*. In this important book, he illustrated more than two hundred surgical instruments. He also showed cases where the surgeon's knife was to be used and when false teeth made of bone were recommended.

Ibn Sina, known as Avicenna, was precocious. By the age of ten, he had memorized the Koran. At fourteen, he knew more than all of his knowledgeable masters. At seventeen, he was called to care for the prince of Persia and succeeded in bringing him back to good health. His two most famous works were an encyclopedia called the *Book of Healing* and the *Canon of Medicine*. His writings were translated into Latin, making him the great master to European physicians from the twelfth to the seventeenth centuries.

Hospitals

Every large city had at least one hospital. At the beginning of the tenth century, Baghdad had at least five of them. Hospitals, which were often housed within the palace, were very modern for their time. Rooms were equipped with comfortable beds. Special areas were reserved for those with contagious diseases, and other zones were designed for those who needed surgery. When a city did not have a separate hospital for women, a section within the public hospital was reserved for them, where all the personnel was female.

Schools of medicine, libraries, pharmacies, mosques, and public baths were attached to each hospital. The administrative staff recorded in logbooks the names of the patients, the care they received, and the food they ate. The cost of medical care was also recorded even though all treatment was free of charge.

Medicines

The study of medicine led to the development of pharmacies. The manuscript of one botanist-pharmacist listed 1,400 "simple" medicines made from single substances such as plants, minerals, or animals. A well-known encyclopedic treatise listed over 760 different drugs.

The first pharmacies opened after the founding of a school of pharmacy. Apothecaries prepared all the potions themselves. In addition to inventing a wide variety of mechanical devices, scholars perfected *al anbik*, or the still, which was used for distilling (creating vapor from liquids). They also discovered acids and *al kohol*, or alcohol. Their research provided key foundations for the study of chemistry.

The Gifts of Islam

The Golden Age of the Arabs was a time of tremendous growth in many areas of learning. Much of this knowledge was shared with Medieval Europe. But the simultaneous expansion of the Arabic empire also brought political and religious enemies.

In the eighth century, Charlemagne battled the Arabs in Spain. From the eleventh to the thirteenth centuries, armies of Christians joined in the Crusades to take back Palestine—the Holy Land—from the Muslims. The Mongols invaded from the north. By the thirteenth century the Golden Age was in decline; the empire had begun to crumble.

But the learning and art and many of the traditions born in this time live on. There are about six hundred million followers of Islam of many different races and from a variety of countries in the world today.

The Fisherman and the Jinnee

from The Thousand and One Nights

Translated by N. J. Dawood

This tale comes from a world-famous story collection called The Thousand and One Nights, *also sometimes called* The Arabian Nights. *Most of the tales in this collection are set in Arabic-speaking areas like Egypt and Baghdad (now the capital of Iraq) or in adjoining lands like Persia (now Iran) where the Muslim religion is also dominant. Of the three interlocking tales in this story, two are set in Persia and all feature characters who are Muslim.*

Once upon a time there was a poor fisherman who had a wife and three children to support.

He used to cast his net four times a day. It chanced that one day he went down to the sea at noon and, reaching the shore, set down his basket, rolled up his shirt sleeves, and cast his net far out into the water. After he had waited for it to sink, he pulled on the cords with all his might; but the net was so heavy that he could not draw it in. So he tied the rope ends to a wooden stake on the beach and, putting off his clothes, dived into the water and set to work to bring it up. When he had carried it ashore, however, he found in it a dead donkey.

"By Allah,[1] this is a strange catch!" cried the fisherman, disgusted at the sight. After he had freed the net and wrung it out, he waded into the water and cast it again, invoking Allah's help. But when he tried to draw it in he found it even heavier than before. Thinking that he had caught some enormous fish, he fastened the ropes to the stake and, diving in again, brought up the net. This time he found a large earthen vessel filled with mud and sand.

Angrily the fisherman threw away the vessel, cleaned his net, and cast it for the third time. He waited patiently, and when he felt the net grow heavy he hauled it in, only to find it filled with bones and broken glass. In despair, he lifted his eyes to heaven and cried: "Allah

---

1. **Allah** (al' lə) the Arabic word for God.

knows that I cast my net only four times a day. I have already cast it for the third time and caught no fish at all. Surely He will not fail me again!"

With this the fisherman hurled his net far out into the sea and waited for it to sink to the bottom. When at length he brought it to land he found in it a bottle made of yellow copper. The mouth was stopped with lead and bore the seal of our master Solomon, son of David.[2] The fisherman rejoiced and said: "I will sell this in the market of the coppersmiths. It must be worth ten pieces of gold." He shook the bottle and, finding it heavy, thought to himself: "I will first break the seal and find out what is inside."

The fisherman removed the lead with his knife and again shook the bottle; but scarcely had he done so when there burst from it a great column of smoke which spread along the shore and rose so high that it almost touched the heavens. Taking shape, the smoke resolved itself into a jinnee of such prodigious[3] stature that his head reached the clouds, while his feet were planted on the sand. His head was a huge dome and his mouth as wide as a cavern, with teeth ragged like broken rocks. His legs towered like the masts of a ship, his nostrils were two inverted bowls, and his eyes, blazing like torches, made his aspect fierce and menacing.

The sight of this jinnee struck terror to the fisherman's heart; his limbs quivered, his teeth chattered together, and he stood rooted to the ground with parched tongue and staring eyes.

"There is no god but Allah and Solomon is His Prophet!" cried the jinnee. Then, addressing himself to the fisherman, he said: "I pray you, mighty Prophet, do not kill me! I swear never again to defy your will or violate your laws!"

"Blasphemous giant," cried the fisherman, "do you presume to call Solomon the Prophet of Allah? Solomon has been dead these eighteen hundred years, and we are now approaching the end of time. But what is your history, pray, and how came you to be imprisoned in this bottle?"

---

2. Solomon . . . David In the Old Testament, David and his son Solomon are both kings of Israel and are considered prophets by Muslims.
3. prodigious (prə dij′ əs) *n.* wonderful; amazing.

On hearing these words the jinnee replied sarcastically: "Well, then; there is no god but Allah! Fisherman, I bring you good news."

"What news?" asked the old man.

"News of your death, horrible and prompt!" replied the jinnee.

"Then may heaven's wrath be upon you, ungrateful wretch!" cried the fisherman. "Why do you wish my death, and what have I done to deserve it? Have I not brought you up from the depths of the sea and released you from your imprisonment?"

But the jinnee answered: "Choose the manner of your death and the way that I shall kill you. Come, waste no time!"

"But what crime have I committed?" cried the fisherman.

"Listen to my story, and you shall know," replied the jinnee.

"Be brief, then, I pray you," said the fisherman, "for you have wrung my soul with terror."

"Know," began the giant, "that I am one of the rebel jinn who, together with Sakhr the Jinnee, mutinied against Solomon, son of David. Solomon sent against me his vizier,[4] Asaf ben Berakhya, who vanquished me despite my supernatural power and led me captive before his master. Invoking the name of Allah, Solomon adjured[5] me to embrace his faith and pledge him absolute obedience. I refused, and he imprisoned me in this bottle, upon which he set a seal of lead bearing the Name of the Most High. Then he sent for several of his faithful jinn, who carried me away and cast me into the middle of the sea. In the ocean depths I vowed: 'I will bestow eternal riches on him who sets me free!' But a hundred years passed away and no one freed me. In the second hundred years of my imprisonment I said: 'For him who frees me I will open up the buried treasures of the earth!' And yet no one freed me. Whereupon I flew into a rage and swore: 'I will kill the man who sets me free, allowing him only to choose the manner of his death!' Now it was you who set me free; therefore prepare to die and choose the way that I shall kill you."

---

4. **vizier** (vi zir′) a high officer in the government; a minister.
5. **adjured** (a joord′) v. commanded; ordered.

"O wretched luck, that it should have fallen on my lot to free you!" exclaimed the fisherman. "Spare me, mighty jinnee, and Allah will spare you; kill me, and so shall Allah destroy you!"

"You have freed me," repeated the jinnee. "Therefore you must die."

"Chief of the jinn," cried the fisherman, "will you thus requite[6] good with evil?"

"Enough of this talk!" roared the jinnee. "Kill you I must."

At this point the fisherman thought to himself: "Though I am but a man and he is a jinnee, my cunning may yet overreach his malice." Then, turning to his adversary, he said: "Before you kill me, I beg you in the Name of the Most High engraved on Solomon's seal to answer me one question truthfully."

The jinnee trembled at the mention of the Name, and, when he had promised to answer truthfully, the fisherman asked: "How could this bottle, which is scarcely large enough to hold your hand or foot, ever contain your entire body?"

"Do you dare doubt that?" roared the jinnee indignantly.

"I will never believe it," replied the fisherman, "until I see you enter this bottle with my own eyes!"

Upon this the jinnee trembled from head to foot and dissolved into a column of smoke, which gradually wound itself into the bottle and disappeared inside. At once the fisherman snatched up the leaden stopper and thrust it into the mouth of the bottle. Then he called out to the jinnee: "Choose the manner of your death and the way that I shall kill you! By Allah, I will throw you back into the sea, and keep watch on this shore to warn all men of your treachery!"

When he heard the fisherman's words, the jinnee struggled desperately to escape from the bottle, but was prevented by the magic seal. He now altered his tone and, assuming a submissive air, assured the fisherman that he had been jesting with him and implored him to let him out. But the fisherman paid no heed to the jinnee's entreaties[7] and resolutely carried the bottle down to

---

6. **requite** (ri kwīt′) *v.* to make return or repayment for.
7. **entreaties** (en trēt′ ēz) *n.* earnest requests.

the sea. "What are you doing with me?" whimpered the jinnee helplessly.

"I am going to throw you back into the sea!" replied the fisherman. "You have lain in the depths eighteen hundred years, and there you shall remain till the Last Judgment![8] Did I not beg you to spare me so that Allah might spare you? But you took no pity on me, and He has now delivered you into my hands."

"Let me out," cried the jinnee in despair, "and I will give you fabulous riches!"

"Perfidious[9] jinnee," retorted the fisherman, "you justly deserve the fate of the king in the tale of Yunan and the doctor."

"What tale is that?" asked the jinnee.

THE TALE OF KING YUNAN
AND DUBAN THE DOCTOR

It is related (began the fisherman) that once upon a time there reigned in the land of Persia a rich and mighty king called Yunan. He commanded great armies and had a numerous retinue of followers and courtiers. But he was afflicted with a leprosy[10] which baffled his physicians and defied all cures.

One day a venerable[11] old doctor named Duban came to the king's capital. He had studied books written in Greek, Persian, Latin, Arabic, and Syriac, and was deeply versed in the wisdom of the ancients. He was master of many sciences, knew the properties of plants and herbs, and was above all skilled in astrology and medicine. When this physician heard of the leprosy with which Allah had plagued the king and of his doctors' vain endeavors to cure him, he put on his finest robes and betook himself to the royal palace. After he had kissed the ground before the king and called down blessings upon him, he told him who he was and said: "Great king, I

---

8. Last Judgment the final judgment of humankind at the end of the world.

9. perfidious (pər fid′ ē əs) *adj*. treacherous.

10. leprosy (lep′ rə sē) *n*. a chronic infectious disease that attacks the skin, flesh, and nerves.

11. venerable (ven′ ər ə b′l) *adj*. worthy of respect by reason of age and dignity or character.

have heard about the illness with which you are afflicted and have come to heal you. Yet will I give you no potion to drink, nor any ointment to rub upon your body."

The king was astonished at the doctor's words and asked: "How will you do that? By Allah, if you cure me I will heap riches upon you, and your children's children after you. Anything you wish for shall be yours and you shall be my companion and my friend."

Then the king gave him a robe of honor and other presents and asked: "Is it really true that you can heal me without draught or ointment? When is it to be? What day, what hour?"

"Tomorrow, if the king wishes," he replied.

The doctor took leave of the king, and hastening to the center of the town rented for himself a house, to which he carried his books, his drugs, and his other medicaments. Then he distilled balsams and elixirs,[12] and these he poured into a hollow polo stick.

Next morning he went to the royal palace and, kissing the ground before the king, requested him to ride to the field and play a game of polo with his friends. The king rode out with his viziers and his chamberlains,[13] and when he had entered the playing field the doctor handed him the hollow club and said: "Take this and grasp it firmly. Strike the ball with all your might until the palm of your hand and the rest of your body begin to perspire. The cure will penetrate your palm and course through the veins and arteries of your body. When it has done its work, return to the palace, wash yourself, and go to sleep. Thus shall you be cured; and peace be with you."

The king took hold of the club and, gripping it firmly, struck the ball and galloped after it with the other players. Harder and harder he struck the ball as he dashed up and down the field, until his palm and all his body perspired. When the doctor saw that the cure had begun its work, he ordered the king to return to the palace. The slaves hastened to make ready the royal bath and hurried to prepare the linens and the towels. The king bathed, put on his night-clothes, and went to sleep.

---

12. **balsams** (bôl′ səmz) **and elixirs** (i lik′ sərz) two potions with supposed healing powers.
13. **chamberlains** (chām′ bər linz) *n.* high officials in the king's court.

Next morning the physician went to the palace. When he was admitted to the king's presence he kissed the ground before him and wished him peace. The king hastily rose to receive him; he threw his arms around his neck and seated him by his side.

For when the king left the bath the previous evening, he looked upon his body and rejoiced to find no trace of the leprosy. His skin had become as pure as virgin silver.

The king regaled the physician sumptuously all day. He bestowed on him robes of honor and other gifts, and when evening came gave him two thousand pieces of gold and mounted him on his own favorite horse. And so enraptured was the king by the consummate skill of his doctor that he kept repeating to himself: "This wise physician has cured me without draught or ointment. By Allah, I will load him with honors and he shall henceforth be my companion and trusted friend." And that night the king lay down to sleep in perfect bliss, knowing that he was clean in body and rid at last of his disease.

Next morning, as soon as the king sat down upon his throne, with the officers of his court standing before him and his lieutenants and viziers seated on his right and left, he called for the physician, who went up to him and kissed the ground before him. The king rose and seated the doctor by his side. He feasted him all day, gave him a thousand pieces of gold and more robes of honor, and conversed with him till nightfall.

Now among the king's viziers there was a man of repellent aspect, an envious, black-souled villain, full of spite and cunning. When this vizier saw that the king had made the physician his friend and lavished on him high dignities and favors, he became jealous and began to plot the doctor's downfall. Does not the proverb say: "All men envy, the strong openly, the weak in secret?"

So, on the following day, when the king entered the council chamber and was about to call for the physician, the vizier kissed the ground before him and said: "My bounteous master, whose munificence[14] extends to all men, my duty prompts me to forewarn you against an evil which threatens your life; nor would I be anything but a base-born wretch were I to conceal it from you."

---

14. **munificence** (my͞o͞o nif′ ə sens) *n.* great generosity.

Perturbed at these ominous words, the king ordered him to explain his meaning.

"Your majesty," resumed the vizier, "there is an old proverb which says: 'He who does not weight the consequences of his acts shall never prosper.' Now I have seen the king bestow favors and shower honors upon his enemy, on an assassin who cunningly seeks to destroy him. I fear for the king's safety."

"Who is this man whom you suppose to be my enemy?" asked the king, turning pale.

"If you are asleep, your majesty," replied the vizier, "I beg you to awake. I speak of Duban, the doctor."

"He is my friend," replied the king angrily, "dearer to me than all my courtiers; for he has cured me of my leprosy, an evil which my physician had failed to remove. Surely there is no other physician like him in the whole world, from East to West. How can you say these monstrous things of him? From this day I will appoint him my personal physician and give him every month a thousand pieces of gold. Were I to bestow on him the half of my kingdom, it would be but a small reward for his service. Your counsel, my vizier, is the prompting of jealousy and envy. Would you have me kill my benefactor and repent of my rashness, as King Sindbad repented after he had killed his falcon?"

THE TALE OF KING SINDBAD
AND THE FALCON

Once upon a time (went on King Yunan) there was a Persian king who was a great lover of riding and hunting. He had a falcon which he himself had trained with loving care and which never left his side for a moment; for even at nighttime he carried it perched upon his fist, and when he went hunting took it with him. Hanging from the bird's neck was a little bowl of gold from which it drank. One day the king ordered his men to make ready for a hunting expedition and, taking with him his falcon, rode out with his courtiers. At length they came to a valley where they laid the hunting nets. Presently a gazelle fell into the snare, and the king said: "I will kill the man who lets her escape!"

They drew the nets closer and closer round the beast. On seeing the king the gazelle stood on her haunches and raised her forelegs to her head as if she wished to salute him. But as he bent forward to lay hold of her, she leaped over his head and fled across the field. Looking round, the king saw his courtiers winking at one another.

"Why are they winking?" he asked his vizier.

"Perhaps because you let the beast escape," ventured the other, smiling.

"On my life," cried the king, "I will chase the gazelle and bring her back!"

At once he galloped off in pursuit of the fleeing animal, and when he had caught up with her, his falcon swooped upon the gazelle, blinding her with his beak, and the king struck her down with a blow of his sword. Then dismounting he flayed the animal and hung the carcass on his saddle-bow.

It was a hot day and the king, who by this time had become faint with thirst, went to search for water. Presently, however, he saw a huge tree, down the trunk of which water was trickling in great drops. He took the little bowl from the falcon's neck and, filling it with this water, placed it before the bird. But the falcon knocked the bowl with its beak and toppled it over. The king once again filled the bowl and placed it before the falcon, but the bird knocked it over a second time. Upon this the king became very angry and, filling the bowl a third time, set it down before his horse. But the falcon sprang forward and knocked it over with its wings.

"Allah curse you for a bird of ill omen!" cried the king. "You have prevented yourself from drinking and the horse also."

So saying, he struck the falcon with his sword and cut off both its wings. But the bird lifted its head as if to say: "Look into the tree!" The king raised his eyes and saw in the tree an enormous serpent spitting its venom down the trunk.

The king was deeply grieved at what he had done and, mounting his horse, hurried back to the palace. He threw his kill to the cook, and no sooner had he sat down, with the falcon still perched on his fist, than the bird gave a convulsive gasp and dropped down dead.

The king was stricken with sorrow and remorse for having so rashly killed the bird which had saved his life.

* * *

When the vizier heard the tale of King Yunan, he said: "I assure your majesty that my counsel is prompted by no other motive than my devotion to you and my concern for your safety. I beg leave to warn you that, if you put your trust in this physician, it is certain that he will destroy you. Has he not cured you by a device held in the hand? And might he not cause your death by another such device?"

"You have spoken wisely, my faithful vizier," replied the king. "Indeed, it is quite probable that this physician has come to my court as a spy to destroy me. And since he cured my illness by a thing held in the hand, he might as cunningly poison me with the scent of a perfume. What should I do, my vizier?"

"Send for him at once," replied the other, "and when he comes, strike off his head. Only thus shall you be secure from his perfidy."

Thereupon the king sent for the doctor, who hastened to the palace with a joyful heart, not knowing what lay in store for him.

"Do you know why I have sent for you?" asked the king.

"Allah alone knows the unspoken thoughts of men," replied the physician.

"I have brought you here to kill you," said the king.

The physician was thunderstruck at these words and cried: "But why should you wish to kill me? What crime have I committed?"

"It has come to my knowledge," replied the king, "that you are a spy sent here to cause my death. But you shall be the first to die."

Then he called out to the executioner, saying: "Strike off the head of this traitor!"

"Spare me, and Allah will spare you!" cried the unfortunate doctor. "Kill me, and so shall Allah kill you!"

But the king gave no heed to his entreaties. "Never will I have peace again," he cried, "until I see you dead. For if you cured me by a thing held in the hand, you will doubtless kill me by the scent of a perfume or by some other foul device."

"Is it thus that you repay me?" asked the doctor. "Will you thus requite good with evil?"

But the king said: "You must die; nothing can now save you."

When he saw that the king was determined to put him to death, the physician wept and bitterly repented the service he had done him. Then the executioner came forward, blindfolded the doctor and, drawing his sword, held it in readiness for the king's signal. But the doctor continued to wail, crying: "Spare me, and Allah will spare you! Kill me, and so shall Allah kill you!"

Moved by the old man's lamentations, one of the courtiers interceded for him with the king, saying: "Spare the life of this man, I pray you. He has committed no crime against you, but rather has he cured you of an illness which your physicians have failed to remedy."

"If I spare this doctor," replied the king, "he will use his devilish art to kill me. Therefore he must die."

Again the doctor cried: "Spare me, and Allah will spare you! Kill me, and so shall Allah kill you!" But when at last he saw that the king was fixed in his resolve, he said: "Your majesty, if you needs must kill me, I beg you to grant me a day's delay, so that I may go to my house and wind up my affairs. I wish to say farewell to my family and my neighbors and instruct them to arrange for my burial. I must also give away my books of medicine, of which there is one, a work of unparalleled virtue, which I would offer to you as a parting gift, that you may preserve it among the treasures of your kingdom."

"What may this book be?" asked the king.

"It holds secrets and devices without number, the least of them being this: that if, after you have struck off my head, you turn over three leaves of this book and read the first three lines upon the left-hand page, my severed head will speak and answer any questions you may ask it."

The king was astonished to hear this and at once ordered his guards to escort the physician to his house. That day the doctor put his affairs in order and next morning returned to the king's palace. There had already assembled the viziers, the chamberlains, the nabobs,[15] and all the chief officers of the realm, so that with their colored robes the court seemed like a garden full of flowers.

The doctor bowed low before the king; in one hand he had an ancient book and in the other a little bowl filled

---

15. **nabobs** (nā′ bäbz) *n.* very rich or important people; aristocrats.

with a strange powder. Then he sat down and said: "Bring me a platter!" A platter was instantly brought in, and the doctor sprinkled the powder on it, smoothing it over with his fingers. After that he handed the book to the king and said: "Take this book and set it down before you. When my head has been cut off, place it upon the powder to stanch the bleeding. Then open the book."

The king ordered the executioner to behead the physician. He did so. Then the king opened the book, and, finding the pages stuck together, put his finger to his mouth and turned over the first leaf. After much difficulty he turned over the second and the third, moistening his finger with his spittle at every page, and tried to read. But he could find no writing there.

"There is nothing written in this book," cried the king.

"Go on turning," replied the severed head.

The king had not turned six pages when the venom (for the leaves of the book were poisoned) began to work in his body. He fell backward in an agony of pain, crying: "Poisoned! Poisoned!" and in a few moments breathed his last.

"Now, treacherous jinnee," continued the fisherman, "had the king spared the physician, he in turn would have been spared by Allah. But he refused, and Allah brought about the king's destruction. And as for you, if you had been willing to spare me, Allah would have been merciful to you, and I would have spared your life. But you sought to kill me; therefore I will throw you back into the sea and leave you to perish in this bottle!"

Civilizations of Africa

Old Song

Traditional

Voices from the past often reflect on life's struggles and triumphs. This poem, written many years ago, has advice about fame that is timeless.

Do not seek too much fame,
but do not seek obscurity.
Be proud.
But do not remind the world of your deeds.
5   Excel when you must,
but do not excel the world.
Many heroes are not yet born,
many have already died.
To be alive to hear this song is a victory.

from Sundiata: An Epic of Old Mali

D. T. Niane

In this translation of an African legend, Mari Djata (also known as Sogolon Djata and as Sundiata) seems to be a very unlikely hero, with his huge head and his inability to stand upright. How Mari Djata overcomes his infirmity and regains his honor is an exciting and instructive tale.

CHARACTERS IN *SUNDIATA*

Balla Fasséké (bä' lä fä sə' kä):   Griot and counselor of Sundiata.

Boukari (bōō kä' rē):   Son of the king and Namandjé, one of his wives; also called Manding (män' diŋ) Boukari.

Dankaran Tourman (dän' kä rän tōō' män):   Son of the king and his first wife, Sassouma, who is also called Sassouma Bérété.

Djamarou (jä mä' rōō):   Daughter of Sogolon and the king; sister of Sundiata and Kolonkan.

Farakourou (fä rä kōō' rōō):   Master of the forges.

Gnankouman Doua (nän kōō' män dōō' ə)   The king's griot; also called simply, Doua.

Kolonkan (kō lōn' kən):   Sundiata's eldest sister.

Namandjé (nä män' jä):   One of the king's wives.

Naré Maghan (nä' rä mäg' hän): Sundiata's father.

Nounfaïri (nōōn' fä ē' rē):   Soothsayer and smith; father of Farakourou.

Sassouma Bérété (sä sōō' mä be re' tä):   The king's first wife.

Sogolon (sô gôlōn'):   Sundiata's mother; also called Sogolon Kedjou (kä' jōō).

Sundiata (sōōn dyä' tä):   Legendary king of Mali; referred to as Djata (dyä' tä) and Sogolon Djata, which means "son of Sogolon." Sundiata is also called Mari (mä' rē) Djata.

Childhood

God has his mysteries which none can fathom. You, perhaps, will be a king. You can do nothing about it. You, on
the other hand, will be unlucky, but you can do nothing
about that either. Each man finds his way already
marked out for him and he can change nothing of it.

Sogolon's son had a slow and difficult childhood. At
the age of three he still crawled along on all-fours while
children of the same age were already walking. He had
nothing of the great beauty of his father Naré Maghan.
He had a head so big that he seemed unable to support
it; he also had large eyes which would open wide whenever anyone entered his mother's house. He was taciturn
and used to spend the whole day just sitting in the middle of the house. Whenever his mother went out he would
crawl on all-fours to rummage about in the calabashes[1]
in search of food, for he was very greedy.

Malicious tongues began to blab. What three-year-old
has not yet taken his first steps? What three-year-old is
not the despair of his parents through his whims and
shifts of mood? What three-year-old is not the joy of his
circle through his backwardness in talking? Sogolon
Djata (for it was thus that they called him, prefixing his
mother's name to his), Sogolon Djata, then, was very different from others of his own age. He spoke little and his
severe face never relaxed into a smile. You would have
thought that he was already thinking, and what amused
children of his age bored him. Often Sogolon would make
some of them come to him to keep him company. These
children were already walking and she hoped that Djata,
seeing his companions walking, would be tempted to do
likewise. But nothing came of it. Besides, Sogolon Djata
would brain the poor little things with his already strong
arms and none of them would come near him any more.

The king's first wife was the first to rejoice at Sogolon
Djata's infirmity. Her own son, Dankaran Touman, was
already eleven. He was a fine and lively boy, who spent
the day running about the village with those of his own
age. He had even begun his initiation in the bush.[2] The

---

1. **calabashes** (kal ə bash' iz) *n*. dried, hollow shells of gourds, used as bowls.
2. **initiation in the bush** education in tribal lore given to twelve-year-old West
African boys so they can become full members of the tribe.

king had had a bow made for him and he used to go behind the town to practice archery with his companions. Sassouma was quite happy and snapped her fingers at Sogolon, whose child was still crawling on the ground. Whenever the latter happened to pass by her house, she would say, "Come, my son, walk, jump, leap about. The jinn[3] didn't promise you anything out of the ordinary, but I prefer a son who walks on his two legs to a lion that crawls on the ground." She spoke thus whenever Sogolon went by her door. The innuendo would go straight home and then she would burst into laughter, that diabolical laughter which a jealous woman knows how to use so well.

Her son's infirmity weighed heavily upon Sogolon Kedjou: she had resorted to all her talent as a sorceress to give strength to her son's legs, but the rarest herbs had been useless. The king himself lost hope.

How impatient man is! Naré Maghan became imperceptibly estranged but Gnankouman Doua never ceased reminding him of the hunter's words. Sogolon became pregnant again. The king hoped for a son, but it was a daughter called Kolonkan. She resembled her mother and had nothing of her father's beauty. The disheartened king debarred Sogolon from his house and she lived in semi-disgrace for a while. Naré Maghan married the daughter of one of his allies, the king of the Kamaras. She was called Namandjé and her beauty was legendary. A year later she brought a boy into the world. When the king consulted soothsayers[4] on the destiny of this son, he received the reply that Namandjé's child would be the right hand of some mighty king. The king gave the newly-born the name of Boukari. He was to be called Manding Boukari or Manding Bory later on.

Naré Maghan was very perplexed. Could it be that the stiff jointed son of Sogolon was the one the hunter soothsayer had foretold?

"The Almighty has his mysteries," Gnankouman Doua would say and, taking up the hunter's words, added, "The silk cotton tree emerges from a tiny seed."

---

3. **jinn** (jin) *n.* supernatural beings that influence human affairs. Their promise was that the son of Sogolon would make Mali a great empire.
4. **soothsayers** (sōōth' sā' ərz) *n.* people who can foretell the future.

One day Naré Maghan came along to the house of Nounfaïri, the blacksmith seer of Niani. He was an old, blind man. He received the king in the anteroom which served as his workshop. To the king's question he replied, "When the seed germinates growth is not always easy; great trees grow slowly but they plunge their roots deep into the ground."

"But has the seed really germinated?" said the king.

"Of course," replied the blind seer. "Only the growth is not as quick as you would like it; how impatient man is."

This interview and Doua's confidence gave the king some assurance. To the great displeasure of Sassouma Bérété the king restored Sogolon to favor and soon another daughter was born to her. She was given the name of Djamarou.

However, all Niani talked of nothing else but the stiff-legged son of Sogolon. He was now seven and he still crawled to get about. In spite of all the king's affection, Sogolon was in despair. Naré Maghan aged and he felt his time coming to an end. Dankaran Touman, the son of Sassouma Bérété, was now a fine youth.

One day Naré Maghan made Mari Djata come to him and he spoke to the child as one speaks to an adult. "Mari Djata, I am growing old and soon I shall be no more among you, but before death takes me off I am going to give you the present each king gives his successor. In Mali every prince has his own griot. Doua's father was my father's griot, Doua is mine and the son of Doua, Balla Fasséké here, will be your griot. Be inseparable friends from this day forward. From his mouth you will hear the history of your ancestors, you will learn the art of governing Mali according to the principles which our ancestors have bequeathed to us. I have served my term and done my duty too. I have done everything which a king of Mali ought to do. I am handing an enlarged kingdom over to you and I leave you sure allies. May your destiny be accomplished, but never forget that Niani is your capital and Mali the cradle of your ancestors."

The child, as if he had understood the whole meaning of the king's words, beckoned Balla Fasséké to approach. He made room for him on the hide he was sitting on and then said, "Balla, you will be my griot."

"Yes, son of Sogolon, if it pleases God," replied Balla Fasséké.

The king and Doua exchanged glances that radiated confidence.

The Lion's Awakening

A short while after this interview between Naré Maghan and his son the king died. Sogolon's son was no more than seven years old. The council of elders met in the king's palace. It was no use Doua's defending the king's will which reserved the throne for Mari Djata, for the council took no account of Naré Maghan's wish. With the help of Sassouma Bérété's intrigues, Dankaran Touman was proclaimed king and a regency council was formed in which the queen mother was all-powerful. A short time after, Doua died.

As men have short memories, Sogolon's son was spoken of with nothing but irony and scorn. People had seen one-eyed kings, one-armed kings, and lame kings, but a stiff-legged king had never been heard tell of. No matter how great the destiny promised for Mari Djata might be, the throne could not be given to someone who had no power in his legs: if the jinn loved him, let them begin by giving him the use of his legs. Such were the remarks that Sogolon heard every day. The queen mother, Sassouma Bérété, was the source of all this gossip.

Having become all-powerful, Sassouma Bérété persecuted Sogolon because the late Naré Maghan had preferred her. She banished Sogolon and her son to a back yard of the palace. Mari Djata's mother now occupied an old hut which had served as a lumber-room of Sassouma's.

The wicked queen mother allowed free passage to all those inquisitive people who wanted to see the child that still crawled at the age of seven. Nearly all the inhabitants of Niani filed into the palace and the poor Sogolon wept to see herself thus given over to public ridicule. Mari Djata took on a ferocious look in front of the crowd of sightseers. Sogolon found a little consolation only in the love of her eldest daughter, Kolonkan. She was four and she could walk. She seemed to understand all her mother's miseries and already she helped her with the housework. Sometimes, when Sogolon was attending to the chores, it was she who stayed beside her sister Djamarou, quite small as yet.

Sogolon Kedjou and her children lived on the queen mother's leftovers, but she kept a little garden in the open ground behind the village. It was there that she passed her brightest moments looking after her onions and gnougous.[5] One day she happened to be short of condiments and went to the queen mother to beg a little baobab leaf.[6]

"Look you," said the malicious Sassouma, "I have a calabash full. Help yourself, you poor woman. As for me, my son knew how to walk at seven and it was he who went and picked these baobab leaves. Take them then, since your son is unequal to mine." Then she laughed derisively with that fierce laughter which cuts through your flesh and penetrates right to the bone.

Sogolon Kedjou was dumbfounded. She had never imagined that hate could be so strong in a human being. With a lump in her throat she left Sassouma's. Outside her hut Mari Djata, sitting on his useless legs, was blandly eating out of a calabash. Unable to contain herself any longer, Sogolon burst into sobs and seizing a piece of wood, hit her son.

"Oh son of misfortune, will you never walk? Through your fault I have just suffered the greatest affront of my life! What have I done, God, for you to punish me in this way?"

Mari Djata seized the piece of wood and, looking at his mother, said, "Mother, what's the matter?"

"Shut up, nothing can ever wash me clean of this insult."

"But what then?"

"Sassouma has just humiliated me over a matter of a baobab leaf. At your age her own son could walk and used to bring his mother baobab leaves."

"Cheer up, Mother, cheer up."

"No. It's too much. I can't."

"Very well then, I am going to walk today," said Mari Djata. "Go and tell my father's smiths to make me the heaviest possible iron rod. Mother, do you want just the leaves of the baobab or would you rather I brought you the whole tree?"

---

5. **gnougous** (no͞o′ go͞oz′) *n.* root vegetables.
6. **baobab** (bā′ ō bab′) **leaf** *n.* baobab is a thick-trunked tree; its leaves are used to flavor foods.

"Ah, my son, to wipe out this insult I want the tree and its roots at my feet outside my hut."

Balla Fasséké, who was present, ran to the master smith, Farakourou, to order an iron rod.

Sogolon had sat down in front of her hut. She was weeping softly and holding her head between her two hands. Mari Djata went calmly back to his calabash of rice and began eating again as if nothing had happened. From time to time he looked up discreetly at his mother, who was murmuring in a low voice, "I want the whole tree, in front of my hut, the whole tree."

All of a sudden a voice burst into laughter behind the hut. It was the wicked Sassouma telling one of her serving women about the scene of humiliation and she was laughing loudly so that Sogolon could hear. Sogolon fled into the hut and hid her face under the blankets so as not to have before her eyes this heedless boy, who was more preoccupied with eating than with anything else. With her head buried in the bedclothes Sogolon wept and her body shook violently. Her daughter, Sogolon Dja-marou, had come and sat down beside her and she said, "Mother, Mother, don't cry. Why are you crying?"

Mari Djata had finished eating and, dragging himself along on his legs, he came and sat under the wall of the hut for the sun was scorching. What was he thinking about? He alone knew.

The royal forges were situated outside the walls and over a hundred smiths worked there. The bows, spears, arrows and shields of Niani's warriors came from there. When Balla Fasséké came to order the iron rod, Farakourou said to him, "The great day has arrived then?"

"Yes. Today is a day like any other, but it will see what no other day has seen."

The master of the forges, Farakourou, was the son of the old Nounfaïri, and he was a soothsayer like his father. In his workshops there was an enormous iron bar wrought by his father, Nounfaïri. Everybody wondered what this bar was destined to be used for. Farakourou called six of his apprentices and told them to carry the iron bar to Sogolon's house.

When the smiths put the gigantic iron bar down in front of the hut the noise was so frightening that So-golon, who was lying down, jumped up with a start. Then Balla Fasséké, son of Gnankouman Doua, spoke.

"Here is the great day, Mari Djata. I am speaking to you, Maghan, son of Sogolon. The waters of the Niger can efface the stain from the body, but they cannot wipe out an insult. Arise, young lion, roar, and may the bush know that from henceforth it has a master."

The apprentice smiths were still there, Sogolon had come out, and everyone was watching Mari Djata. He crept on all-fours and came to the iron bar. Supporting himself on his knees and one hand, with the other hand he picked up the iron bar without any effort and stood it up vertically. Now he was resting on nothing but his knees and held the bar with both his hands. A deathly silence had gripped all those present. Sogolon Djata closed his eyes, held tight, the muscles in his arms tensed. With a violent jerk he threw his weight on to it and his knees left the ground. Sogolon Kedjou was all eyes and watched her son's legs, which were trembling as though from an electric shock. Djata was sweating and the sweat ran from his brow. In a great effort he straightened up and was on his feet at one go—but the great bar of iron was twisted and had taken the form of a bow!

Then Balla Fasséké sang out the "Hymn to the Bow," striking up with his powerful voice:

> "Take your bow, Simbon.
> Take your bow and let us go.
> Take your bow, Sogolon Djata."

When Sogolon saw her son standing she stood dumb for a moment, then suddenly she sang these words of thanks to God, who had given her son the use of his legs:

> "Oh day, what a beautiful day.
> Oh day, day of joy:
> Allah[7] Almighty, you never created a finer day.
> So my son is going to walk!"

Standing in the position of a soldier at ease, Sogolon Djata, supported by his enormous rod, was sweating great beads of sweat. Balla Fasséké's song had alerted the whole palace and people came running from all over to see what had happened, and each stood bewildered

---

7. **Allah** (al' ə) Muslim name for God.

before Sogolon's son. The queen mother had rushed there and when she saw Mari Djata standing up she trembled from head to foot. After recovering his breath Sogolon's son dropped the bar and the crowd stood to one side. His first steps were those of a giant. Balla Fasséké fell into step and pointing his finger at Djata, he cried:

> "Room, room, make room!
> The lion has walked:
> Hide antelopes,
> Get out of his way."

Behind Niani there was a young baobab tree and it was there that the children of the town came to pick leaves for their mothers. With all his might the son of Sogolon tore up the tree and put it on his shoulders and went back to his mother. He threw the tree in front of the hut and said. "Mother, here are some baobab leaves for you. From henceforth it will be outside your hut that the women of Niani will come to stock up."

Children of Wax

Alexander McCall Smith

In this folk tale, a young boy wants to do something that he knows will cause him great harm. Watch for the cause of his wish and for the effects the wish has on him and on his family.

Not far from the hills of the Matopos[1] there lived a family whose children were made out of wax. The mother and the father in this family were exactly the same as everyone else, but for some reason their children had turned out to be made of wax. At first this caused them great sorrow, and they wondered who had put such a spell on them, but later they became quite accustomed to this state of affairs and grew to love their children dearly.

It was easy for the parents to love the wax children. While other children might fight among themselves or forget to do their duty, wax children were always dutiful and never fought with one another. They were also hard workers, one wax child being able to do the work of at least two ordinary children.

The only real problem which the wax children gave was that people had to avoid making fires too close to them, and of course they also had to work only at night. If they worked during the day, when the sun was hot, wax children would melt.

To keep them out of the sun, their father made the wax children a dark hut that had no windows. During the day no rays of the sun could penetrate into the gloom of this hut, and so the wax children were quite safe. Then, when the sun had gone down, the children would come out of their dark hut and begin their work. They tended the crops and watched over the cattle, just as ordinary children did during the daytime.

There was one wax child, Ngwabi, who used to talk about what it was like during the day.

"We can never know what the world is like," he said to his brothers and sisters. "When we come out of our hut everything is quite dark and we see so little."

---

1. **the hills of the Matopos** the blue granite mountains of Matabeleland, a part of Zimbabwe in eastern Africa.

Ngwabi's brothers and sisters knew that what he said was right, but they accepted they would never know what the world looked like. There were other things that they had which the other children did not have, and they contented themselves with these. They knew, for instance, that other children felt pain: wax children never experienced pain, and for this they were grateful.

But poor Ngwabi still longed to see the world. In his dreams he saw the hills in the distance and watched the clouds that brought rain. He saw paths that led this way and that through the bush, and he longed to be able to follow them. But that was something that a wax child could never do, as it was far too dangerous to follow such paths in the night-time.

As he grew older, this desire of Ngwabi's to see what the world was really like when the sun was up grew stronger and stronger. At last he was unable to contain it any more and he ran out of the hut one day when the sun was riding high in the sky and all about there was light and more light. The other children screamed, and some of them tried to grab at him as he left the hut, but they failed to stop their brother and he was gone.

Of course he could not last long in such heat. The sun burned down on Ngwabi and before he had taken more than a few steps he felt all the strength drain from his limbs. Crying out to his brothers and sisters, he fell to the ground and was soon nothing more than a pool of wax in the dust. Inside the hut, afraid to leave its darkness, the other wax children wept for their melted brother.

When night came, the children left their hut and went to the spot where Ngwabi had fallen. Picking up the wax, they went to a special place they knew and there Ngwabi's eldest sister made the wax into a bird. It was a bird with great wings and for feathers they put a covering or leaves from the trees that grew there. These leaves would protect the wax from the sun so that it would not melt when it became day.

After they had finished their task, they told their parents what had happened. The man and woman wept, and each of them kissed the wax model of a bird. Then they set it upon a rock that stood before the wax children's hut.

The wax children did not work that night. At dawn, they were all in their hut, peering through a small crack that there was in the wall. As the light came up over the hills, it made the wax bird seem pink with fire. Then, as the sun itself rose over the fields, the great bird which they had made suddenly moved its wings and launched itself into the air. Soon it was high above the ground, circling over the children's hut. A few minutes later it was gone, and the children knew that their brother was happy at last.

Our History

Mbella Sonne Dipoko

Sometimes things are not what they seem and change is not always positive. This poem has a unique perspective on history.

To pre-colonial Africa

And the waves arrived
Swimming in like hump-backed divers
With their finds from far-away seas.

Their lustre gave the illusion of pearls
5   As shorewards they shoved up mighty canoes
And looked like the carcass of drifting whales.

And our sight misled us
When the sun's glint on the spear's blade
Passed for lightning
10   And the gun-fire of conquest
The thunderbolt that razed the forest.

So did our days change their garb
From hides of leopard skin
To prints of false lions
15   That fall in tatters
Like the wings of whipped butterflies.

The Judgment of the Wind

Harold Courlander and Wolf Leslau

The conflict in this folk tale from Eritrea and Ethiopia involves a human being and nature. The resolution of the conflict has its own special message.

A great snake hid in the forest and preyed upon many living creatures who happened to pass his way. He sometimes went out of the forest and ate goats and cattle of villagers who lived nearby. At last a party of hunters went out to destroy him so that their cattle would be safe. With their spears and shields and hunting knives in their hands they looked for the snake where they found signs of him. Hearing them approach, he fled into a cotton field where a farmer was working.

The farmer was about to drop his tools and run away, but the snake said: "Brother, enemies are following me to kill me. Hide me so that I shan't die." The farmer thought for a moment and then said:

"Though you have a bad reputation, one must have sympathy for the hunted." And he hid the snake in a large pile of cotton standing in his field. When the hunters came along they asked:

"Have you seen the serpent that kills our cattle?"

"I have not seen him," the farmer replied, and the hunters went on.

The snake came out from under the cotton.

"They are gone," the farmer said. "You are safe."

But the snake did not go away. He took hold of the farmer.

"What are you doing?" the farmer asked.

"I am hungry," the snake said. "I shall have to eat you."

"What? I save your life and then you wish to destroy mine?"

"I am hungry," the snake replied. "I have no choice."

"You are ungrateful," the farmer said.

"I am hungry," the snake said.

"Since it is like this, let us have our case judged," the farmer said.

"Very well. Let the tree judge us."

So they went before the huge sycamore tree which grew at the side of the road. Each of them stated his case, while the tree listened.

Then the tree said to the farmer:

"I stand here at the edge of the road and give shade. Tired travelers come and sit in my shade to rest. And then when they are through they cut off my branches to make ax handles and plows. Man is ungrateful for the good I do him. Therefore, since it is this way, I cannot judge in your favor. The snake is entitled to eat you."

The snake and the man went then to the river, and again they told their story. The river listened, and then it said to the farmer:

"I flow here between my banks and provide man with water. Without me, man would suffer; he would not have enough to drink. In the dry season when there are no rains, man comes and digs holes in my bed to find water for himself and his cattle. But when the heavy rains come I am filled to the brink. I cannot hold so much water, and I overflow onto man's fields. Then man becomes angry. He comes to me and curses me and throws stones at me. He forgets the good I do him. I have no use for man. Therefore, since this is man's nature, I cannot judge in your favor. The snake may eat you."

The snake and the man went to the grass, and once more they told their story. The grass listened, and then it said to the farmer:

"I grow here in the valley and provide food for man's cattle. I give myself to man to make roofs for his houses, and to make baskets for his kitchen. But then man puts the torch to me when I am old, and burns me. And after that he plows me under and plants grain in my place, and wherever I grow among the grain he digs me out and kills me. Man is not good. Therefore, I cannot judge in your favor. The snake may eat you."

The snake took hold of the farmer and they went away from the grass.

"The judgment is very cruel," the farmer said.

But on the road they met the wind. And though he had no hope, the farmer once more told his story. The wind listened, and then it said:

"All things live according to their nature. The grass grows to live and man burns it to live. The river flows to live, and overflows its banks because that is its nature; it cannot help it. And man grieves when his planted fields are flooded, for they are his life. The tree cherishes its branches because they are its beauty. And the snake eats whatever it finds, for that, too, is his nature. So you see one cannot blame the tree, the grass, and the river for their judgment, nor can one blame the snake for his hunger."

The farmer became even more sad, for he saw no way out for him. But the wind went on:

"So this is not a matter for judgment at all, but for all things acting according to their nature. Therefore, let us dance and sing in thanks because all things are as they are."

And the wind gave the farmer a drum to play, and he gave the snake a drum to play also. In order to hold his drum the snake had to let go of the farmer.

"As your nature is to eat man, eat man," the wind sang to the snake.

The wind turned to the farmer:

"As your nature is not to be eaten, do not be eaten!" it sang.

"Amen!" the farmer replied with feeling. And as the snake was no longer holding him, he threw down his drum and fled safely to his village.

African Musical Instruments

from The Music of Africa

Dr. Fred Warren with Lee Warren

As this selection shows, African musical instruments such as the drum, the xylophone, and the mbira play a unique role in a part of the world where making music is part of living.

Where music is found to be woven into the very fabric of people's lives, it is likely that the people will be personally involved both in the process of making the instruments as well as the music itself. And, just as the quality of craftsmanship in music making is not shared equally by all tribes or the individuals in them, so, too, are there significant differences in the art of making instruments and the kind of instruments made among both individuals and groups.

Environment has affected the kinds of instruments produced in various parts of Africa. If there were no trees or reeds from which to make musical instruments, the people turned to singing only. This is especially noticeable in the southern tip of Africa where only one percent of the entire country was covered by natural woods. Few drums are to be found in South Africa; their music is almost exclusively vocal with simple accompaniments such as hand-clapping and stamping.

Among the earliest recorded observations about African music were those made and written down by the mid-sixteenth-century Portuguese explorers and missionaries. Travelling in Central and Southern Africa, they remarked on the instruments which accompanied the chiefs upon their journeys, the presence of numerous musicians in the royal households, and the continual singing and dancing in which everyone participated.

The three kinds of musical instruments most frequently mentioned were the *drum*, the *xylophone* and the *mbira*, the last being a peculiarly African instrument consisting of a number of short metal reeds and which has no European equivalent. (In later times, the mbira was misnamed the "kaffir piano." A *Kaffir* is a member of one of the Bantu tribes of South Africa.)

The Drum

The most widely used instrument in Africa is the *drum*. Africans drum when they are happy and they drum when they are sad. On important state occasions such as the welcoming of a visiting dignitary from a foreign land, the drum can be the most important musical instrument played, with the drummer's status, accordingly, impressively high. An African child will drum on almost anything he can put his hands and fingers on. He will drum on tables, chairs, boxes, packing cases and kerosene tins. To say that Africans are fond of drumming is an understatement. It's more accurate to say the only time he doesn't drum is when he is asleep!

Why do Africans find drumming so exciting? For part of the answer we have to look at the role that drums play in an African's life, and remember that what a drummer plays has a meaning. In Africa, drums *say* something and an African drums for a *purpose*. Take the *talking* drums of the Ashanti people of Ghana, for example. The drummer actually talks with the *atumpan* drum, and similar stories can be told of drums found in other parts of Africa. The talking drums of Africa are essentially language drums.

You will remember that most African languages are tonal languages. A higher-pitched drum corresponds to the high-pitched syllable and a lower-pitched drum to the low-pitched syllable. This enables the drummer to send messages. For instance, a European coming into the forest would be described as "A man from the outside world coming to the forest"; a native would be described as "returning home." Talking drums can be heard as far away as six or seven miles, and from that point the message can be relayed another six or seven miles, and so on.

When the African was brought to the United States as a slave, he brought with him his music and dance, his history and his religion; he brought with him his memories and his way of life. This cultural heritage was systematically and deliberately destroyed. Religious practices, along with the music and dance, the drums and the rattles and the bells, all of which were an integral part of African religion and the African way of life, were banned in many parts of America. They were forbidden because of a fear of "subversive activities." There were, after all, some one hundred and thirty major slave revolts which occurred between 1663 and 1865. Legislation was enacted, making it unlawful for the African to play his drums, and for the slaves to gather even for the purpose of dancing. In 1817, for example, the Municipal Council of New Orleans issued an ordinance forbidding slave gatherings for the purpose of dancing except on Sundays and only in places designated by the Mayor. Congo Square (today known as Beauregard Square) was established as the place for such dances, but only under police supervision.

Undoubtedly, such modern inventions in the twentieth century as the telephone and other communication systems have taken the place of the drums as means of communication between Africans. However, up until a relatively short time ago, the talking drums of Africa were an effective way for Africans to communicate with each other. A highly skilled drummer or a master drummer can perform messages on the drums because he is able to play the variety of rhythms which are part of the vocabulary of any language, as well as the rising and falling pitch levels of the African tonal languages.

It takes years of practice and experience to become a *master drummer* and, once having achieved the status, the master drummer is publicly recognized as an outstanding artist. The fact is that a good African master drummer is a distinguished musician, judged by any standards, African or Western. The African talking drums are capable of producing a wide range of tones which all fall within the range of the adult male's speaking voice. But let us take a look at how a drum actually talks.

To begin with, a good drummer can produce different tones by the way he plays the drum. It can be played with the palms of the hand, the fingers, a stick or any combination of these. Or, a drummer can produce a wide range of tones of different pitches with the *donno* drum in West Africa. It is commonly referred to as the *hourglass* drum because of its shape. The hourglass is a double-headed drum which is held in the left armpit. The left arm squeezes the strings which hold the drum heads together, thereby tightening and loosening the drum heads and raising and lowering the pitch.

When the drumming is associated with dancing, singing or some kind of drama, the African generally uses a full ensemble of drums, or a drum orchestra. Often rattles and bells are added. When an African wishes to "speak," however, he uses only one drum or a pair of drums. When a pair of drums is used—for example, the atumpan drums—one of them speaks with a low voice (it is called a male drum), and the other with a high voice (this is the female drum).

African drums talk by imitating the way African people talk. First, they imitate the rhythm of the words and phrases which make up the sentences of African languages. This is why African children are taught to play drums by means of words and sentences. You can easily demonstrate for yourself how this works by handclapping the rhythm of the words of a familiar poem or song, syllable by syllable. If the rhythm is clearly articulated, it will make the poem or song recognizable to your listener.

Secondly, the African drummer imitates the various tones or pitch level—the high, the low and those in-between—of the language. For example, in the language of Twi (pronounced "chwee") the question, *Wo din de sen* means "What is your name?" There are four syllables in this sentence; the first is a low tone, the second high, the third low and the fourth high. And so, the drummer will play his male and female drums as follows:

1	2	3	4
male	female	male	female
Wo	din	de	sen
	(What is your name?)		

You can see how important it is to learn how to listen to the talking drums, as well as play them.

Sometimes other instruments are added to the drums. Basically, however, a traditional African orchestra can consist of an ensemble of drums—drums of every size and shape—just as the basic ingredient of the traditional Western orchestra is an ensemble of strings. An African drum orchestra can produce a variety of different tonal qualities as well as pitch levels. Some of the drums have a high pitch, others have a low pitch, and others are in-between. Some drums have a hard piercing tone, others have a clear ringing tone, and others sound heavy or dull.

In addition, there are orchestras which correspond to our Western chamber music ensembles. Some of them concentrate on stringed instruments, others on brass and woodwinds. In Africa, it is possible to have an orchestra of four horns plus rhythm; three flutes plus rhythm or three xylophones plus rhythm.

There is one example of an African instrument ensemble where the drums are completely absent. This is a string orchestra. In its traditional setting in Nigeria, the string ensemble is a trio, consisting of a string player, a singer chanting in monotone and a third musician supplying rhythmic accompaniment on a large gourd known as a calabash.

In the musical ensembles which consist primarily of wind or string instruments, the emphasis is on melodic improvisation rather than rhythmic improvisation.

And so now another myth about Africa can be laid to rest—the assumption that African musical instruments consist only of drums. Actually, most of the varieties of musical instruments known to man are to be found in Africa. They include examples of the four categories of instruments which have been set up by musicologists and anthropologists:

1) *Idiophones*—Instruments whose entire bodies vibrate, such as rattles, bells, xylophones, hand pianos, etc.
2) *Membranophones*—Instruments with vibrating membranes or parchment skins, such as drums.
3) *Aerophones*—Instruments which enclose a body of vibrating air, such as flutes and trumpets.
4) *Chordophones*—Instruments with vibrating strings, such as fiddles, lutes, zithers, etc.

In Western music, we classify musical instruments as *percussion* (membranophones and idiophones); *strings* (chordophones); and *woodwinds* and *brass* (aerophones).

One instrument has strangely escaped classification by the scholars in spite of the fact that it may very well be an even more widely used percussion instrument than the drum. It is the human body. Not merely torso, not only limbs, but the *body* has been used as a percussion instrument in Africa more effectively than probably anywhere else in the world. An amusing challenge is to think of the different ways in which you can turn yourself into a "percussion" instrument: you might try clapping your hands, stamping your feet, clacking your tongue, slapping your chest or thigh. You might even try tapping your open mouth while singing and listening for the changes in the resonance of your voice. Try singing a song and improvising several different patterns of rhythmic accompaniment, using your own body exclusively. The next step is to share the experience: Gather your friends some evening and divide them into handclappers, knee slappers, foot stampers, finger clickers, tongue clackers, or any other "body musician," each one playing a different rhythm while everyone sings a familiar song. Imagine the distinction of establishing the first "Body Percussion Ensemble" in your neighborhood!

The Xylophone
Another instrument commonly found in many parts of Africa is the *xylophone*, several types of which are indigenous to West, Central, East and Southeast Africa. Differences exist in the musical functions they perform, and the type of musical ensemble in which they participate. Xylophones are played alone; they are played along with drums; they are played as an accompaniment to singing and dancing; they are played in orchestras of xylophones.

There are xylophones which can play only several different notes and there are xylophones which can play about thirty different notes. There may be one, two, three or as many as six performers on a single xylophone, and a solo musician may use only one or as many as four beaters or mallets in performance. African xylophones are constructed in a variety of ways, and from a variety of materials. Some instruments, known as *log xylophones*, consist of a set of wooden keys laid across banana trunks. Banana trunks make excellent cushions for the keys to rest on and enable the keys to vibrate freely. In addition, banana trunks, because they are hollow inside, are excellent resonators. Sometimes, wooden keys are simply laid across the performer's legs, sometimes they are laid across two trees that have been cut down. In West Africa, a commonly found xylophone consists of wooden keys, supported on a wooden frame, with each key having its own gourd or calabash resonator hanging beneath.

There is strong evidence that the xylophone may also have originated in Africa. Reportedly, it was in use in Mali in the thirteenth century and this predates its first appearance in Europe by a couple of hundred years. It is almost certain that an African xylophone was brought to the Americas on the first slave ships which sailed from Mozambique to South America. Have you heard of the *marimba*? It is one of the most popular instruments in Latin America and has been incorporated into the music of the United States and Europe. *Marimba* is an African (Bantu) word for the wooden xylophone with resonators found along the East Africa coast. That makes the African xylophone the ancestor of our marimba.

The Mbira

Second only to the drum as the most popular folk instrument in Africa is the *mbira*. It is a small instrument with a number of metal reeds of varying length which are attached to a sounding board or box and which you pluck with your thumbs. The pitch is determined by the length of the metal reed and the number of reeds will vary, anywhere from seven to eight, to fifteen or more. The mbira, which has over one hundred different African names, originated in Africa. It is sometimes referred to as a "thumb piano" or "hand piano." An intimate instrument, the mbira is ideally appropriate to personal music making. It produces a soft and gentle sound and is also especially suited for fast playing. The first non-Africans to "discover" the mbira were Portuguese explorers in the 16th century. Father Dos Santos, a Portuguese priest and missionary, wrote the following about the mbira in 1586:

> It is all made of irons about a palm in length, tempered in the fire so that each has a different sound . . . They strike the keys as lightly as a good player strikes those of the harpsichord. Thus the iron rods being shaken, and the blows resounding above the hollow of the bowl . . . they produce altogether a sweet and gentle harmony of accordant sounds . . . It is very soft and makes but little noise.

Interestingly enough, the mbira, *invented by Africans*, has a delicate and sensitive tonal quality, and is completely different from the "big" sound we have been brought up to expect from African instruments. Come to think of it, we don't remember seeing a single mbira in any of the Tarzan pictures.

The few instruments we described are a mere sampling of the many the African uses as tools to fashion his music. It is not unreasonable to conclude that in the hands of an African just about anything can be, and is, used as a musical instrument. In a society where the making of music is part of the very process of living, this should offer no surprise; for, in reality, the sounds of African music are the sounds of Africans at work and at play.

The Ancient Americas

The Historical Background

from Everyday Life of the Maya

Ralph Whitlock

This summary of Mayan history gives the context for a brilliant and sophisticated civilization.

The first men to set foot on the American continent were doubtless unaware that they were doing so. They were almost certainly hunters following herds of caribou and mammoths eastwards from north-eastern Siberia over tundra[1] that is now submerged beneath the Bering Sea. The likeliest period for the beginning of the trek was around 29,000 B.C., when, early in the Pleistocene Age, so much of the water in the northern seas was locked in a vast sheet of ice that the sea-level dropped by several hundred feet.

The migration into America was neither deliberate nor large-scale. Smaller family or tribal groups drifted, in the course of many generations, across the tundra in pursuit of game. The movement doubtless lasted for many thousands of years, until the 'land bridge' was eventually broken by the rising seas, and involved many peoples entirely unconnected with each other. They wandered on, with the passing of the centuries, until by about 9000 B.C. some had reached the Antarctic tip of South America.

The development of civilization on the American continent followed the same pattern as in the Old World. For millennia men gained their living by hunting and fishing, gradually perfecting new tools and weapons, such as grooved stone tips for hunting spears and woven nets for catching birds and fish. They also collected berries, seeds and roots in season. Among the earliest plants to be cultivated seem to have been squashes and beans, with maize, or corn, appearing soon afterwards. Maize, which grows plentifully in the wild in Central America, would be an obvious choice for women looking for seeds to grind. It was certainly under cultivation and making an important contribution to the diet of tribes living in central southern Mexico by 5000 B.C.

---

1. **tundra** (tun' drǝ) *n.* a vast, treeless plain.

With cultivation Man ceases, after a time, to be nomadic.[2] He puts a fence around his cultivated fields, builds a permanent house to live in, and combines with neighbours to form a settlement which is defensible against marauding animals and human enemies. Such villages grow into towns; and towns combine to form states. A surplus in the amount of food produced enables some of the citizens to specialize, in such varied spheres as weaving and religion, ironwork and oratory, art and soldiering. In Middle America the countryside seems to have been studded with farms and villages by about 2000 B.C. In the following millennium a number of tribes made parallel and more or less simultaneous advances towards civilization. Their origins and their relationship to each other remain obscure, though our knowledge of the period is steadily increasing.

Early Inhabitants of Central America

One of the most gifted and most enigmatic of these early peoples were the Olmecs, whose civilization sprang up, apparently suddenly, along the northern shores of the Isthmus of Tehuantepec around 1200 B.C. This is a little to the west of the indisputable Mayan area, but some authorities think that the Olmecs may have been a Mayan tribe. Through the mists which obscure the mysterious Olmecs we see emerging several characteristics of early civilizations that have their counterparts in the Old World and were later to develop considerably in America. Most important is the appearance of a social system dominated by priests and kings, perhaps often united in the same personages. Another interesting parallel with the Old World is the use made by the Olmecs of irrigation by the rivers which flow into the Gulf of Mexico. These, like the Nile, bring down silt after the rains, in floods which the Olmecs harnessed to their agriculture.

The Olmecs, like Stone Age peoples in other regions, undertook the transport of huge blocks of stone over considerable distances. Their favorite stone was basalt, quarried from the Tuxtla mountains, which run parallel to the coast. Archaeologists have found great basalt heads, often weighing as much as 20 tons. The Olmecs

---

2. **nomadic** (nō mad′ ik) *adj.* having no permanent home.

seem also to have invented the wheel, or to have acquired a knowledge of it from some outside source, and they mounted clay figures, apparently toys, to roll on wheels. Why they never developed this invention for practical purposes is still a mystery.

The Olmecs are thought to have been the inventors of the Long Count, the system of reckoning which enabled the Maya to become such proficient mathematicians and astronomers. They are also credited with the invention of writing, again transmitted to the Maya. Clearly, the civilizations of the Olmecs and the Maya were intimately related, and many experts believe that they were simply different facets of the same phenomenon.

Before we enter the time zone of the full-fledged Mayan civilization it will be helpful to consider a few other early indigenous cultures of Middle America which influenced it. Near Oaxaca, capital of Oaxaca state in southern central Mexico, the hilltop of Monte Alban was occupied and levelled by the Zapotec people as early as about 600 B.C. The bas-relief sculpture known as 'The Dancers,' on the huge masonry blocks in the foundations of a wall, belongs to this early period. The great days of the Zapotecs came later, however, between 300 and 900 A.D., which coincides with the peak period of many of the Mayan cities.

Twenty-five miles north-east of Mexico City, the ruins of Teotihuacan were regarded by the Aztecs with some awe just before the Spanish conquest. Teotihuacan was a popular place of pilgrimage for the Aztec aristocracy who, however, had no knowledge of its history. To them it was 'the home of the gods,' and they worshipped at the mouldering shrines. Teotihuacan, still an impressive site, was not, however, exceedingly old. It was probably founded about the beginning of the Christian era and was destroyed by invaders some 750 years later. Thus it was one of the civilizations that developed independently and more or less simultaneously with the Mayan.

Teotihuacan was not a Mayan city. For archaeologists, however, it provides a vital clue to the history of the area, for its influence is clearly traceable in the ruins of Kaminaljuyu, an early Mayan site on the outskirts of Guatemala City. Here, as at Teotihuacan, are raised platforms crowned by temple pyramids; here are rich ornaments and painted pottery, much of it actually brought (no doubt on men's backs) from Teotihuacan itself, nearly 900 miles away.

Kaminaljuyu seems to have begun in a humble way in the fifth or fourth century B.C. and to have developed a brilliant culture by the first or second century A.D. Thereafter it declined a little, perhaps eclipsed by other Mayan cities farther north, and about A.D. 400 it fell under the control of Teotihuacan. The Teotihuacan invaders set about creating a miniature Teotihuacan at Kaminaljuyu, despite being handicapped by having only clay instead of stone to work with. Teotihuacan rulers definitely lived at Kaminaljuyu and were buried there, with great pomp and elaborate provisions for their future life. Their dominion seems to have lasted till Teotihuacan itself was destroyed, about A.D. 750.

Distant as is Kaminaljuyu from Teotihuacan it by no means marks the limits of Teotihuacan influence. Tikal, in the heart of the Peten and only 30 miles from the Belize border with Guatemala, also fell under the city's control. Tikal, like so many of the cities of the Mayan region, had its origins about 600 B.C. and eventually became the largest of all the Mayan cities. It has six temple pyramids, one of which is 210 feet high, and one scientist has estimated that its probable population at its zenith was 50,000. Stelae at Tikal dating from around A.D. 500 show Teotihuacan warriors and the Teotihuacan rain-god. But it has not yet been resolved whether this and similar discoveries are to be interpreted as evidence of trade or of conquest.

It is obvious, therefore, that the Mayan civilization did not evolve in a vacuum. All around the Maya lands were other related peoples, developing on parallel lines. Between them and the Maya there was a constant interchange of goods and ideas, both by trade and by war. Whether or not the Aztecs and the Incas had any knowledge of each other, the Aztecs and the Maya were certainly aware of one another's existence. The Aztecs, however, achieved power in Mexico when the Maya were already in decline.

A Brief Summary of Mayan History
Students of Mayan history divide it into several periods as follows:

The *Formative Period* lasted from 1500 or 1000 B.C. to around A.D. 150. During this time the Maya of the

Guatemalan highlands and the Pacific coastal region seem to have developed most quickly, though towards the end of the period temples were being erected in Yucatan and the Peten.

The *Proto-Classic Period* occupied the years from A.D. 150–300, and laid the foundations of the brilliant Classic Period that was to follow. Some authorities dispense with the Proto-Classic period and consider it part of the Formative.

The *Classic Period*, extending from A.D. 300–925, saw the high flowering of the Mayan civilization, though from about A.D. 800 to 925 there was evidence of some decline.

The *Inter-regnum* lasted for some 50 years in the tenth century A.D., when Maya society sank to the cultural level which had prevailed approximately 900 years earlier.

The *Post-Classic Period* saw the revival of Mayan culture and the growth of new cities and city states, particularly in Yucatan. This period lasted until the Spanish conquest.

The independence of the Maya finally came to an end with the fall of the city of Tayasal, capital of the Itza people, in the Peten, in 1697.

It must be remembered that the early dating is almost entirely archaeological rather than documentary. It rests largely on a comparison of artefacts and styles. The earliest date recorded in inscriptions is the equivalent of 31 B.C., on a stelae at Chiapa de Corzo, in the Mexican state of Chiapas. This is outside the limits of strictly Mayan territory, though it uses the Long Count, a form of calendar afterwards associated with the Maya. The earliest inscriptions so far discovered in recognized Mayan lands are dated A.D. 292 and 320, dates on the threshold of the splendid Classic Period.

The Mayan sites of the Classic Period were not cities in the contemporary European sense but were primarily cult centres. The distribution of peasant dwellings in the immediate vicinity of the temple pyramids was only slightly more concentrated than in the more distant countryside. The construction of the cities' temples and palaces required stone, and it is natural that, given a fairly even distribution of population over the whole Mayan region, the cities should have proliferated where stone was most easily obtained and worked.

Two important Classic sites in the Peten were Tikal and Uaxactun. The ruins of Tikal, probably the most impressive of all Mayan sites in Guatemala, cover more than 25 square miles. It has eight mighty pyramids, one of them 229 feet high, unnumbered stelae, palaces and altars (for no more than a quarter of the area has yet been excavated), and a grand plaza measuring 400 feet by 250 feet.

Uaxactun, only 35 miles away, is somewhat smaller but shares many of the same characteristics. Both are in low-lying, humid country, now densely afforested and very sparsely populated. The mosquito-infested jungles seem to us a poor place for the building of temples and civilized city-states. In the Mayan Classic Period, however, most of the land was probably cleared and cultivated, the clearing being, in any case, inevitable, if only to provide wood for lime-burning to make lime mortar. This material was used in the construction of nearly all Mayan buildings.

The earliest date mentioned on inscriptions at Uaxactun is A.D. 328; at Tikal, on the Leiden plaque which was found in the vicinity, A.D. 320, or, if one excludes that on the grounds that this may not have been its home locality, A.D. 416. These are the two oldest identified sites in the lowlands. Others with early dates include Balakbal and Uolantun, both of the early fifth century and both situated quite near Tikal. Later in the century the Mayan civilization spread outwards and by early in the sixth century had reached Chichen Itza, far in the north of Yucatan, and Copan, on the Guatemala–Honduras border. The expansion continued until nearly the end of the eighth century, by which time virtually the whole of the central and lowland Maya region was studded with temples and site centres (which for convenience are usually called cities, with the reservations already expressed).

The Classic Period which saw the expansion and florescence[3] of the Mayan civilization is generally referred to as the Old Empire, but it was not strictly an empire. The Mayan political system was based on the independent city-state, in which respect it was similar to the organization of city-states in medieval Europe and classical

---

3. **florescence** (flō rés əns) n. blooming.

Greece. Each state had as its head a hereditary ruler or chief. Military authority was in the hands of a war chief, who was elected for a three-year period. There was a hereditary priestly caste which was exceedingly influential. Certain authorities consider that, in some instances at least, the religious authority was combined, at its highest level, with the secular in the person of the hereditary ruler.

Each state made its own alliances with its neighbours. The Mayan people, however, shared a common culture and religion and spoke related languages. A basis therefore existed for a closer political association, and this was achieved in the heyday of the Classic Period by a system of confederations, on much the same lines as the Hanseatic League or the league of Greek cities. Some of the largest cities, such as Tikal, gathered into their orbit a number of smaller centres, whose own chiefs served as an aristocratic caste to assist the chief ruler in the business of government.

As the civilization of the Classic Period gathered momentum, the principal Mayan cities sent out 'colonists' who deliberately founded other centres. It is probably more correct to think of these 'colonists,' not as peasants setting out to form new agricultural settlements, but as priests and nobles establishing new centres of worship.

Paul Rivet, a great French authority on the Maya, asserts that between A.D. 534 and 633 the Maya founded ten new cities, five of them in the centre of their area and five on the fringes. One was the city of Tulum, on the distant eastern coast of Yucatan. In the next century 14 more new cities were added, among them Chakanputun, on the Gulf coast of Yucatan. Another period of expansion extended from A.D. 731–90, when three splendid new centres were founded at Nakum, Seibal and Bonampak, all in the central region.

Soon afterwards decline set in. After about 850 few new sites were created and the older ones were gradually abandoned. As the tenth century wore on all the magnificent civilization that had been the Old Empire faded away.

Why this should have happened is still a mystery. There is no trace of the large-scale destruction and fires which would have marked an invasion or an earthquake. Geology suggests no dramatic change of climate. An epidemic is a possibility, but the two likeliest scourges, yellow fever and malaria, are thought only to have been introduced to the Americas at the time of the Spanish conquest. The explanation generally accepted at present is that the soil was exhausted by overcropping and wasteful agricultural techniques. Tribes employed the slash-and-burn system, a technique which requires plenty of land. The very success of the Mayan civilization of the Old Empire could, by increasing the population and therefore the pressure on the land, have provided the seeds of its own demise.

The founding of new cities which characterized Mayan activity during the height of the Classic Period may have been motivated by a realization of the dangers of the situation. Viewed through the mists of more than a thousand years, the scene is one of swirling motion. New colonists are thrown out to the fringes of the settled territory, there to establish new centres; in the next century the activity moves back to the heartland and we see new cities being built there.

To give an instance the outline history of which seems fairly clear, the Itza people moved from the central Mayan area northwestwards into Yucatan early in the sixth century A.D. and there established the city of Chichen Itza, about 50 miles inland from the north coast of the peninsula. Nearly 200 years later (the recorded date is A.D. 692) they moved on 150 or 200 miles to found the city of Chakanputun, on the west coast. About A.D. 930 they started moving back again, accompanied by a warlike Indian tribe from central Mexico, who provided the leader, a man named Kukulkan. By 987 they were safely reinstated in Chichen Itza. Not content with occupying the old site, they founded several other cities, including Mayapan which became the last great Mayan 'capital,' and, in 1007, Uxmal.

The civilization that grew up around these settlements, popularly known as the New Empire, represents the last brilliant flowering of the Maya genius. For 100 years or so Mayan arts and architecture flourished as in the great days of the Old Empire, or Classic Period. Then it was interrupted by civil war, the two chief protagonists being the citizens of Chichen Itza and of Mayapan. It seems that Chichen Itza was controlled by the Itza people, who were Mayan, while at Mayapan Indians from Mexico's central plateau were predominant. The latter called in mercenary auxiliaries from their homeland and finally defeated the Itza in 1194. Then, for some 250 years, relative peace prevailed. It was, however, a restless peace, for Mayapan seems to have ruled harshly. In 1441 the subject peoples revolted, killed their ruler and sacked the city of Mayapan.

Deterioration set in rapidly. Yucatan split into numerous little city-states, waging almost incessant war. Urban life declined, and with it most civilized arts. A destructive hurricane which hit the peninsula in 1464 hastened the process. Epidemics also seem to have played their part.

The Itza people decamped and trekked south to the neighbourhood of Tikal, where they occupied Tayasal, a site which they had abandoned in the ninth century. There, hidden by unhealthy jungles which were by then almost uninhabited, they retained their independence until 1697, when the Spanish commander, Martin de Ursaa, finally took Tayasal.

Such is a brief, perhaps over-brief, summary of Mayan history. Although the Mayan passion for the calendar has provided us with plenty of dates, the accompanying script has not yet been deciphered, and many of the events are subject to different interpretations by different experts. The situation is rendered more confused by the duplication of names; there are, for instance, two Kukulkans, separated by several centuries. The first of these heroes had, by a natural metamorphosis, become a god, and, to increase the confusion, Kukulkan in Mayan means exactly the same as Quetzalcoatl—'feathered serpent.'

The Spanish Conquest

The Spaniards first landed in Yucatan in 1511 but, being preoccupied with the much richer cities of Mexico, did not begin its conquest until 1527–8. The Mayan cities of northern Yucatan, then numbering 16 or 18 and in a state of chronic anarchy,[4] were in no condition to offer an organized or united resistance. Nevertheless, they did not fall easily. Resorting to guerilla warfare, the Maya harassed the Spaniards for several decades.

---

4. **anarchy** (an´ ər kē) *n.* complete absence of government.

After subduing and pacifying Mexico, Cortes despatched two of his lieutenants to deal with the kingdoms farther south. The able but ruthless Pedro de Alvarado was given the task of conquering Guatemala, which he did against desperate resistance. Here, as in Aztec Mexico, treachery and rivalry among the Indian tribes contributed to the Spanish victory. Guatemala, too, had its people who hated their neighbours worse than the Spaniards, whom they were prepared to help in order to settle old scores.

At the same time, another of Cortes's henchmen, Cristobal de Olid, was sent to subdue Honduras. De Olid, however, decided that this was a heaven-sent opportunity to set up a kingdom of his own. He reckoned without his commander. Starting from Tuzantepetl, near the northern coast of the Isthmus of Tehuantepec, Cortes, with a small army of Spaniards and Mexican auxiliaries, made an epic march across the unknown and harsh interior of Yucatan, to Nito, on the Caribbean coast. It was a desperate trek, through marshes, lagoons and jungles where, wrote Cortes, 'the overhanging foliage threw so deep a shade that the soldiers could not see where to set their feet.' Though his followers were ragged and fever-racked, the indomitable Cortes on reaching Honduras promptly put an end to the rebellion.

Then it was the turn of the Maya of Yucatan. Cortes's route had taken him across the broad base of the peninsula, through sparsely inhabited country. The remnants of Mayan tribes whom he found there told him they were descended from an ancient and mighty nation. Cortes also knew that in northern Yucatan there were cities and civilized men, though possibly not much gold. Francisco de Montejo was sent to deal with them.

Advancing from the west, Montejo met at first with little success. After his army had been broken down by a war of ambushes and attrition, he embarked on ships and sailed around to the other side of the peninsula, where he made a base at Chetumal. Driven from there, he took his flotilla[5] down to Ulua, in Honduras, leaving the Maya victors in the first round. The campaign had begun in 1527 and it was now 1535.

---

5. **flotilla** (flō til' ə) *n.* fleet of boats.

Under Montejo's son a new campaign was launched in 1542. Thanks largely to internecine[6] feuds among the Maya, it was eventually successful. By 1546 the northern cities had been subdued, with horrific slaughter, and half a million Maya had been sold into slavery.

One Mayan tribe, the Itza, escaped by retreating to their ancestral home in the wastes of the Peten. There they maintained a small independent state until 1697. A Spanish missionary then negotiated the surrender of the Itza to a Spanish army, but at the last moment the truce was broken, by hotheads on both sides, and the last Mayan stronghold perished, as had so many other Indian cities, in a holocaust of fire and blood.

When all was over, the Maya settled down to a continuing sullen resentment against their conquerors. It is not, indeed, until the present century that many of the indigenous peoples of Yucatan have become at all reconciled to government by distant Mexico. Even now it is likely that resentment still smoulders in the secret Indian soul. That and apathy, bred by centuries of oppression and injustice, have militated against any revival of the old artistic genius of the Maya. There would seem to be no other reason why the present-day Maya should not have latent gifts as pronounced as those of their ancestors.

---

6. **internecine** (in tər nē′ sin) *adj.* involving conflict within a group.

How Coyote Stole Fire

Gail Robinson and Douglas Hill

In this Native American myth explaining the origins of fire, Coyote feels sorry for the sufferings of human beings during the cold, dark winter.

Long ago, when man was newly come into the world, there were days when he was the happiest creature of all. Those were the days when spring brushed across the willow tails, or when his children ripened with the blueberries in the sun of summer, or when the goldenrod bloomed in the autumn haze.

But always the mists of autumn evenings grew more chill, and the sun's strokes grew shorter. Then man saw winter moving near, and he became fearful and unhappy. He was afraid for his children, and for the grandfathers and grandmothers who carried in their heads the sacred tales of the tribe. Many of these, young and old, would die in the long, ice-bitter months of winter.

Coyote, like the rest of the People, had no need for fire. So he seldom concerned himself with it, until one spring day when he was passing a human village. There the women were singing a song of mourning for the babies and the old ones who had died in the winter. Their voices moaned like the west wind through a buffalo skull, prickling the hairs on Coyote's neck.

"Feel how the sun is now warm on our backs," one of the men was saying. "Feel how it warms the earth and makes these stones hot to the touch. If only we could have had a small piece of the sun in our teepees during the winter."

Coyote, overhearing this, felt sorry for the men and women. He also felt that there was something he could do to help them. He knew of a faraway mountaintop where the three Fire Beings lived. These Beings kept fire to themselves, guarding it carefully for fear that man might somehow acquire it and become as strong as they. Coyote saw that he could do a good turn for man at the expense of these selfish Fire Beings.

So Coyote went to the mountain of the Fire Beings and crept to its top, to watch the way that the Beings guarded their fire. As he came near, the Beings leaped to their feet and gazed searchingly round their camp. Their eyes glinted like bloodstones, and their hands were clawed like the talons of the great black vulture.

"What's that? What's that I hear?" hissed one of the Beings.

"A thief, skulking in the bushes!" screeched another.

The third looked more closely, and saw Coyote. But he had gone to the mountaintop on all-fours, so the Being thought she saw only an ordinary coyote slinking among the trees.

"It is no one, it is nothing!" she cried, and the other two looked where she pointed and also saw only a gray coyote. They sat down again by their fire and paid Coyote no more attention.

So he watched all day and night as the Fire Beings guarded their fire. He saw how they fed it pine cones and dry branches from the sycamore trees. He saw how they stamped furiously on runaway rivulets[1] of flame that sometimes nibbled outwards on edges of dry grass. He saw also how, at night, the Beings took turns to sit by the fire. Two would sleep while one was on guard; and at certain times the Being by the fire would get up and go into their teepee, and another would come out to sit by the fire.

Coyote saw that the Beings were always jealously watchful of their fire except during one part of the day. That was in the earliest morning, when the first winds of dawn arose on the mountains. Then the Being by the fire would hurry, shivering, into the teepee calling, "Sister, sister, go out and watch the fire." But the next Being would always be slow to go out for her turn, her head spinning with sleep and the thin dreams of dawn.

Coyote, seeing all this, went down the mountain and spoke to some of his friends among the People. He told them of hairless man, fearing the cold and death of winter. And he told them of the Fire Beings, and the warmth and brightness of the flame. They all agreed that man should have fire, and they all promised to help Coyote's undertaking.

Then Coyote sped again to the mountaintop. Again the Fire Beings leaped up when he came close, and one cried out, "What's that? A thief, a thief!"

---

1. **rivulets** (riv′ yoo litz) *n.* little streams.

But again the others looked closely, and saw only a gray coyote hunting among the bushes. So they sat down again and paid him no more attention.

Coyote waited through the day, and watched as night fell and two of the Beings went off to the teepee to sleep. He watched as they changed over at certain times all the night long, until at last the dawn winds rose.

Then the Being on guard called, "Sister, sister, get up and watch the fire."

And the Being whose turn it was climbed slow and sleepy from her bed, saying, "Yes, yes, I am coming. Do not shout so."

But before she could come out of the teepee, Coyote lunged from the bushes, snatched up a glowing portion of fire, and sprang away down the mountainside.

Screaming, the Fire Beings flew after him. Swift as Coyote ran, they caught up with him, and one of them reached out a clutching hand. Her fingers touched only the tip of the tail, but the touch was enough to turn the hairs white, and coyote tail-tips are white still. Coyote shouted, and flung the fire away from him. But the others of the People had gathered at the mountain's foot, in case they were needed. Squirrel saw the fire falling, and caught it, putting it on her back and fleeing away through the tree tops. The fire scorched her back so painfully that her tail curled up and back, as squirrels' tails still do today.

The Fire Beings then pursued Squirrel, who threw the fire to Chipmunk. Chattering with fear, Chipmunk stood still as if rooted until the Beings were almost upon her. Then, as she turned to run, one Being clawed at her, tearing down the length of her back and leaving three stripes that are to be seen on chipmunks' backs even today. Chipmunk threw the fire to Frog, and the Beings turned towards him. One of the Beings grasped his tail, but Frog gave a mighty leap and tore himself free, leaving his tail behind in the Being's hand—which is why frogs have had no tails ever since.

As the Beings came after him again, Frog flung the fire on to Wood. And Wood swallowed it.

The Fire Beings gathered round, but they did not know how to get the fire out of Wood. They promised it gifts, sang to it and shouted at it. They twisted it and struck it and tore it with their knives. But Wood did not give up the fire. In the end, defeated, the Beings went back to their mountaintop and left the People alone.

But Coyote knew how to get fire out of Wood. And he went to the village of men and showed them how. He showed them the trick of rubbing two dry sticks together, and the trick of spinning a sharpened stick in a hole made in another piece of wood. So man was from then on warm and safe through the killing cold of winter.

Loo-Wit, The Fire-Keeper

Joseph Bruchac

This myth reveals how the Nisqually Indians explained the earth's formations, characteristics, and weather when scientific knowledge was unknown. It also reveals the Nisqually belief that greed and disrespect for the earth lead to misfortune.

When the world was young, the Creator gave everyone all that was needed to be happy.

The weather was always pleasant. There was food for everyone and room for all the people. Despite this, though, two brothers began to quarrel over the land. Each wanted to control it. It reached the point where each brother gathered together a group of men to support his claim. Soon it appeared there would be a war.

The Creator saw this and was not pleased. He waited until the two brothers were asleep one night and then carried them to a new country. There a beautiful river[1] flowed and tall mountains rose into the clouds. He woke them just as the sun rose, and they looked out from the mountaintop to the land below. They saw what a good place it was. It made their hearts good.

"Now," the Creator said, "this will be your land." Then he gave each of the brothers a bow and a single arrow. "Shoot your arrow into the air," the Creator said. "Where your arrow falls will be the land of your people, and you shall be a great chief there."

The brothers did as they were told. The older brother shot his arrow. It arched over the river and landed to the south in the valley of the Willamette River. There is where he and his people went, and they became the Multnomahs.[2] The younger brother shot his arrow. It flew to the north of the great river. He and his people went there and became the Klickitats.[3]

Then the Creator made a Great Stone Bridge across the river. "This bridge," the Creator said, "is a sign of

---

1. a beautiful river Columbia River, which flows between the present-day states of Oregon and Washington.
2. Multnomahs Native American people who were nearly killed off by disease in the 1800's.
3. Klickitats a Native American tribe of Washington; now part of the Yakima Nation.

peace. You and your peoples can visit each other by crossing over this bridge. As long as you remain at peace, as long as your hearts are good, this bridge will stand."

For many seasons the two people remained at peace. They passed freely back and forth across the Great Stone Bridge. One day, though, the people to the north looked south toward the Willamette and said, "Their lands are better than ours." One day, though, the people to the south looked north toward the Klickitat and said, "Their lands are more beautiful than ours." Then, once again, the people began to quarrel.

The Creator saw this and was not pleased.

The people were becoming greedy again. Their hearts were becoming bad. The Creator darkened the skies and took fire away. Now the people grew cold. The rains of autumn began and the people suffered greatly.

"Give us back fire," they begged. "We wish to live again with each other in peace."

Their prayers reached the Creator's heart. There was only one place on earth where fire still remained. An old woman name Loo-Wit had stayed out of the quarreling and was not greedy. It was in her lodge only that fire still burned. So the Creator went to Loo-Wit.

"If you share your fire with all the people," the Creator said, "I will give you whatever you wish. Tell me what you want."

"I want to be young and beautiful," Loo-Wit said.

"That is the way it will be," said the Creator.

"Now take your fire to the Great Stone Bridge above the river. Let all the people come to you and get fire. You must keep the fire burning there to remind people that their hearts must stay good."

The next morning, the skies grew clear and the people saw the sun rise for the first time in many days. The sun shone on the Great Stone Bridge, and there the people saw a young woman as beautiful as the sunshine itself. Before her, there on the bridge, burned a fire. The people came to the fire and ended their quarrels. Loo-Wit gave each of them fire. Now their homes again became warm and peace was everywhere.

One day, though, the chief of the people to the north came to Loo-Wit's fire. He saw how beautiful she was and wanted her to be his wife. At the same time, the chief of the people to the south also saw Loo-Wit's beauty. He, too, wanted to marry her. Loo-Wit could not decide which of the two she liked better. Then the chiefs began to quarrel. Their peoples took up the quarrel, and fighting began.

When the Creator saw the fighting, he became angry. He broke down the Great Stone Bridge. He took each of the two chiefs and changed them into mountains. The chief of the Klickitats became the mountain we now know as Mount Adams. The chief of the Multnomahs became the mountain we now know as Mount Hood. Even as mountains, they continued to quarrel, throwing flames and stones at each other. In some places, the stones they threw almost blocked the river between them. That is why the Columbia River is so narrow in the place called The Dalles today.

Loo-Wit was heartbroken over the pain caused by her beauty. She no longer wanted to be a beautiful young woman. She could no longer find peace as a human being.

The Creator took pity on her and changed her into a mountain also, the most beautiful of the mountains. She was placed so that she stood between Mount Adams and Mount Hood, and she was allowed to keep the fire within herself which she had once shared on the Great Stone Bridge. Eventually, she became known as Mount St. Helens and she slept peacefully.

Though she was asleep, Loo-Wit was still aware, the people said. The Creator had placed her between the two quarreling mountains to keep the peace, and it was intended that humans, too, should look at her beauty and remember to keep their hearts good, to share the land and treat it well. If we humans do not treat the land with respect, the people said, Loo-Wit will wake up and let us know how unhappy she and the Creator have become again. So they said long before the day in the 1980's when Mount St. Helens woke again.

from Morning Girl

Michael Dorris

Without a mirror, knowing what you look like would be pretty difficult. Here is how one young girl discovered the truth about her own appearance.

The water is never still enough. Just when I can almost see my face, when my eyes and my nose and my mouth are about to settle into a picture I can remember, a fish rises for air or a leaf drops to the surface of the pond or Star Boy tosses a pebble into my reflection and I break into shining pieces. It makes no sense to him that I'm curious about what people see when they look at me.

"They see *you*," he said, as if that answered my question. We were searching for ripe fruit on the trees behind our house.

"But what *is* me?" I asked him. "I wouldn't recognize myself unless I was sitting on the bottom of a quiet pool, looking up at me looking down."

"You are . . . *you*." He lost his patience and walked away to find his friend Red Feathers.

But what did "you" mean? I knew my hands very well. I study them when I trim my nails with the rough edge of a broken shell, making them smooth and flat. I could spread my fingers and press them into wet sand to see the shape they leave. Once I tried to do that with my head, but all I got was a big shallow hole and dirty hair.

I knew the front of my body, the bottoms of my feet. I knew the color of my arms—tan as the inside of a yam[1] after the air has dried it—and if I stretched my tongue I could see its pink tip.

"Tell me about my face," I asked Mother one day when we were walking along the beach.

She stopped, turned to me in confusion. "What *about* your face?"

"Is it long and wrinkled, like Grandmother's, or round as a coconut, like Star Boy's? Are my eyes wise like yours or ready to laugh like Father's? Are my teeth as crooked as the trunks of palm trees?"

---

1. yam (yam) *n.* a vegetable that grows on vines in tropical climates.

Mother cocked her head to the side and made lines in her forehead. "I don't think I've ever looked at you that way," she said. "To me you've always been yourself, different from anyone else."

"But I want to *know*," I begged her.

Mother nodded. "I remember that feeling. Try this."

She took my hand and guided it to my neck. "Touch," she told me. "Very softly. No, close your eyes and think with your fingers. Now compare." She placed my other hand on her face, the face I knew better than any other.

I traced the line of her chin. Mine was smaller, pointier. I followed her lips with one thumb, my own with the other. Hers seemed fuller.

"Your mouth is wider," I cried, unhappy with myself.

"That's because I'm smiling, Morning Girl."

And suddenly my mouth was wide, too, and my cheeks were hills on either side.

Next I found the lashes of our eyes, then moved above them. Even without watching I could see the curved shape of Mother's dark brows. They made her look surprised at everything, surprised and delighted.

"Mine are straight," I said.

"Like your grandfather's."

He had always looked tired. I liked surprised better.

"Now, here." Mother cupped my fingers around the tip of my nose. I could feel the breath rush in and out of my nostrils. I could smell the fruit I had picked with Star Boy.

Finally we moved to the ears, and in the dark they were as delicate and complicated as the inside of a spiral shell, but soft.

"Our ears are the same," I told Mother, and she felt with her own hand, testing and probing every part.

"You're right." She sounded as pleased as I was.

I opened my eyes and memorized her ears. At least *that* part I would now recognize.

"Did this help you?" she asked me. "Do you know Morning Girl any better?"

"Oh yes," I said. "She has a chin like a starfish and brows like white clouds on the horizon. Her nose works. Her cheeks swell into mountains when she smiles. The only thing right about her is her ears."

Mother covered her mouth, the way she does when she laughs and doesn't want anyone to stare. "That's my Morning Girl," she said. "That's her exactly."

The next day, as I was getting up and Star Boy was about to go to sleep on his mat, I leaned close to him.

"What does my chin look like?" I demanded.

He blinked, frowned, made his eyes small while he decided. "A starfish," he finally said.

I was very worried until I saw he was making a joke.

"I heard Mother telling Father," he confessed when I pinched him. "But I don't know." He rubbed his arm, showed me where I had made it turn red. "To me it looks more like the end of the rock that juts out into the ocean near the north end of the island. The one they call 'The Giant Digging Stick.'"

"You don't have to be curious about *your* face," I whispered. "All you have to do is wait for a jellyfish to float on shore and get stranded when the tide leaves. Sometimes I see one and I think it's you, buried in the sand up to your neck."

When I went outside, Father was sitting on a log, fixing a shark's tooth to use as a hook at the end of his fishing lance.[2]

"Who is this?" he asked the lance. "Who is this with my wife's ears stuck onto the side of her head?"

"You laugh at me, too," I said. "But why is it so strange to want to know what everyone else already knows? Why should my own face be a secret from me?"

"There *is* a way," Father said kindly, and motioned me to stand beside him. He knelt down so that we would be the same size. "Look into my eyes," he told me. "What do you see?"

I leaned forward, stared into the dark brown circles, and it was like diving into the deepest pools. Suddenly I saw two tiny girls looking back. Their faces were clear, their brows straight as canoes, and their chins as narrow and clean as lemons. As I watched, their mouths grew wide. They were pretty.

"Who are they?" I couldn't take my eyes off those strange new faces. "Who are these pretty girls who live inside your head?"

"They are the answer to your question," Father said. "And they are always here when you need to find them."

---

2. **lance** (lans) *n.* a spear.

from Relation of Alvar Nuñez Cabeza de Vaca

Alvar Nuñez Cabeza de Vaca

Cabeza de Vaca was a Spanish adventurer whose views and beliefs were dramatically changed as a result of his experiences living with Native Americans. As this selection indicates, Cabeza de Vaca reluctantly came to understand something about the people whose land he traveled through.

from Chapter VII
The Character of the Country

The country where we came on shore to this town and region of Apalachen, is for the most part level, the ground of sand and stiff earth. Throughout are immense trees and open woods, in which are walnut, laurel and another tree called liquid-amber, cedars, savins, evergreen oaks, pines, red-oaks and palmitos like those of Spain. There are many lakes, great and small, over every part of it; some troublesome of fording, on account of depth and the great number of trees lying throughout them. Their beds are sand. The lakes in the country of Apalachen are much larger than those we found before coming there.

In this Province are many maize fields; and the houses are scattered as are those of the Gelves. There are deer of three kinds, rabbits, hares, bears, lions and other wild beasts. Among them we saw an animal with a pocket on its belly, in which it carries its young until they know how to seek food; and if it happen that they should be out feeding and any one come near, the mother will not run until she has gathered them in together. The country is very cold. It has fine pastures for herds. Birds are of various kinds. Geese in great numbers. Ducks, mallards, royal-ducks, fly-catchers, night-herons and partridges abound. We saw many falcons, gerfalcons, sparrow-hawks, merlins, and numerous other fowl.

Two hours after our arrival at Apalachen, the Indians who had fled from there came in peace to us, asking for their women and children, whom we released; but the detention of a cacique by the Governor produced great excitement, in consequence of which they returned for battle early the next day [June 26], and attacked us with such promptness and alacrity that they succeeded in setting fire to the houses in which we were. As we sallied they fled to the lakes near by, because of which and the large maize fields, we could do them no injury, save in the single instance of one Indian, whom we killed. The day following, others came against us from a town on the opposite side of the lake, and attacked us as the first had done, escaping in the same way, except one who was also slain.

We were in the town twenty-five days [July 19], in which time we made three incursions, and found the country very thinly peopled and difficult to travel for the bad passages, the woods and lakes. We inquired of the cacique we kept and the natives we brought with us, who were the neighbors and enemies of these Indians, as to the nature of the country, the character and condition of the inhabitants, of the food and all other matters concerning it. Each answered apart from the rest, that the largest town in all that region was Apalachen; the people beyond were less numerous and poorer, the land little occupied, and the inhabitants much scattered; that thenceforward were great lakes, dense forests, immense deserts and solitudes. We then asked touching the region towards the south, as to the towns and subsistence in it. They said that in keeping such a direction, journeying nine days, there was a town called Aute, the inhabitants whereof had much maize, beans and pumpkins, and being near the sea, they had fish, and that those people were their friends.

In view of the poverty of the land, the unfavorable accounts of the population and of everything else we heard, the Indians making continual war upon us, wounding our people and horses at the places where they went to drink, shooting from the lakes with such safety to themselves that we could not retaliate, killing a lord of Tescuco, named Don Pedro, whom the Commissary brought with him, we determined to leave that place and go in quest of the sea, and the town of Aute of which we were told. . . .

The Indians we had so far seen in Florida are all archers. They go naked, are large of body, and appear at a distance like giants. They are of admirable proportions, very spare and of great activity and strength. The bows they use are as thick as the arm, of eleven or twelve palms in length, which they will discharge at two hundred paces with so great precision that they miss nothing.

Having got through this passage, at the end of a league we arrived at another of the same character, but worse, as it was longer, being half a league in extent. This we crossed freely, without interruption from the Indians, who, as they had spent on the former occasion their store of arrows, had nought with which they dared venture to engage us. Going through a similar passage the next day [July 21], I discovered the trail of persons ahead, of which I gave notice to the Governor, who was in the rear guard, so that though the Indians came upon us, as we were prepared they did no harm. After emerging upon the plain they followed us, and we went back on them in two directions. Two we killed, and they wounded me and two or three others. Coming to woods we could do them no more injury, nor make them further trouble. . . .

from Chapter VIII
We Go from Aute

The next morning we left Aute, and traveled all day before coming to the place I had visited. The journey was extremely arduous. There were not horses enough to carry the sick, who went on increasing in numbers day by day, and we knew of no cure. It was piteous and painful to witness our perplexity and distress. We saw on our arrival how small were the means for advancing farther. There was not any where to go; and if there had been, the people were unable to move forward, the greater part being ill, and those were few who could be on duty. I cease here to relate more of this, because any one may suppose what would occur in a country so remote and malign, so destitute of all resource, whereby either to live in it or go out of it; but most certain assistance is in God, our Lord, on whom we never failed to place reliance. One thing occurred, more afflicting to us than all the rest, which was, that of the persons mounted, the greater part commenced secretly to plot, hoping to secure a better fate for themselves by abandoning the Governor and the sick, who were in a state of weakness and prostration. But, as among them were many hidalgos and persons of gentle condition, they would not permit this to go on, without informing the Governor and the officers of your Majesty;

and as we showed them the deformity of their purpose, and placed before them the moment when they should desert their captain, and those who were ill and feeble, and above all the disobedience to the orders of your Majesty, they determined to remain, and that whatever might happen to one should be the lot of all, without any forsaking the rest.

After the accomplishment of this, the Governor called them all to him, and of each apart he asked advice as to what he should do to get out of a country so miserable, and seek that assistance elsewhere which could not here be found, a third part of the people being very sick, and the number increasing every hour; for we regarded it as certain that we should all become so, and could pass out of it only through death, which from its coming in such a place was to us all the more terrible. These, with many other embarrassments being considered, and entertaining many plans, we coincided in one great project, extremely difficult to put in operation, and that was to build vessels in which we might go away. This appeared impossible to every one: we knew not how to construct, nor were there tools, nor iron, nor forge, nor tow, nor resin, nor rigging; finally, no one thing of so many that are necessary, nor any man who had a knowledge of their manufacture; and, above all, there was nothing to eat, while building, for those who should labor. Reflecting on all this, we agreed to think of the subject with more deliberation, and the conversation dropped from that day, each going his way, commending our course to God, our Lord, that he would direct it as should best serve Him. . . .

During this time some went gathering shell-fish in the coves and creeks of the sea, at which employment the Indians twice attacked them and killed ten men in sight of the camp, without our being able to afford succor. We found their corpses traversed from side to side with arrows; and for all some had on good armor, it did not give adequate protection or security against the nice and powerful archery of which I have spoken. According to the declaration of our pilots under oath, from the entrance to which we had given the name *Bahia de la Cruz* to this place, we had traveled two hundred and eighty leagues or thereabout. Over all that region we had not seen a single mountain, and had no information of any whatsoever.

from *Relation of Alvar Nuñez Cabeza de Vaca* 117

Before we embarked there died more than forty men of disease and hunger, without enumerating those destroyed by the Indians. By the twenty-second of the month of September, the horses had been consumed, one only remaining; and on that day we embarked in the following order: In the boat of the Governor went forty-nine men; in another, which he gave to the Comptroller and the Commissary, went as many others; the third, he gave to Captain Alonzo del Castillo and Andrés Dorantes, with forty-eight men; and another he gave to two captains, Tellez and Peñalosa, with forty-seven men. The last was given to the Assessor and myself, with forty-nine men. After the provisions and clothes had been taken in, not over a span of the gunwales remained above water; and more than this, the boats were so crowded that we could not move: so much can necessity do, which drove us to hazard our lives in this manner, running into a turbulent sea, not a single one who went, having a knowledge of navigation. . . .

from Chapter X
The Assault from the Indians

The morning having come [October 31], many natives arrived in canoes who asked us for the two that had remained in the boat. The Governor replied that he would give up the hostages when they should bring the Christians they had taken. With the Indians had come five or six chiefs, who appeared to us to be the most comely persons, and of more authority and condition than any we had hitherto seen, although not so large as some others of whom we have spoken. They wore the hair loose and very long, and were covered with robes of marten such as we had before taken. Some of the robes were made up after a strange fashion, with wrought ties of lion skin, making a brave show. They entreated us to go with them, and said they would give us the Christians, water, and many other things. They continued to collect about us in canoes, attempting in them to take possession of the mouth of that entrance; in consequence, and because it was hazardous to stay near the land, we went to sea, where they remained by us until about mid-day. As they would not deliver our people, we would not give up theirs; so they began to hurl clubs at us and to throw stones with slings, making threats of shooting arrows, although we had not seen among them all more than three or four bows. While thus engaged, the wind beginning to freshen, they left us and went back. . . .

from Chapter XXXII
The Indians Give Us the Hearts of Deer

. . . We were in this town three days. A day's journey farther was another town, at which the rain fell heavily while we were there, and the river became so swollen we could not cross it, which detained us fifteen days. In this time Castillo saw the buckle of a sword-belt on the neck of an Indian and stitched to it the nail of a horse shoe. He took them, and we asked the native what they were: he answered that they came from heaven. We questioned him further, as to who had brought them thence: they all responded, that certain men who wore beards like us, had come from heaven and arrived at that river; bringing horses, lances, and swords, and that they had lanced two Indians. In a manner of the utmost indifference we could feign, we asked them what had become of those men: they answered us that they had gone to sea, putting their lances beneath the water, and going themselves also under the water; afterwards that they were seen on the surface going towards the sunset. For this we gave many thanks to God our Lord. We had before despaired of ever hearing more of Christians. Even yet we were left in great doubt and anxiety, thinking those people were merely persons who had come by sea on discoveries. However, as we had now such exact information, we made greater speed, and as we advanced on our way, the news of the Christians continually grew. We told the natives that we were going in search of that people, to order them not to kill nor make slaves of them, nor take them from their lands, nor do other injustice. Of this the Indians were very glad.

We passed through many territories and found them all vacant: their inhabitants wandered fleeing among the mountains, without daring to have houses or till the earth for fear of Christians. The sight was one of infinite pain to us, a land very fertile and beautiful, abounding in springs and streams, the hamlets deserted and burned, the people thin and weak, all fleeing or in concealment. As they did not plant, they appeased their keen hunger by eating roots, and the bark of trees. We bore a share in the famine along the whole way, for poorly could these unfortunates provide for us, themselves being so reduced they looked as though they would willingly die. They brought shawls of those they had concealed because of the Christians, presenting them to us; and they related how the Christians, at other times had come through the land destroying and burning the towns, carrying away half the men, and all the women and the boys, while those who had been able to escape were wandering about fugitives. We found them so alarmed they dared not remain anywhere. They would not, nor could they till the earth; but preferred to die rather than live in dread of such cruel usage as they received. Although these showed themselves greatly delighted with us, we feared that on our arrival among those who held the frontier and fought against the Christians, they would treat us badly, and revenge upon us the conduct of their enemies; but when God our Lord was pleased to bring us there, they began to dread and respect us as the others had done, and even somewhat more, at which we no little wondered. Thence it may at once be seen, that to bring all these people to be Christians and to the obedience of the Imperial Majesty, they must be won by kindness, which is a way certain, and no other is. . . .

from Chapter XXXIII
We See Traces of Christians

When we saw sure signs of Christians, and heard how near we were to them, we gave thanks to God our Lord, for having chosen to bring us out of a captivity so melancholy and wretched. The delight we felt let each one conjecture, when he shall remember the length of time we were in that country, the suffering and perils we underwent. That night I entreated my companions that one of them should go back three days' journey after the Christians who were moving about over the country, where we had given assurance of protection. Neither of them received this proposal well, excusing themselves because of weariness and exhaustion; and although either might have done better than I, being more youthful and athletic, yet seeing their unwillingness, the next morning I took the negro with eleven Indians, and following the Christians by their trail, I traveled ten leagues, passing three villages, at which they had slept.

The day after I overtook four of them on horseback, who were astonished at the sight of me, so strangely habited as I was, and in company with Indians. They stood staring at me a length of time, so confounded that they neither hailed me nor drew near to make an inquiry. I bade them take me to their chief: accordingly we went together half a league to the place where was Diego de Alcaraz, their captain.

After we had conversed, he stated to me that he was completely undone; he had not been able in a long time to take any Indians; he knew not which way to turn, and his men had well begun to experience hunger and fatigue. I told him of Castillo and Dorantes, who were behind, ten leagues off, with a multitude that conducted us. He thereupon sent three cavalry to them, with fifty of the Indians who accompanied him. The negro returned to guide them, while I remained. I asked the Christians to give me a certificate of the year, month and day, I arrived there, and of the manner of my coming, which they accordingly did. From this river to the town of the Christians, named San Miguel, within the government of the province called New Galicia, are thirty leagues.

from Chapter XXXIV
Of Sending for the Christians

Five days having elapsed, Andrés Dorantes and Alonzo del Castillo arrived with those who had been sent after them. They brought more than six hundred persons of that community, whom the Christians had driven into the forests, and who had wandered in concealment over the land. Those who accompanied us so far, had drawn them out, and given them to the Christians, who thereupon dismissed all the others they had brought with them. Upon their coming to where I was, Alcaraz begged that we would summon the people of the towns on the margin of the river, who straggled about under cover of the woods, and order them to fetch us something to eat. This last was unnecessary, the Indians being ever diligent to bring us all they could. Directly we sent out messengers to call them, when there came six hundred souls, bringing us all the maize in their possession. They fetched it in certain pots, closed with clay, which they had concealed in the earth. They brought us whatever else they had; but we, wishing only to have the provision, gave the rest to the Christians, that they might divide among themselves. After this we had many high words with them; for they wished to make slaves of the Indians we brought.

In consequence of the dispute, we left at our departure many bows of Turkish shape we had along with us and many pouches. The five arrows with the points of emerald were forgotten among others, and we lost them. We gave the Christians a store of robes of cowhide and other things we brought. We found it difficult to induce the Indians to return to their dwellings, to feel no apprehension and plant maize. They were willing to do nothing until they had gone with us and delivered us into the hands of other Indians, as had been the custom; for if they returned without doing so, they were afraid they should die, and going with us, they feared neither Christians nor lances. Our countrymen became jealous at this, and caused their interpreter to tell the Indians that we were of them, and for a long time we had been lost; that they were the lords of the land who must be obeyed and served, while we were persons of mean condition and small force. The Indians cared little or nothing for what was told them; and conversing among themselves said the Christians lied: that we had come whence the sun rises, and they whence it goes down; we healed the sick, they killed the sound; that we had come naked and barefooted, while they had arrived in clothing and on horses with lances; that we were not covetous of anything, but all that was given to us, we directly turned to give, remaining with nothing; that the others had the only purpose to rob whomsoever they found, bestowing nothing on any one.

In this way they spoke of all matters respecting us, which they enhanced by contrast with matters respecting concerning the others, delivering their response through the interpreter of the Spaniards. To other Indians they made this known by means of one among them through whom they understood us. Those who speak that tongue we discriminately call Primahaitu, which is like saying Vasconyados. We found it in use over more than four hundred leagues of our travel, without another over that whole extent. Even to the last, I could not convince the Indians that we were of the Christians; and only with great effort and solicitation we got them to go back to their residences. We ordered them to put away apprehension, establish their towns, plant and cultivate the soil. . . .

Civilizations of
China and Japan

Watching the Reapers

Po Chü-i

In some ways and in some places, the work of tilling the soil has not changed in thousands of years, as this selection shows.

Tillers of the soil have few idle months;
In the fifth month their toil is double-fold.
A south-wind visits the fields at night:
Suddenly the hill is covered with yellow corn.
5   Wives and daughters shoulder baskets of rice;
Youths and boys carry the flasks of wine.
Following after they bring a wage of meat
To the strong reapers toiling on the southern hill,
Whose feet are burned by the hot earth they
    tread,
10   Whose backs are scorched by flames of the
    shining sky.
Tired they toil, caring nothing for the heat,
Grudging the shortness of the long summer day.
A poor woman follows at the reapers' side
With an infant child carried close at her breast.
15   With her right hand she gleans the fallen grain;
On her left arm a broken basket hangs.
And *I* to-day . . . by virtue of what right
Have I never once tended field or tree?
My government-pay is three hundred tons;
20   At the year's end I have still grain in hand.
Thinking of this, secretly I grew ashamed;
And all day the thought lingered in my head.

Hailibu the Hunter

Retold by John Minford

In folk tales like this one, characters sometimes gain magical powers, like the ability to understand the language of animals. The choices that Hailibu makes let him enter nature's magical circle.

Once upon a time there was a hunter whose name was Hailibu. He was always ready to help others. Instead of keeping his game all to himself, he always used to share it out among his neighbors. This made him very popular.

One day Hailibu went hunting deep in the mountains. On the outskirts of a thick forest, he spotted a little white snake coiled in slumber under a tree. Not wanting to wake her, he tiptoed past. Just at this moment, a grey crane few overhead, swooped down on the sleeping snake, seized her in its claws, and soared up into the sky again. Waking up with a shock, the little white snake screamed, "Help! Help!" Hailibu quickly took an arrow, bent his bow, and shot at the grey crane as it rose up the wall of the mountain. The crane swerved to one side, dropped the little white snake, and flew away. Hailibu said to the snake, "You poor little thing. Go home to your parents." She nodded her head to show him her gratitude and then disappeared into some thick undergrowth. Hailibu put his arrows in their quiver, slung his bow over his shoulder, and went home.

Next day, when passing by the place again, Hailibu saw a little white snake crawling up toward him, escorted by a whole retinue of snakes. Amazed, he was about to walk round them and continue on his way when the little white snake said to him, "How are you, my saviour? You probably cannot recognize me. I am the Dragon King's daughter. Yesterday you saved my life. My parents asked me especially to come here and invite you home, so that they can express their gratitude to you in person." The snake continued, "When you get there, don't accept anything my parents offer you but ask for the precious stone my father keeps in his mouth. With that precious stone in your mouth, you will be able to understand the language of the whole animal kingdom. But you must never tell what you hear to anyone else, or your body will turn to stone from head to foot, and you will die."

On hearing this, Hailibu nodded and followed the white snake. The way led into a deep valley, and the farther he walked, the colder he felt. They found themselves in front of a large door, and the little white snake said, "My parents are waiting for you outside, at the entrance to their storeroom. Here they are now." While she was speaking, the Dragon King stepped forward to greet him and said with great respect, "You saved my dear daughter. I thank you from the bottom of my heart. This is the storeroom where I keep my treasure. Allow me to show you around. Take whatever you want. Don't stand on ceremony,[1] please!" With these words, he opened the storeroom and led Hailibu in. It was full of pearls and jewels, brilliant and glittering. The old Dragon King led him from one room to the next. After they had gone through all the 108 rooms without Hailibu having chosen a single piece of the treasure, the old Dragon King said with embarrassment, "Dear sir! Don't you fancy any of the precious things in my storeroom?" Hailibu answered, "They are fine enough but they can only be used for decoration. They are of no use to hunters like myself. If Your Majesty really wishes to give me something as a remembrance, please give me the precious stone in your mouth!" On hearing these words, the Dragon King lowered his head, pondered for a while, then reluctantly spat the precious stone out of his mouth and handed it to Hailibu.

So Hailibu became the owner of the precious stone. As he took his leave of the Dragon King and went on his way, the little white snake followed him out. She warned him again and again, "With the precious stone you can know everything. But you must not divulge the slightest part of what you know. If you do, danger will befall you! Never forget this!"

From then on, it became very easy for Hailibu to hunt in the mountains, for he understood the language of the birds and beasts and knew exactly which animals were on the other side of the mountain. Several years passed in this way. One day he went hunting in the mountains as usual. Suddenly he heard a flock of birds discussing among themselves as they flew through the air: "We must

---

1. **Don't stand on ceremony** don't be formal.

move somewhere else as soon as possible! Tomorrow the mountains around here are going to erupt; the fields will be flooded and goodness knows how many animals will be drowned!"

On hearing the news, Hailibu was very concerned and no longer in the mood for hunting. He hurried home and said to his neighbors: "We must move somewhere else as quickly as possible! We cannot live here any longer! You must believe me! Don't wait until it is too late!"

They were all puzzled by what he had said. Some thought there was no such impending calamity at all; some thought that Hailibu had gone mad. No one believed him. Hailibu, with tears on his cheeks, said to them in despair, "Do I have to die in order to convince you?"

A few old men said to him, "We all know you have never lied to us before. But now you are saying all this about the mountains erupting and the fields being flooded. Won't you tell us what makes you so sure it will happen?"

Hailibu thought to himself: "Disaster is imminent. How can I escape alone and leave all the villagers to perish? If necessary, I shall have to sacrifice myself in order to save them." So he told the villagers the whole story of how he had acquired the precious stone and used it for hunting; how he had heard a flock of birds discussing the disaster and seen them making their escape. He also told them that he was not allowed to tell what he had heard to anyone else; otherwise, his body would turn to stone and he would die. While he was speaking, he turned little by little into stone. The villagers, seeing what had happened, felt great sorrow. They moved to another place at once, driving their herds and flocks with them. While they were hurrying away, the sky became overcast and it poured rain that whole night. The next morning, they heard a rumbling peal of thunder and a great crash which seemed to shake the earth to its very foundations. The mountains erupted, belching forth a great flood of water. Deeply moved, the villagers said, "Had Hailibu not sacrificed his life for us, we would have been drowned by the flood!"

Afterwards, the villagers found the stone into which Hailibu had been transformed and placed it on the top of the mountain. Generation after generation, they have offered sacrifices to this stone in memory of Hailibu, the hero who gave his life to save others. People say that there is still a place called "Hailibu Stone."

Ancient Airs

Li Po

Many people, even poets like Li Po in this poem, wonder what will happen to the things that are important to them after they are gone.

The great odes have had no revival,
Who will continue the effort after I am gone?
The ways of ancient kings were overgrown with
    weeds,
Brambles thrived everywhere in the Warring
    States.
5   Dragons and tigers tore at one another,
Long battles did not end with the power-crazed
    Ch'in.
How the true voice grew weak and dim,
Then sorrow and lament inspired the *sao* poets.
Yang and Ma aroused the ebbing tide,
10   And new currents began to flow everywhere.
Though their rise and fall alternate time and
    again,
Still, the great tradition suffered a great decline.
Ever since the time of the Chien-an masters,
Fine phrases and ornate style have been
    overpraised.
15   Our great age has restored the ancient tradition,
As His Majesty values only what is pure and true.
A host of talents flock to the enlightened court;
Availing themselves of the happy trend, they all
    leap to recognition.
Style and substance lend each other brilliance,
20   Like myriad stars blinking in an autumn sky.

The Old Man Who Made the Trees Bloom

from Japanese Tales and Legends

Retold by Helen and William McAlpine

This story proves that even people who seem to be thoroughly evil may be reformed by continuing goodness and kindness from others.

One morning, long, long ago, an old woodcutter, who lived in a small hamlet by the side of a great forest, was on his daily journey to cut down trees for the lord of the province, when he noticed a little white dog lying by the side of the path. It was thin and wasted and near to death from cold and hunger. Moved to pity by the creature's suffering, he picked it up, put it tenderly into the breast of his kimono, and carried it back to his house. His wife hurried out to meet him when she saw him return so early, and asked what was the matter. In reply he uncovered the little dog and showed it to her.

'You poor little dog!' she cried in sympathy. 'Who has been so cruel to you? And how intelligent you look with your clear bright eyes and alert lively ears! An old couple like us might well like to have you in our house.'

'Indeed! Indeed!' murmured the old man, who was only too willing to have it as a pet. They both went inside, laid it on the straw-matted floor, and began at once to attend to its sickness.

Under their tender care the little dog grew well and strong. His bright eyes grew brighter, his ears stood erect at the slightest noise, his nose was forever twitching from side to side with eager curiosity, and his coat gleamed with whiteness, so much so indeed, that they called him 'Shiro,' which means 'white.' As the old couple had no children of their own, Shiro became as dear to them as a son and he followed the old couple wherever they went.

One winter day the old man, his spade over his shoulder, went to his field to dig some vegetables. Shiro, always happy on such occasions, jumped and frolicked in great circles round him and made sudden raids into the ditch and undergrowth. When they reached the field, he careered as madly as ever and barked in delight as he hurled himself over the brambly bushes. Suddenly he stopped. His ears went stiff and erect and his whole body became alive and tense. With his nose to the ground he moved slowly to the fence near the corner of the field. His nose twitched and sniffed over a little mound of earth. All at once he began digging furiously, sending the earth through his hind legs in a continuous cascade. His loud excited barking attracted the old man's attention at the other end of the field, and thinking that Shiro must have discovered something very extraordinary to make him behave in such a way, he came hurriedly to see what it was all about. Taking his spade, he started digging in the hole scraped by Shiro, but hardly had he removed two clods when a shower of golden coins poured into the air as though from an invisible fountain. The old man fell back in wonderment and hurried away to bring his wife to see the miraculous sight.

Their neighbour, an ill-tempered and avaricious man, had also been attracted by Shiro's barking, and from the other side of the bamboo fence separating their fields he had witnessed this unbelievable wonder. His mean eyes glistened with covetousness[1] and he could hardly control his grasping hands. Cunningly he put on a friendly voice and begged the old couple to lend him their dog for the day. Gentle and kindhearted and wishing to be of service, the old man lifted Shiro and, telling him to be a good dog, handed him over the fence to his neighbour. Sensing the man's ugly nature, Shiro refused to follow his temporary master. He crouched on the ground, his trembling body gathered up in fear. The neighbour coaxed and shouted, shouted and coaxed, but only succeeded in further increasing Shiro's fear. Growing more and more angry, he tied a straw rope round Shiro's neck and dragged him forcibly to a corner of his field where he bound him to a tree, so tightly and with such a short lead that the poor creature was forced to lie in an agonizing position. His throat was so constricted by the rope that his weak barks could not be heard by his own master.

'Now then,' shouted the vicious neighbour, 'where is it buried? Where is it buried? Seek it out for me or I'll kill you, you vile hound.'

---

1. **covetousness** (kuv′ ət əs nəs) *n.* greed.

Furiously he struck the ground before Shiro's nose. The blade slid into the earth and scraped against some metal object. The surly man stood still. His eyes widened in avid expectation. The next moment he was clawing the earth with both hands in a frenzy of greed. When he unearthed nothing but old tins, rags, wooden clogs, and broken tiles, his fury became uncontrollable. He picked up his spade and struck viciously at Shiro, who was whining and cowering in terror at the foot of the tree. The blow cut him cruelly, but it also severed the rope that held him, and Shiro ran in anguished circles, dazed by the blow and howling pitifully. Attracted by his cries his master hurried to the fence, and when he saw what had happened was beside himself with grief. Shiro crawled through the fence and his master gathered him tenderly in his arms.

'Shiro, my poor Shiro, what terrible thing has happened to you? Will you ever forgive me? Will you ever forgive my cruel mistake?' the old man sobbed. But Shiro could only shiver and cling more tightly to him.

Sadly the old man returned home with his pet. He bathed and tended his wound and fed him with thin gruel. But despite all his efforts, the spade of their wicked neighbour had wounded him so severely that he died that same evening.

The old couple were overwhelmed by their loss. They did not sleep that night, and early next morning, with great sorrow and mourning bitterly, they buried their little pet in the corner of the field where Shiro's miracle had happened. Over his grave the old man constructed a small tombstone, and beside it he planted a young pine tree. Every day, the old couple went to the grave, and standing side by side with bowed heads, they mourned for their friend.

The tree grew with incredible swiftness. In a week's time, its branches shadowed Shiro's grave; in a fortnight's time it would take two people with their arms stretched round to span its trunk; and within a month its topmost leaves seemed to sweep the sky, so tall had it grown. Each day the old man, gazing upon this new wonder, said:

'Wife, truly another miracle. Our little Shiro is dead, but his spirit has entered into this tree. His gaiety and exuberance could not be killed. It has become the sap of this magnificent tree and is prancing madly in its leaves and branches. I am sure of it.' And they gazed upon the tree with renewed astonishment.

The news of the growing tree soon spread. From distant mountain and valley people came and gathered round it daily. They craned their necks and strained their eyes to see its topmost branches, now dimmed in the haze of the sky. They shook their heads and whispered to each other that it was not true, but raised their heads to look again and could not doubt their eyes.

One day in the winter the old woman said to her husband:

'Husband, do you remember how our little Shiro loved rice cake—mochi-cake? Would it not be a fine idea to fashion a good mortar from the trunk of Shiro's tree and make mochi-cake to offer on his tomb?'

'What a fine idea, indeed! What a fine idea!' her husband replied excitedly. 'We will certainly do as you say.' And immediately he began sharpening his large axe.

The following morning and all the afternoon he worked, and slowly his blade ate into the great trunk. At last, with one powerful final swing, the great tree creaked and fell to the earth with a roar so mighty that it was heard in the furthermost corners of Japan. A fine and beautiful mortar came to shape under the skilful hands of the old man, and was soon ready to receive the glistening white rice for pounding. With hearts full of love and tenderness for the memories of their little friend, the old couple began to beat the rice with their pestles to turn it into a fine powder before cooking. But hardly had they broken more than a rice-bowl full of the grains, when before their amazed eyes the whole pile turned into a glittering heap of golden coins.

How they marvelled! And how eagerly they talked about their good fortune to the neighbours, who were all overjoyed that such riches should fall to them. All, that is, except the mean irascible[2] man who had so cruelly killed Shiro. He could hardly contain his greed as he listened to the story of the old man and schemed, there and then, to gain possession of the magic mortar and have it for his own. Next day he went to the house of the old couple, and cringing and fawning and feigning great sorrow, said:

'Ever since the death of your little dog, I have been filled with a great melancholy. A great melancholy, good

---

2. **irascible** (i ras′ ə bəl) *adj.* easily angered; quick-tempered.

neighbours, because I feel I was to blame. Night and day I have thought that if only there was some way in which I could show how deeply I feel about it and do something to show my repentance, how gladly I would do it, but I was too ashamed. Today, in all humbleness, I have come to ask your forgiveness. I would so much like to make some fine mochi-cakes and offer them on the tomb of little Shiro. But, alas, my mortar is too old and despicable and I am too poor to buy a new one. Would you, kind neighbours, lend me yours for a little while to make my small offering for our little friend?'

The fond and foolish old couple were deeply moved by this deceitful talk, and believing that he was sincerely repentant, they allowed the scheming rascal to take the mortar with him, and he gleefully rolled and tumbled it before him to his house.

On arriving home, he lost no time in preparing to make the cakes. Together with his equally avaricious wife, he poured the rice into the mortar and they set about pounding it. On and on they pounded but no gold appeared and they both shouted angrily:

'Turn into gold, you miserable grains! Turn into gold!' And they hammered and hammered more vigorously than ever. 'Don-don, don-don,' went their pestles, and the grains went flying in all directions, but not a single coin of gold flew out. They were about at the end of their strength, when suddenly the pounded rice in the mortar began to move and transform itself.

'It is changing,' cried the old knave.

'We shall be rich,' cried his shrewish wife.

And they danced with delight round and round the mortar. But to their horror, instead of a fine heap of glittering gold appearing, there came nothing but old tins, rags, wooden clogs, and broken tiles, just like the rubbish he had dug up in the field. In a great rage he seized his hatchet and with one blow split the mortar in two. His wife seized another hatchet and in a frenzy they both hacked and chopped the two halves to pieces. Lighting a fire in the kiln oven, they flung the pieces in and watched until they were consumed to ashes.

Next day, the old man came to ask for the return of his mortar, but the neighbour gave him a surly greeting.

'The mortar was cracked and useless. At the first stroke of my pestle it fell apart, so I chopped it up for firewood and burnt it to ashes. If they are of any use to you, help yourself. There they are in the kiln.'

With these curt words the neighbour crabbedly turned his back and refused to say another word.

The old man was desolate. He looked first at his neighbour and then at the kiln. His eyes rested on the ashes. There was no anger in his heart, only a deep sadness.

'First my dear Shiro, now my wonderful new mortar,' he lamented to himself. 'A coldhearted and unfeeling man! Yet, what is to be done? Nothing, no, nothing can restore them to me. Only ashes left. But they are the ashes of my little dog; for truly the mortar was made from his divine and wonderful spirit. I will take them and bury them beside him. He will be overjoyed to know that his spirit has been restored to him.'

The old man gathered the ashes into a rice basket and turned slowly homewards, wondering what his wife would think of this new disaster. He had hardly travelled more than half-way, when out of a pine grove a gentle breeze arose, danced momentarily among the trees, and the next instant was swirling round the rice basket and lifting the ashes high into the air. The breeze died as quickly as it had risen and the ashes floated down like snowflakes on the cold naked branches of the wintry trees. But wonderful to behold, wherever they alighted, the naked branches burst into a profusion of blooms and leaves, and soon everywhere about the dazed old man, the cheerlessness of winter was transformed into the gaiety of spring and the air was filled with the perfume of opening blossoms. The old man turned slowly to gaze upon this new wonder. He stretched out his hand to touch the leaves and petals to assure himself of their reality. He turned slowly round and round, his eyes drinking in the young greenness and his nostrils filled with the fragrance of May. Suddenly he was running excitedly to the village.

'Look! Look! Old Flowerman can make the trees bloom! Old Flowerman can make the trees bloom! Look! Look!' he cried, throwing handfuls of the ash on every tree and bush, and watching how the trees and the bushes opened in bloom where it fell.

It happened that the lord of the province, accompanied by his retainers, was making a tour of the village. Attracted by the shouts of the old man and the crowd of people surrounding him, the lord reined in his horse and asked one of his followers to find out what the excitement was.

Meanwhile the old man, in his unbounded joy at the new beautiful power he possessed, had climbed a cherry-tree, and singing all the while to himself, scattered the ash on every branch, and the pink and white blossoms spread their radiance about him.

The retainer called to him, and descending from the tree, the old man was taken into the presence of his lord. Humbly and simply he told his story, and when he demonstrated the miracle of the ash, the lord was filled with great pleasure and said:

'Wonderful! Truly wonderful! A man who causes flowers to follow his shadow! Where is there another who possesses such a gift of beauty? Old man, I shall reward you,' and he dismounted from his horse.

A retainer brought an offering table and on it placed a rare brocade bag filled with golden coins. The lord himself held it out and the old man, bowing first to the ground, took the brocade bag with humble reverence.

He could hardly wait to get home to tell his wife of the miracle of the ash and the honour that had been done him by the lord of the province, and as he hurried along clasping the precious bag, he was filled with delight and smiling with pleasure.

The greedy neighbour was a witness to the whole happening and was filled with bitterness and resentment. He hurried back to his house and opened the kiln door. Sure enough, there were traces of the ash in the oven and on the floor. He called to his wife and they both scooped up what was left into a basket. With the basket under his arm he hurried out and waited by the roadside for the return of the lord and his train. The sound of the horses' hooves told him that the retinue was approaching. He quickly climbed the nearest tree and began singing to himself and calling out, 'Old Flowerman can make the trees blossom! Old Flowerman can make the trees blossom! Look! Look!' just as the old man had done.

The lord trotted his horse to the tree and, looking up, said:

'What! Have we another worker of miracles in the village? This is certainly not the same old man as I saw just now. You there, are you another who can make the trees bloom? If so, demonstrate your powers at once.'

'Yes, my lord, I will do so at once,' replied the ill-natured neighbour.

Straightaway he began sprinkling the ash over the branches. But instead of settling and bringing forth flowers, the ash flew helter-skelter in all directions and enveloped the lord and his retainers in a choking cloud of dust. It entered and inflamed their eyes, it clogged their mouths and made them cough violently, and it terrified the lord's horse so that it reared and whinnyed in fright. The lord was greatly outraged and his retainers indignantly dragged the unfortunate fool from the tree and thrust him to his knees. The man grovelled and whined despicably and beat his forehead on the ground and wept bitterly.

'I have been evil and wicked,' he cried abjectly. 'I have killed my neighbour's dog in a fit of rage and smashed to pieces his beautiful mortar. There has been nothing but envy and covetousness in my heart, and because of them I have greatly wronged my good neighbour. Now I have insulted my lord. Forgive me! Forgive me! If only you will, from this moment I shall mend my ways and my evil thoughts. Only I pray give me another chance.'

The lord was still very angry. He severely reprimanded the ill-tempered man, but at last he forgave him on the condition that, if he did not change his ways from this very day, he would be severely punished.

As the weeks and months passed the old couple grew more serene and happy, and their good fortune for ever grew. Their neighbour and his wife slowly changed their character and their ways. Their envy gave place to kindness; their ill-temper to gentleness; and their unneighbourliness to a warm lasting friendship with the old couple. On every festival and anniversary, all four went to the temple and to the grave of Shiro and offered prayers and mochi-cakes for the everlasting peace of his spirit, and the remainder of their days were spent in generous goodwill to each other and to the people of the village.

Tanka

Ki no Tsurayuki

Translated by Geoffrey Bownas

This poem reflects a traditional Buddhist emphasis on contemplation of nature as a path to wisdom and understanding of life.

When I went to visit
The girl I love so much,
That winter night
The river blew so cold
That the plovers[1] were crying.

---

1. plovers (pluv′ ərz) *n.* wading shore birds with short tails, long, pointed wings, and short, stout beaks.

from The Pillow Book

Sei Shōnagon

Translated by Ivan Morris

The Pillow Book is a collection of thoughts, feelings, and observations about life, written by a tenth-century court attendant at the Japanese imperial court. This selection contains a description of the beauty of different seasons and an account of two pampered court pets.

IN SPRING IT IS THE DAWN

In spring it is the dawn that is most beautiful. As the light creeps over the hills, their outlines are dyed a faint red and wisps of purplish cloud trail over them.

In summer the nights. Not only when the moon shines, but on dark nights too, as the fireflies flit to and fro, and even when it rains, how beautiful it is!

In autumn the evenings, when the glittering sun sinks close to the edge of the hills and the crows fly back to their nests in threes and fours and twos; more charming still is a file of wild geese, like specks in the distant sky. When the sun has set, one's heart is moved by the sound of the wind and the hum of the insects.

In winter the early mornings. It is beautiful indeed when snow has fallen during the night, but splendid too when the ground is white with frost; or even when there is no snow or frost, but it is simply very cold and the attendants hurry from room to room stirring up the fires and bringing charcoal, how well this fits the season's mood! But as noon approaches and the cold wears off, no one bothers to keep the braziers[1] alight, and soon nothing remains but piles of white ashes.

---

1. braziers (brā′ zhərz) *n.* metal pans or bowls used to hold burning coals or charcoal.

THE CAT WHO LIVED
IN THE PALACE

The cat who lived in the Palace had been awarded the headdress of nobility and was called Lady Myōbu. She was a very pretty cat, and His Majesty saw to it that she was treated with the greatest care.

One day she wandered onto the veranda, and Lady Uma, the nurse in charge of her, called out, "Oh, you naughty thing! Please come inside at once." But the cat paid no attention and went on basking sleepily in the sun. Intending to give her a scare, the nurse called for the dog, Okinamaro.

"Okinamaro, where are you?" she cried. "Come here and bite Lady Myōbu!" The foolish Okinamaro, believing that the nurse was in earnest, rushed at the cat, who, startled and terrified, ran behind the blind in the Imperial Dining Room, where the Emperor happened to be sitting. Greatly surprised, His Majesty picked up the cat and held her in his arms. He summoned his gentlemen-in-waiting. When Tadataka, the Chamberlain,[2] appeared, His Majesty ordered that Okinamaro be chastised and banished to Dog Island. The attendants all started to chase the dog amid great confusion. His Majesty also reproached Lady Uma. "We shall have to find a new nurse for our cat," he told her. "I no longer feel I can count on you to look after her." Lady Uma bowed; thereafter she no longer appeared in the Emperor's presence.

The Imperial Guards quickly succeeded in catching Okinamaro and drove him out of the Palace grounds. Poor dog! He used to swagger about so happily. Recently, on the third day of the Third Month,[3] when the Controller First Secretary paraded him through the Palace grounds, Okinamaro was adorned with garlands of willow leaves, peach blossoms on his head, and cherry blossoms round his body. How could the dog have imagined that this would be his fate? We all felt sorry for him. "When Her Majesty was having her meals," recalled one of the ladies-in-waiting, "Okinamaro always used to be in attendance and sit opposite us. How I miss him!"

---

2. **Chamberlain** (chām′ bər lin) *n.* a high official in the emperor's court.
3. **the third day of the Third Month** the day of the Jòmi Festival, an event during which the dogs in the palace were often decorated with flowers.

It was about noon, a few days after Okinamaro's banishment, that we heard a dog howling fearfully. How could any dog possibly cry so long? All the other dogs rushed out in excitement to see what was happening. Meanwhile a woman who served as a cleaner in the Palace latrines[4] ran up to us. "It's terrible," she said. "Two of the Chamberlains are flogging a dog. They'll surely kill him. He's being punished for having come back after he was banished. It's Tadataka and Sanefusa who are beating him." Obviously the victim was Okinamaro. I was absolutely wretched and sent a servant to ask the men to stop; but just then the howling finally ceased. "He's dead," one of the servants informed me. "They've thrown his body outside the gate."

That evening, while we were sitting in the Palace bemoaning Okinamaro's fate, a wretched looking dog walked in; he was trembling all over, and his body was fearfully swollen.

"Oh dear," said one of the ladies-in-waiting. "Can this be Okinamaro? We haven't seen any other dog like him recently, have we?"

We called to him by name, but the dog did not respond. Some of us insisted that it was Okinamaro, others that it was not. "Please send for Lady Ukon,"[5] said the Empress, hearing our discussion. "She will certainly be able to tell." We immediately went to Ukon's room and told her she was wanted on an urgent matter.

"Is this Okinamaro?" the Empress asked her, pointing to the dog.

"Well," said Ukon, "it certainly looks like him, but I cannot believe that this loathsome creature is really our Okinamaro. When I called Okinamaro, he always used to come to me, wagging his tail. But this dog does not react at all. No, it cannot be the same one. And besides, wasn't Okinamaro beaten to death and his body thrown away? How could any dog be alive after being flogged by two strong men?" Hearing this, Her Majesty was very unhappy.

When it got dark, we gave the dog something to eat; but he refused it, and we finally decided that this could not be Okinamaro.

---

4. **latrines** (lə trēnz') *n.* lavatories.
5. **Lady Ukon** (o͞o kôn') one of the ladies in the Palace Attendants' Office, a bureau of female officials who waited on the emperor.

On the following morning I went to attend the Empress while her hair was being dressed and she was performing her ablutions.[6] I was holding up the mirror for her when the dog we had seen on the previous evening slunk into the room and crouched next to one of the pillars. "Poor Okinamaro!" I said. "He had such a dreadful beating yesterday. How sad to think he is dead! I wonder what body he has been born into this time. Oh, how he must have suffered!"

At that moment the dog lying by the pillar started to shake and tremble, and shed a flood of tears. It was astounding. So this really was Okinamaro! On the previous night it was to avoid betraying himself that he had refused to answer to his name. We were immensely moved and pleased. "Well, well, Okinamaro!" I said, putting down the mirror. The dog stretched himself flat on the floor and yelped loudly, so that the Empress beamed with delight. All the ladies gathered round, and Her Majesty summoned Lady Ukon. When the Empress explained what had happened, everyone talked and laughed with great excitement.

The news reached His Majesty, and he too came to the Empress's room. "It's amazing," he said with a smile. "To think that even a dog has such deep feelings!" When the Emperor's ladies-in-waiting heard the story, they too came along in a great crowd. "Okinamaro!" we called, and this time the dog rose and limped about the room with his swollen face. "He must have a meal prepared for him," I said. "Yes," said the Empress, laughing happily, "now that Okinamaro has finally told us who he is."

The Chamberlain, Tadataka, was informed, and he hurried along from the Table Room. "Is it really true?" he asked. "Please let me see for myself." I sent a maid to him with the following reply: "Alas, I am afraid that this is not the same dog after all." "Well," answered Tadataka, "whatever you say, I shall sooner or later have occasion to see the animal. You won't be able to hide him from me indefinitely."

Before long, Okinamaro was granted an Imperial pardon and returned to his former happy state. Yet even now, when I remember how he whimpered and trembled in response to our sympathy, it strikes me as a strange and moving scene; when people talk to me about it, I start crying myself.

---

6. **ablutions** (ab lōo′ shənz) *n.* washings of the body.

Barbarians from the West

from China: From Manchu to Mao (1699–1976)

John R. Roberson

For years, the sophisticated, cultured society of China considered visitors from the West to be barbarians, as this selection shows.

On April 26, 1699, the emperor of China made a bow-and-arrow shot so spectacular that it is still remembered today. The emperor was Kang Xi, one of China's best in all ways; the occasion was an imperial visit to the city of Hangzhou, on a tour of the southern provinces of the empire. Since archery on horseback was his favorite sport, an archery competition was one of numerous entertainments scheduled during his stay.

That day the best archers in the Imperial Bodyguard demonstrated their skill. Then it was the emperor's turn. First he rode across the width of the range and shot as his horse passed in front of the target. His arrow hit the mark. Then he turned to a more difficult exercise—shooting as his horse galloped down the range straight toward the target. Just as he was about to release his arrow, for some reason his horse swerved to the left. The crowd of spectators was horrified. Both the emperor's hands were occupied with the bow and arrow. Would he be thrown from his horse?

Kang Xi stayed in the saddle. He quickly changed his grip on the bow, took new aim, and hit the target squarely again. A shiver of relief and admiration ran through the crowd. Among those present were the emperor's mother, seven of his sons, numerous ministers of state, royal secretaries, court historians, and officials of the province and city. All these dignitaries were seated in exact order of their rank in the imperial hierarchy.

Outside the archery range, ordinary citizens jostled each other for a glimpse of the emperor. Word of his feat quickly spread to them. Kang Xi was always solicitous of their welfare, and they loved him for it. When he went on tour, the people decorated the route he traveled with arches covered with silk brocade and poles decorated with brightly colored streamers, ribbons, and bows. At night, Chinese paper lanterns, some in the shapes of fish or dragons, shone along the way.

Perhaps somewhere on the very outskirts of the crowd were a few foreigners—Roman Catholic scholar-priests who had come to China from faraway Europe. As non-Chinese, they were considered the lowest ranking people present. Their activities and travel were closely restricted. But in Kang Xi's glorious sixty-year reign, the influence of the foreigners in China was to grow and grow.

Kang Xi was the first emperor to recognize that there were certain things mighty China could learn from Europe, and he was the first to sign a treaty with a Western nation (the 1689 Treaty of Nerchinsk with Russia). From his time on, the dominant theme in China's history is the impact of Western nations on the world's oldest continuous civilization.

Still, on that triumphant spring day in 1699, no one would have believed that two centuries later Europeans would control the Chinese capital for a few months. Or that the empress of China would hide in a lowly peasant's cart to escape from the city.

Kang Xi had been emperor of China since 1661, since he was eight years old. At first a council of ministers ruled for him, but by the time he was fourteen he was considered wise enough to guide his empire himself. Confidence in his ability was completely justified.

The young ruler was strong, well built, and somewhat taller than others his age. But people noticed most his eyes—large, bright eyes that lighted up his face and gave an indication of the intelligence behind them. Strength and courage enabled him to lead his imperial armies time after time to victory over invaders on China's borders and over rebels at home. Intelligence and hard work enabled him to give his country good, stable government, and with it prosperity.

More than a dozen times he toured his empire, for as he said, "One should see everything for oneself." He stopped to chat with many people en route, ranging from the poorest peasant, farming land belonging to someone else, through landowners, scholars, provincial officials and governors. He asked about crops and local problems, and sometimes joined fishermen fishing. He even talked with the European missionaries.

Kang Xi was particularly concerned with China's vast system of canals. Through a thousand years the Chinese had developed these canals to provide irrigation for their crops, flood control, and water transportation. The chief highway of the empire, in fact, was the Grand Canal stretching from Tianjin in the north to Hangzhou, 850 miles to the south.

The emperor was very fond of maps, and on tour would sometimes spread a map in front of him and point out details of the canal system to his officials. He wanted very much to have a good map of his entire empire, whose borders he had expanded farther than any emperor before him. One of the Europeans in Peking, the Jesuit scholar Ferdinand de Verbiest, had drawn a map of the world that particularly impressed the emperor. As a result, in 1708 Kang Xi commissioned the Jesuit missionaries to map his empire. The task took nearly ten years, as the mapmakers studied the best European and Chinese maps of that day, and actually surveyed the land in some areas themselves.

When the new map was finished, it showed China with approximately the same boundaries it has today. In the semitropical south, a fertile land of terraced rice fields carefully tended and irrigated, China bordered on what is now Vietnam. Inland, the boundary was marked by the snowy Himalayan Mountains, the world's highest range, separating China from Burma and India. Tibet, astride the Himalaya, would soon be added to the empire by Kang Xi. Farther north was Outer Mongolia, bordering on Russia. (Because of the terrain and the scattered population, the exact boundaries in the west and northwest remained inexact.) From Mongolia, east to the Pacific, China's northern boundary was marked by the Amur River, under the terms of the treaty Kang Xi had signed with the Russians. On the north bank was Siberia; on the south bank, Manchuria, the home of the Manchu tribe that had conquered all China and made Kang Xi's father emperor in 1644.

Kang Xi ruled all this vast territory by force when he had to. But he much preferred to earn the allegiance of his people by ruling well. He saw to it that promotions were awarded on the basis of knowledge and merit, and rooted out corruption at all levels of government. He lived modestly himself, and repeatedly reduced the taxes on his people. He encouraged education and the arts, and assembled a group of scholars to compile a great encyclopedia to make available in one place the accumulated wisdom of the centuries.

In all these ways Kang Xi sought to fulfill the Chinese view of the ideal society—a view set forth more than two thousand years before by China's most revered philosopher, Confucius.

In the view of Confucius, the structure of a nation was shaped like a pyramid. The emperor was at the peak, and the people formed the broad base. The whole structure was held together by "right relationships" between its parts, between those below and those above. Good sons and daughters revered their parents, in a close-knit family. The head of the family respected the landowning gentry in the village, who in turn owed allegiance to the village and provincial officials. And so the pyramid was built, right up to its tip, the emperor.

In the Confucian ideal, force played no part in these relationships. The emperor would rule as long as he was good and wise, and his heirs would succeed him. If the emperor did not measure up, the whole structure would fall apart, and China would seek a new emperor worthy to found a new dynasty.

Kang Xi was determined to measure up. And China under his rule did seem to enjoy "right relationships," all through society.

There was one problem. The Confucian view of the world made no adequate provision for non-Chinese. It assumed that China was the center of the world, the only civilized nation, and that all other people were simple barbarians who would gladly pay tribute to the Chinese emperor in return for the opportunity to sample a bit of Chinese culture. By Kang Xi's time, this assumption, held for thousands of years, was being challenged.

The challengers came from Europe—a continent the Chinese were only vaguely aware of, located somewhere bordering what they called the Great Western Ocean (the Atlantic). Some seemed civilized enough. The European priests wanted to learn about Chinese culture, and talk about astronomy and mathematics and religion—particularly about their own religion, Christianity. Various emperors before Kang Xi had allowed them to maintain a sort of school in Peking, and Kang Xi conferred a great honor by allowing them to instruct him personally in mathematics.

But other Europeans were rough sea captains and sailors, who knew nothing of the etiquette of accepted behavior in China. They came determined to establish trade. For Europeans had sampled Chinese silks and tea, and a great demand for such luxuries had developed. Kings and merchants both saw prospects of enormous profits from commerce with rich China, with its millions of inhabitants.

The Chinese were glad enough to sell their products, as long as they were paid in good silver money. But they thought it wise to keep close control over these foreign merchants. So they limited their trading activities to only one port, Canton, on China's south coast, the port farthest away from the court and capital at Peking. This cautious policy Kang Xi continued.

The reign of Kang Xi lasted for sixty years. In 1722, at the age of sixty-eight, the emperor caught a fatal cold while pursuing his archery—hunting on horseback on the wild Steppes of Mongolia.

Kang Xi's son succeeded him for a comparatively brief reign of fourteen years. He was followed by his son, Qian Long, who achieved another sixty-year reign. From the beginning of Kang Xi's rule to the end of Qian Long's was a span of 134 years. The Manchu Dynasty, called in Chinese the Qing, or "bright," lasted until 1911, in all, 267 years. But after the standard of excellence established by the first Manchu emperors, especially by Kang Xi, it was downhill all the way.

Zealous Chinese today maintain that European meddling was responsible for the decline. Ardent Westerners maintain that the West's chief goal was to benefit China by bringing her into contact with the rest of the world. There is some truth in both positions, though neither gives the whole story.

Whatever their motives, Westerners became more and more active in China during the reign of Qian Long. The China trade grew enormously. In the eighteenth century, England and Holland were the chief seafaring nations of Europe. Then, their ships competed with new rivals, the Yankee sea captains from New England. Clipper ships built in America were the swiftest on the seas, and each year they loaded the first Chinese tea harvest on board and raced to London. This first tea of the season commanded premium prices among Englishmen, some of whom would drink twenty cups in an evening.

One port in so vast a country was hardly adequate for the potential trade, and the merchants constantly sought to have China's policy changed. In 1793, King George III of England, still smarting from the loss of his American colonies, sent a delegation to Qian Long to ask, as one ruler to another, that additional ports be opened to English merchants. The emperor's reply was patient but firm:

> Yesterday your ambassador petitioned my ministers to memorialize me regarding your trade with China, but his proposal is not consistent with our dynastic usage and cannot be entertained. . . . Our Celestial Empire possesses all things in prolific abundance and lacks no product within its own borders. There was, therefore, no need to import the manufactures of outside barbarians in exchange for our own produce. . . . Nevertheless, I do not forget the lonely remoteness of your island, cut off from the world by intervening wastes of sea, nor do I overlook your excusable ignorance of the usages of Our Celestial Empire. I have consequently commanded my ministers to enlighten your ambassador on the subject, and have ordered the departure of the mission. . . .

Subsequent delegations had even less success.

Qian Long's claim that his empire possessed all things and lacked for nothing was very nearly true. China enjoyed a long period of peace, disturbed by only minor rebellions and border skirmishes. The arts flourished. Literature reached new heights, and Chinese kilns produced some of the most beautiful porcelain ever seen.

It was a Golden Age. And yet it produced its own problems. The population increased rapidly, creating the need for increased production of food. But China was already farming all of her land that was suitable for agriculture. In years when crops were poor, thousands starved.

Part of each year's crop, in both good years and bad, went to feed the army. The soldiers grew fat and lazy, and their discipline lax. Even the elite Manchu regiments, so proud and powerful when their forebears conquered China in 1644, grew soft. The Manchus, both military and civilian, had maintained their separate identity in all the years since the conquest, wearing their hair loose while requiring the Chinese to braid theirs in a pigtail called a queue. Manchus could marry only other Manchus. And yet the longer they ruled in China, the more they appreciated Chinese ways, and the more like Chinese they became.

Qian Long himself grew soft, and fond of the easy life. The end of his reign was far different from that of his grandfather. Kang Xi had kept vigorous and alert to the very end, riding his horses, studying his mathematics, traveling and keeping a close eye on all his empire. He died at sixty-eight. Qian Long reigned to the age of eighty-five. First he grew weary of the duties of office, and then so senile that he did not know what was happening in the government. The Confucian doctrine proved all too true, that the ruler at the top of the pyramid of society sets the tone of the whole.

Europe and Japan
in the Middle Ages

King Arthur: The Marvel of the Sword

Mary MacLeod

In this selection, the author mixes the magical legend of King Arthur with historical details. Even the legendary King Arthur was once a teenager!

When Uther[1] Pendragon, King of England, died, the country for a long while stood in great danger, for every lord that was mighty gathered his forces, and many wished to be king. For King Uther's own son, Prince Arthur, who should have succeeded him, was but a child, and Merlin, the mighty magician, had hidden him away.

Now a strange thing had happened at Arthur's birth.

Some time before, Merlin had done Uther a great service, on condition that the King should grant him whatever he wished for. This the King swore a solemn oath to do. Then Merlin made him promise that when his child was born it should be delivered to Merlin to bring up as he chose, for this would be to the child's own great advantage. The King had given his promise so he was obliged to agree. Then Merlin said he knew a very true and faithful man, one of King Uther's lords, by name Sir Ector,[2] who had large possessions in many parts of England and Wales, and that the child should be given to him to bring up.

On the night the baby was born, while it was still unchristened, King Uther commanded two knights and two ladies to take it, wrapped in a cloth of gold, and deliver it to a poor man whom they would find waiting at the postern gate of the Castle. This poor man was Merlin in disguise, although they did not know it. So the child was delivered unto Merlin and he carried him to Sir Ector, and made a holy man christen him, and named him Arthur; and Sir Ector's wife cherished him as her own child.

Within two years King Uther fell sick of a great malady, and for three days and three nights he was speechless. All the Barons[3] were in sorrow, and asked Merlin what was best to be done.

---

1. **Uther** (yo͞o thər)
2. **Ector** (ek′ tôr)
3. **Barons** (bar′ ənz) *n.* members of the lowest rank of British nobility.

All the Barons[3] were in sorrow, and asked Merlin what was best to be done.

"There is no remedy," said Merlin. "God will have His Will. But look ye all, Barons, come before King Uther to-morrow, and God will make him speak."

So the next day Merlin and all the Barons came before the King, and Merlin said aloud to King Uther:

"Sir, after your days shall your son Arthur be King of this realm and all that belongs to it?"

Then Uther Pendragon turned and said in hearing of them all: "I give my son Arthur God's blessing and mine, and bid him pray for my soul, and righteously and honorably claim the crown, on forfeiture of my blessing."

And with that, King Uther died.

But Arthur was still only a baby, not two years old, and Merlin knew it would be no use yet to proclaim him King. For there were many powerful nobles in England in those days, who were all trying to get the kingdom for themselves, and perhaps they would kill the little Prince. So there was much strife and debate in the land for a long time.

When several years had passed, Merlin went to the Archbishop of Canterbury[4] and counseled him to send for all the lords of the realm,[5] and all the gentlemen of arms, that they should come to London at Christmas, and for this cause—that a miracle would show who should be rightly King of the realm. So all the lords and gentlemen made themselves ready, and came to London, and long before dawn on Christmas Day they were all gathered in the great church of St. Paul's to pray.

When the first service was over, there was seen in the churchyard a large stone, four-square, like marble, and in the midst of it was like an anvil of steel, a foot high. In this was stuck by the point a beautiful sword, with naked blade, and there were letters written in gold about the sword, which said thus:

Whoso pulleth this sword out of this stone and anvil is rightly King of all England.

---

3. **Barons** (bar′ ənz) *n.* members of the lowest rank of British nobility.
4. **Canterbury** (kan′ tər ber′ ē) *n.* cathedral and sacred shrine in Canterbury, a town southeast of London. In medieval times, many English people made pilgrimages or journeys to Canterbury.
5. **realm** (relm) *n.* kingdom.

Then the people marveled, and told it to the Archbishop.

"I command," said the Archbishop, "that you keep within the church, and pray unto God still; and that no man touch the sword till the service is over."

So when the prayers in church were over, all the lords went to behold the stone and the sword; and when they read the writing some of them—such as wished to be king—tried to pull the sword out of the anvil. But not one could make it stir.

"The man is not here, that shall achieve the sword," said the Archbishop, "but doubt not God will make him known. But let us provide ten knights, men of good fame, to keep guard over the sword."

So it was ordained, and proclamation was made that everyone who wished might try to win the sword. And upon New Year's Day the Barons arranged to have a great tournament, in which all knights who would joust[6] or tourney[7] might take a part. This was ordained to keep together the Lords and Commons, for the Archbishop trusted that it would be made known who should win the sword.

On New Year's Day, after church, the Barons rode to the field, some to joust, and some to tourney, and so it happened that Sir Ector, who had large estates near London, came also to the tournament; and with him rode Sir Kay, his son, with young Arthur, his foster brother.

As they rode, Sir Kay found he had lost his sword, for he had left it at his father's lodging, so he begged young Arthur to go and fetch it for him.

"That will I, gladly," said Arthur, and he rode fast away.

But when he came to the house, he found no one at home to give him the sword, for everyone had gone to see the jousting. Then Arthur was angry and said to himself: "I will ride to the churchyard, and take the sword with me that sticketh in the stone, for my brother, Sir Kay, shall not be without a sword this day."

When he came to the churchyard he alighted,[8] and tied his horse to the stile, and went to the tent. But he

---

6. joust (jowst) v. to take part in a combat between two knights on horseback with lances.

7. tourney (tōor′ nē) v. to compete; to take part in a tournament.

8. alighted (a līt′ əd) v. dismounted; got down off a horse.

found there no knights, who should have been guarding the sword, for they were all away at the joust. Seizing the sword by the handle he lightly and fiercely pulled it out of the stone, then took his horse and rode his way, till he came to Sir Kay his brother, to whom he delivered the sword.

As soon as Sir Kay saw it, he knew well it was the sword of the Stone, so he rode to his father Sir Ector, and said:

"Sir, lo, here is the Sword of the Stone, wherefore[9] I must be King of this land."

When Sir Ector saw the sword he turned back, and came to the church, and there they all three alighted and went into the church, and he made his son swear truly how he got the sword.

"By my brother Arthur," said Sir Kay, "for he brought it to me."

"How did you get this sword?" said Sir Ector to Arthur. And the boy told him.

"Now," said Sir Ector, "I understand you must be King of this land."

"Wherefore I?" said Arthur. "And for what cause?"

"Sir," said Ector, "because God will have it so; for never man could draw out this sword but he that shall rightly be King. Now let me see whether you can put the sword there as it was, and pull it out again."

"There is no difficulty," said Arthur, and he put it back into the stone.

Then Sir Ector tried to pull out the sword, and failed; and Sir Kay also pulled with all his might, but it would not move.

"Now you shall try," said Sir Ector to Arthur.

"I will, well," said Arthur, and pulled the sword out easily.

At this Sir Ector and Sir Kay knelt down on the ground.

"Alas," said Arthur, "mine own dear father and brother, why do you kneel to me?"

"Nay, nay, my lord Arthur, it is not so; I was never your father, nor of your blood; but I know well you are of higher blood than I thought you were."

---

9. **wherefore** why.

Then Sir Ector told him all, how he had taken him to bring up, and by whose command; and how he had received him from Merlin. And when he understood that Ector was not his father, Arthur was deeply grieved.

"Will you be my good, gracious lord, when you are King?" asked the knight.

"If not, I should be to blame," said Arthur, "for you are the man in the world to whom I am the most beholden, and my good lady and mother your wife, who has fostered and kept me as well as her own children. And if ever it be God's will that I be King, as you say, you shall desire of me what I shall do, and I shall not fail you: God forbid I should fail you."

"Sir," said Sir Ector, "I will ask no more of you but that you will make my son, your foster brother Sir Kay, seneschal[10] of all your lands."

"That shall be done," said Arthur, "and by my faith, never man but he shall have that office while he and I live."

Then they went to the Archbishop and told him how the sword was achieved, and by whom.

On Twelfth Day all the Barons came to the stone in the churchyard, so that anyone who wished might try to win the sword. But not one of them all could take it out, except Arthur. Many of them therefore were very angry, and said it was a great shame to them and to the country to be governed by a boy not of high blood, for as yet none of them knew that he was the son of King Uther Pendragon. So they agreed to delay the decision till Candlemas, which is the second day of February.

But when Candlemas came, and Arthur once more was the only one who could pull out the sword, they put it off till Easter; and when Easter came, and Arthur again prevailed in the presence of them all, they put it off till the Feast of Pentecost.

Then by Merlin's advice the Archbishop summoned some of the best knights that were to be—such knights as in his own day King Uther Pendragon had best loved, and trusted most—and these were appointed to attend young Arthur, and never to leave him night or day till the Feast of Pentecost.

---

10. **seneschal** (sen' ə shəl) *n.* person in charge of household arrangements.

When the great day came, all manner of men once more made the attempt, and once more not one of them all could prevail but Arthur. Before all the Lords and Commons there assembled he pulled out the sword, whereupon all the Commons cried out:

"We will have Arthur for our King! We will put him no more in delay, for we all see that it is God's will that he shall be our King, and he who holdeth against it, we will slay him."

And therewith they knelt down all at once, both rich and poor, and besought pardon of Arthur, because they had delayed him so long.

And Arthur forgave them, and took the sword in both his hands, and offered it on the altar where the Archbishop was and so he was made knight by the best man there.

After that, he was crowned at once, and there he swore to his Lords and Commons to be a true King, and to govern with true justice from thenceforth all the days of his life.

Lochinvar

Sir Walter Scott

In this poem, a loyal and romantic knight cannot let his beloved Ellen marry another, even if it means disrupting her wedding.

O, young Lochinvar is come out of the West,
Through all the wide Border his steed[1] was the
    best,
And save his good broadsword[2] he weapons had
    none;
He rode all unarmed, and he rode all alone.
5   So faithful in love, and so dauntless in war,
There never was knight like the young Lochinvar.

He stayed not for brake, and he stopped not for
    stone,
He swam the Eske river[3] where ford there was
    none;
But, ere he alighted at Netherby[4] gate,
10   The bride had consented, the gallant came late:
For a laggard in love, and a dastard in war,
Was to wed the fair Ellen of brave Lochinvar.

So boldly he entered the Netherby hall,
Among bridesmen and kinsmen, and brothers
    and all;
15   Then spoke the bride's father, his hand on his
    sword
(For the poor craven[5] bridegroom said never a
    word),
"O come ye in peace here, or come ye in war,
Or to dance at our bridal, young Lord Lochinvar?"

"I long wooed your daughter, my suit you
    denied;—

---

1. steed (stēd) *n.* horse.
2. broadsword *n.* sword with a wide double-edged blade used for slashing rather than thrusting.
3. Eske river (esk) *n.* river near border between England and Scotland.
4. Netherby *n.* name of the manor where the poem is set.
5. craven (krā′ vən) *adj.* very cowardly.

20 Love swells like the Solway, but ebbs like its
   tide—
   And now I am come, with this lost love of mine,
   To lead but one measure, drink one cup of wine.
   There are maidens in Scotland more lovely by far,
   That would gladly be bride to the young
     Lochinvar."
25 The bride kissed the goblet[6] the knight took it up,
   He quaffed off the wine, and he threw down the
     cup,
   She looked down to blush, and she looked up to
     sigh,
   With a smile on her lips and a tear in her eye.
   He took her soft hand, ere her mother could
     bar—
30 "Now tread we a measure!" said young Lochinvar.

   So stately his form, and so lovely her face,
   That never a hall such a galliard[7] did grace;
   While her mother did fret, and her father did
     fume,
   And the bridegroom stood dangling his bonnet
     and plume;[8]
35 And the bridesmaidens whispered, "'Twere better
     by far
   To have matched our fair cousin with young
     Lochinvar."

   One touch to her hand, and one word in her ear,
   When they reached the hall door, and the charger
     stood near;
   So light to the croupe the fair lady he swung,
40 So light to the saddle before her he sprung!
   "She is won! we are gone, over bank, bush, and
     scaur;[9]
   They'll have fleet steeds that follow," quoth young
     Lochinvar.
   There was mounting 'mong Græmes of the
     Netherby clan;

---

6. goblet (gäb' lit) *n.* drinking cup.
7. galliard (gal' yərd) *n.* lively French dance.
8. plume (plo͞om) *n.* decoration made of a large feather or feathers.
9. scaur (skär) *n.* steep, rocky hill.

Forsters, Fenwicks, and Musgraves,[10] they rode
   and they ran;
45   There was racing, and chasing, on Cannobie Lee,
But the lost bride of Netherby ne'er did they see.
So daring in love, and so dauntless in war,
Have ye e'er heard of gallant like young
   Lochinvar?

---

10. Græmes . . . Forsters, Fenwicks, and Musgraves family names.

Grendel

from Beowulf, the Warrior

Ian Serraillier

In this poem, the legendary Grendel, symbolic of the forces of evil, finally meets his match in the epic hero Beowulf.

Hrothgar, King of the Danes, glorious in battle,
Built him a huge hall—its gleaming roof
Towering high to heaven—strong to withstand
The buffet of war. He called it Heorot
And lived there with his Queen. At time of
    feasting
He gave to his followers rings and ornaments
And bracelets of bright gold, cunningly wrought,
Graved with runes and deeds of dead heroes.
Here they enjoyed feasts and high fellowship,
Story and song and the pride of armed peace.
But away in the treacherous fens, beyond the
    moor,
A hideous monster lurked, fiend from hell,
Misbegotten son of a foul mother,
Grendel his name, hating the sound of the harp,
The minstrel's song, the bold merriment of men
In whose distorted likeness he was shaped
Twice six feet tall, with arms of hairy gorilla
And red ferocious eyes and ravening jaws.
He, one night, when the warriors of Hrothgar lay
Slumbering after banquet, came to Heorot,
Broke down the door, seized in his fell grip
A score and more of the sleeping sons of men
And carried them home for meat. At break of day
The hall of Heorot rang loud and long
With woe of warriors and grief of the great King.
Thereafter, from dark lake and dripping caves
Night after night over the misty moor
Came Grendel, gross and grim, famished for flesh.
Empty the beds, no man dared sleep at Heorot,
But Grendel smelt them out of their hiding place,
And many a meal he made of warriors.

For twelve years he waged war with Hrothgar,
Piling grief upon grief. For twelve years
He haunted great Heorot.

Now there lived overseas
In the land of the Geats a youth of valiance
abounding,
Mightiest yet mildest of men, his name Beowulf,
Who, hearing of Grendel and minded to destroy
him,
Built a boat of the stoutest timber and chose
him
Warriors, fourteen of the best. In shining
armour
They boarded the great vessel, beached on the
shingle¹
By the curling tide. Straightway they shoved her
off.
They ran up the white sail. And the wind caught
her,
The biting wind whipped her over the waves.
Like a strong bird the swan-boat winged her way
Over the grey Baltic, the wintry whale-road,
Till the lookout sighted land—a sickle of fair
sand
And glittering white cliffs. The keel struck
The shingle. The warriors sprang ashore.
But the watchman of the Danes, the lone cliff
guardian,
Seeing them from afar, spurred his charger and
came
Galloping down to the shore. He branished his
spear
And over the wind and wave-roar loud he
shouted:
'Strangers from the whale-road, who are you that
dare,
Unbidden, unheralded, so boldly trespass here?
Upon your flashing shields and the points of your
spears
I see the glint of death.'

---

1. **shingle** (shiŋ′ gəl) *n.* beach.

And Beowulf answered:
'We are from Sweden, O guardian of the shore.
    Fear not,
For in loyalty we come—from friendly fields
That tremble to the tale of your suffering and
    horror
Unspeakable. Crowding sail, hot haste we are
    come
With stout spears of ashwood and shields to
    protect you.
God grant we rid you of Grendel the grim
    monster!'
    The watchman lowered his spear, and from
        smiling lips
The wind blew to Beowulf fair words of greeting:
'Whoever serves my King is welcome here.
Come, noble warriors, let me show you the way,
And my men will look to your boat.'

    They left her at anchor,
The broad-bellied ship afloat on the bobbing tide,
And followed him over the cliff toward Heorot. As
    they marched,
The boar-head glared from their helmets, the iron
    rings
Rang on their mailcoats. And the watchman said,
    'Behold
The huge hall, wide-gabled, the gleaming roof
Towering high to heaven. Follow the street
To the studded door, where Wulfgar, herald of the
    King,
Will receive you. May God Almighty prosper your
    venture
And hold you safe!' He wheeled about on his
    horse
And galloped away to the shore.

    Thus came the warriors
To Heorot and, heavy with weariness, halted by
    the door
They propped their spears by a pillar; from
    blistered hands
Their shields slid clattering to the floor. Then
    Wulfgar,

Herald of the King, having demanded their
    errand,
Ran to his royal master and quick returning
Urged them within. The long hall lay before them,
The floor paved with stone, the roof high-raftered.
In mournful state upon his throne sat brooding
Aged Hrothgar, grey-haired and bowed with grief.
Slowly he raised his eyes, leaden, lustreless,
And gazed upon the youth as with ringing step
Boldly he strode forth till he stood at his feet.
    'O noble Hrothgar, giver of treasure,
Lord of the rousing war-song, we bring you
    greeting.
Because we grieve deep for your desolation,
Over the long paths of the ocean have we
    laboured,
I and my warriors, to rid you of the brute
That nightly robs you of rest. I am no weakling.
With my trusty blade I have slain a monster
    brood
And blindly at night many a foul sea-beast
That writhed and twisted in the bounding wave.
I beg you to grant my wish. I shall not fail.'
    Then Hrothgar stretched out his arms in
        welcome
And took him by the hand and said, 'Beowulf,
I knew you as a child, and who has not exulted
In your fame as a fighter? It is a triumph song
That ocean thunders to her farthest shore,
It is a whisper in the frailest sea-shell.
Now, like your princely father long ago,
In the brimming kindness of your heart you have
    come
To deliver us.'

    But Unferth bristled at these words—
Unferth, who sat always at the feet of Hrothgar,
A grovelling, jealous man who could not bear
That anyone should win more fame then he.
    'Braggart!' he cried. 'Are you not that Beowulf
Who failed against Breca in the swimming match?
Seven nights you wallowed in the wintry sea—
Some sport that was!—sport for jeering waves
That jollied you like spindrift from crest to crest

Till, sick with cold, you shrieked for mercy. Who
    heard?
Not Breca, who long since had battled to land,
But the sea, tired at last of its puny plaything,
Spewed you ashore.'

    Angrily Beowulf answered:
'That's a drunkard's tale! True, Breca was first
Ashore, but I could have raced him had I wished.
We were boys then, with our full share of folly,
Plunging—sword in hand—giddily to battle
With monster whales, when a storm came
    sweeping down
And gruesome waves ground and trampled us
    under.
It was Breca that cried for help—I fought to save
    him,
But a fierce north-easter whipped us apart
And I saw him no more. In the dark and bitter cold,
The icy brine was heaving murkily with monsters.
Glad was I of my sword and mail-coat—for a
    serpent
Had wound his sinewy coils about my waist,
And squeezing, dragged me below. But before he
    could break me,
I slew him—nine others too before the raging
    floodtide
Rolled me to land. . . .
I am not aware that you, brave Unferth, can boast
Such a record. If you be as bold as you proclaim,
Tell me, how comes it that Grendel is still alive?
Ha, I know a coward when I see one! Soon,
If the King be willing, I shall grapple with Grendel
And show you what courage means.'

    Then Hrothgar, marking
The warrior's blazing eyes, and hasty hand
Fingering his sword-hilt, with mild words melted
    his anger.
'Noble Beowulf, pay no heed to Unferth,
An envious, wayward man, unworthy of note.
Right gladly I grant your wishes—but first, one
    word
Of warning. That sword you spoke of—it will avail

Nothing with Grendel, whose life is proof against
All weapons whatsoever, wrought by man.
You must go for him with your hands, your bare
    hands.'

    Thus spake King Hrothgar and from his
        bounteous heart
Wished the youth well. Soon as the benches
Had been cleared away for banquet, he called for
    his Queen,
The gracious Wealhtheow who, proudly entering,
Was proudly hailed by royal clarion of trumpets.
A gown of broidered gold she wore, behind her
A long train, dark as the night sky,
Illumined with galaxy of stars that, as she glided
Forward to greet her guests, trembled in the
    torchlight.
The mead cup glowed in her hands, strong to
    revive them
Weary from wandering over the surging sea.
Kneeling, she offered it first to Beowulf, next
To his warriors each in turn, and lastly to the
    Danes.
They drank and they feasted, the jewelled goblets
    clashed
In the great hall. There was loud revelry of heroes,
Bold merriment of men, and minstrel song
And the soothing voice of the harp—until twilight,
The drowsy hour of Grendel's coming, the black
    shape
Stealing over the dusky moor. Then the Danes
Man by man uprose and, clearing the banquet,
Brought for their guests soft couches, pillow-
    strewn,
With fleeces of thick wool. When the Queen had
    departed,
They hurried each to his secret hiding place;
And last of all, murmuring abundant blessing
On Beowulf—grave and reluctant, the noble
    Hrothgar.

    Straightway Beowulf stripped off his armour,
        his mailcoat,
His shining helmet. His shield and precious sword

Gave he to his servant, and in the ring of warriors
Lay down to rest. But spent as they were—
For tumult of Grendel and his havoc, like
    runaway hooves
Making riot in their brains—they could not sleep.
Under their fleeces in terror they sweated and
    trembled,
Wide-awake, till at last, outworn with weariness,
Heavy-lidded, they slept—all but Beowulf.
Alone, he watched.

    Over the misty moor
From the dark and dripping caves of his grim lair,
Grendel with fierce ravenous stride came
    stepping.
A shadow under the pale moon he moved,
That fiend from hell, foul enemy of God,
Toward Heorot. He beheld it from afar, the
    gleaming roof
Towering high to heaven. His tremendous hands
Struck the studded door, wrenched it from the
    hinges
Till the wood splintered and the bolts burst apart.
Angrily he prowled over the polished floor,
A terrible light in his eyes—a torch flaming!
As he scanned the warriors, deep-drugged in
    sleep,
Loud loud he laughed, and pouncing on the
    nearest
Tore him limb from limb and swallowed him
    whole,
Sucking the blood in streams, crunching the
    bones.
Half-gorged, his gross appetite still unslaked,
Greedily he reached his hand for the next—little
    reckoning
For Beowulf. The youth clutched it and firmly
    grappled.

    Such torture as this the fiend had never
      known.
In mortal fear, he was minded to flee to his lair,
But Beowulf prisoned him fast. Spilling the
    benches,

They tugged and heaved, from wall to wall they
    hurtled.
And the roof rang to their shouting, the huge hall
Rocked, the strong foundations groaned and
    trembled.
Then Grendel wailed from his wound, his shriek
    of pain
Roused the Danes in their hiding and shivered to
    the stars.
The warriors in the hall spun reeling from their
    couches,
In dull stupor they fumbled for their swords,
    forgetting
No man-made weapon might avail. Alone, Beowulf
Tore Grendel's arm from his shoulder asunder,
Wrenched it from the root while the tough sinews
    cracked.
And the monster roared in anguish, well knowing
That deadly was the wound and his mortal days
    ended.
Wildly lamenting, away into the darkness he
    limped,
Over the misty moor to his gloomy home.
But the hero rejoiced in his triumph and wildly
    waved
In the air his blood-soaked trophy.

    And the sun,
God's beacon of brightness, banishing night,
Made glad the sky of morning. From near and far
The Danes came flocking to Heorot to behold
The grisly trophy—Grendel's giant arm
Nailed to the wall, the fingertips outspread,
With nails of sharpened steel and murderous
    spikes
Clawing the roof. Having drunk their fill of
    wonder,
Eagerly they followed his track to the lake, and
    there
Spellbound they stared at the water welling with
    blood,
Still smoking hot where down to the joyless deep
He had dived, downward to death. And they
    praised Beowulf

And swore that of all men under the sun, beyond
    measure
Mightiest was he and fittest to govern his people.

    Meanwhile, in the hall at Heorot the grateful
        King,
All glooming gone, his countenance clear and
    cloudless
As the sky in open radiance of the climbing sun,
Gave thanks to God for deliverance. 'Beowulf,' he
    said,
'Bravest of men, I shall love you now as my son.
All I have is yours for the asking. Take
What treasure you will. But first let us feast and
    be merry.'

    Straightway they washed the blood from the
        floor, propped up
The battered door; the drooping walls they draped
With embroidery, bright hangings of woven gold.
There was drinking and feasting again, revelry of
    heroes,
And the jewelled goblets clashed. At last the King,
Aged Hrothgar, grey-haired giver of treasure,
Ordered gifts to be brought. To Beowulf he gave
A sword and mailcoat and banner of gleaming
    gold;
A plated helmet so tough no steel might cleave it;
Eight prancing horses with golden harness
And bridles of silver, the proudest saddled with
    his own
Battle-seat, all set with splendid jewels,
Most cunningly inlaid; to each of the warriors
A sword and bountiful recompense of gold
For their friend that Grendel slew.
    Then the minstrel sang
Of rousing deeds of old. Like flames in the
    firelight
The heart leapt to hear them. And when he had
    done
And the harp lay silent, the Queen of the Danes
    spoke out:
'Beowulf, dearest youth, son of most favoured
And fortunate of mothers, this your deed is

matchless

Greater than all these. In the farthest corners

Of the earth your name shall be known. Wherever
the ocean

Laps the windy shore and the wave-worn
headland,

Your praise shall be sung.'

And now the feast was ended.

With final clarion of trumpets they left the hall,

Hrothgar and his gracious Queen, leading
Beowulf

To a stately chamber to rest. But the Danes
remained

Clearing the banquet, they brought couches
spread

With pillows and warm coverlets, and lay down,

Each with his broad shield at his head, his
mailcoat,

His spear and shining helmet—as was the custom

Long ere Grendel came. Now fearless of monster,

Their minds were at ease, quiet as the summer
sea,

The sparkling water, unmurmuring and serene

Under the moon. In comfort of spirit, in blessed

Trust and tranquillity they sank to rest.

The Bayeux Tapestry

Norman Denny and Josephine Filmer-Sankey

History has not been recorded only in books. This selection describes a historic event captured on a strip of linen 230 feet long.

The Bayeux Tapestry is a very old version of what we are apt to think of as a modern thing. It is a strip-cartoon, one of the earliest and certainly the greatest that is known to us, and it was made within a few years of the tremendous historical event it records: the Norman invasion of England, which took place just nine centuries ago.

The French still call it "Queen Matilda's Tapestry"—*La Tapisserie de la Reine Matilde*. Matilda was the wife of Duke William of Normandy, "William the Conqueror," and she became Queen of England after the Conquest. For a long time she was believed to be the designer and maker of the tapestry, but we now know that this was not the case. It was made to the order of Bishop Odo, William's half-brother, to be hung in Odo's Cathedral at Bayeux, a little town in Normandy some ten miles from the sea.

Bishop Odo ordered it to be made, but there is no reason to suppose that he had any share in its making. For the design, an artist was needed. We do not know who he was; but that he was a great artist is proved by the splendid life and vigor of his drawings, the skill with which he told the story, and the picture he has given us of the life of the time.

We must note an important point. The Bayeux Tapestry, although it is always referred to as such, is not really a tapestry at all. A tapestry is a cloth made on a loom, with its pattern or design woven into it. The Bayeux Tapestry is a piece of embroidery (needlework), the pictures being stitched in woolen threads of eight different colors on a long strip of bleached linen. The designer may have drawn them first on parchment, but it seems more likely that he drew them on the linen strip, which he then handed over to the craftsmen (or women) who did the embroidering.

It is an immense work. The strip of linen is about two hundred and thirty feet long and twenty inches wide. It was made in eight sections, afterwards stitched together, probably embroidered by separate teams of craftsmen. Nothing is now known of these people; but at the time when the work was carried out (probably between A.D. 1070 and 1080) there was a School of Embroidery at Canterbury, in Kent,[1] which was famous throughout Europe for needlework of this kind. We cannot be sure, but it looks as though this is where the work was done. In short, although the tapestry is Norman in origin, and represents the Norman point of view, it was probably executed by English hands.

After its completion the tapestry was taken to Bayeux Cathedral, where it was preserved among the church's greatest treasures, being hung round the nave on feast-days and special occasions. There it remained for seven centuries, untroubled, meticulously cared for, and (it would seem) largely disregarded by the scholars and historians who might have been expected to take more interest in something that was at once a great work of art, a wonderful story and a unique historical document. Then more notice was taken of it, and its life became more adventurous. It narrowly escaped destruction in the early days of the French Revolution[2] and later was taken to Paris to be exhibited there by order of Napoleon[3] (who was planning another invasion of England at the time). During the next hundred years or so it underwent many vicissitudes[4] and changed its dwelling many times, suffering considerable damage in the process. But by 1945 it was installed in what we must hope will be its permanent home, in the former Palace of the Bishops of Bayeux. Beautifully restored and beautifully lighted, housed under glass in a frame work running round three sides of a long gallery specially designed for it, it is on show for all the world to see.

---

1. **Kent** a county in southeast England.
2. **French Revolution** the revolution in France from 1789 to 1799.
3. **Napoleon Bonaparte** French military leader and conquerer, became emperor of France, 1804–1815.
4. **vicissitudes** (vi sis′ ə to͞od) *n.* changes.

Tanka

Translated by Geoffrey Bownas

Priest Jakuren

*This poem uses fleeting images from nature to express
an important idea about human experience.*

> One cannot ask loneliness
> How or where it starts.
> On the cypress-mountain,[1]
> Autumn evening.

---

1. cypress-mountain Cypress trees are cone-bearing evergreen trees, native to
North America, Europe, and Asia.

The Boy Who Drew Sheep

Anne Rockwell

Writers of historical biographies like this one must imagine some of the details, but they usually base what they imagine on historical evidence.

More than seven hundred years ago, in a valley in Italy, there lived a farmer named Bondone. He had a wife and a house, some pigs, a few cows, fig and olive trees, many, many woolly sheep, and a son to help him on the farm. The boy was named Giotto.[1] When he was nine years old, his father entrusted the flock of sheep to him. Each morning, before the sun was up, Giotto and his dog led the sheep up into the hills where they nibbled all day at the meadow grass; and in the evening, when the moon rose, he led them safely home again.

Alone as he was, with no playmates or companions but his dog and sheep, Giotto began to pass the long days by scratching pictures with a sharp pebble on the large stones that jutted up here and there in the meadow. First he drew the things that came into his head, but after a while he decided to draw something that he had actually seen. And so he began to make a picture of one of his sheep. He worked and worked, but the drawing never seemed quite right. So when he finished one he would begin another. The time passed quickly this way, and wherever he wandered with his flock, the rocks were scratched with pictures of sheep: old and solemn rams, gentle ewes, and curly baby lambs.

One day a group of gentlemen on horseback came riding up into the hills where Giotto herded his flock. Both men and horses were dressed in the finest and shiniest silk and leather. Each gentleman carried a hawk on his wrist, and each hawk wore a little leather mask on his face. The men were hunting. But Giotto did not notice them, so busy was he with his newest drawing. Not far from where he sat, a little spring of fresh, cold water gushed up between two rocks. One of the gentlemen rode over all alone, and he and his horse drank from the cool

---

1. **Giotto** (jŏt′ tō)

water. While he was at the spring, he noticed the boy. So he walked quietly over and looked at the drawing.

Giotto must have been surprised to see the well-dressed stranger, for few people came into his hills. The gentleman introduced himself as Cimabue, a citizen of the city of Florence.[2] He congratulated Giotto on his fine drawing and said that he too was an artist. He painted pictures on the walls of the churches of Florence. The man looked again at Giotto's drawing and then offered to teach Giotto all of the many things he knew about picture painting. Giotto would have to come and work for him in his workshop, of course, if this were to happen. Giotto was surprised by this, for where he lived most men were farmers and shepherds, as their fathers had been and their sons would be, and there were no artists.

That evening, when the boy led the sheep back to the valley, Cimabue went with him. For a long time he spoke with Giotto's mother and father. He told them that of all the boys who had ever worked in his workshop (and there were many), none could draw so well, without any lessons, as their son Giotto.

The farmer Bondone was a practical man. He didn't want his son to waste his time in foolishness. But as he looked at the stranger's elegant clothes, which must have cost a great deal of money, he began to think that perhaps the stranger was right: Giotto should go and learn to paint pictures. Perhaps he too would grow rich. And so, before the family went to bed that night, it was settled. Giotto would go to Florence and become an apprentice in Cimabue's workshop.

Early next morning Giotto, instead of heading for the hills with his sheep, said good-bye to them and to his dog and to his mother and father. He climbed up in back of Cimabue on the painter's high-stepping horse, and the two of them set off toward Florence.

Many hours later they reached the gates of the city. Tall towers bristled proudly against the sky, and inside the strong walls were more people together than Giotto had seen in his whole life. Knights in armor rode through the busy streets; well-dressed merchants talked together of business; market stalls were filled to overflowing with

---

2. Florence the Italian city often called the birthplace of the Renaissance since many of the period's great artists lived or worked there.

sweet figs and melons and other good things from the hills.

On every corner, or so it seemed, women sat chatting and spinning wool into long skeins.[3] Iron hooks projected from nearly all of the houses in Florence. Across these iron hooks lay cross-pieces of wood. And from these wooden cross-pieces hung great skeins of purple, crimson, gold, and deep blue wool, drying in the air. For the city of Florence was rich from wool, wool from the sheep that shepherds such as Giotto had raised in the hills. This good wool of Florence was sold to the world and the city's wool merchants were rich and proud.

The city was grand and glorious. Its churches were filled with pictures painted by artists such as Cimabue, artists all other cities in the world would have liked to have. The pictures covered the plaster walls of churches or hung from strong wooden panels. They gleamed with brilliant red and blue and paper-thin coatings of real gold, bright as the sun.

Cimabue took Giotto to the workshop, which stood on one of Florence's narrow, busy streets. There the boy was introduced to the other apprentices. Some of them were boys nearly as young as Giotto; others were almost men; and one or two were grown men without workshops of their own. They managed the workshop of Cimabue. The apprentices lived together behind the workshop. Giotto was welcomed as one of them, and his training began.

First he learned to make charcoal sticks for drawing. He cut up several willow switches into lengths just a little longer than his longest finger. Then he carefully sharpened each end to a point with his knife. Next he tied all of the willow sticks into several neat bundles. These bundles went into an earthenware casserole, with a cover. When the bundles were in, he sealed the cover of the casserole tight shut with a shaped piece of clay, so the inside was airtight. Last of all, he carefully carried the pot to the baker's shop. He gave it to the baker, who placed it at the entrance of one of the great ovens that he was lighting that night for the baking of fine loaves of bread early in the morning. And that night, all night long, the casserole sat in the baker's oven, while the boy

---

3. **skeins** (skānz) *n.* loose thick coils.

slept and dreamed that the charcoal sticks would turn out well. For if the fire was too hot, or the willow bundles improperly packed, the charcoal would be too burnt, and it would crumble when it was put to paper or parchment. Then the boy who made it might be whipped. But if he was lucky and had done his work well, the sticks would be hard and black, and there would be charcoal for drawing for many weeks, and praise for him, too. When Giotto brought his first charcoal back to the workshop, he *was* lucky, for the sticks were perfect, black and sharp and crisp. He also brought breakfast . . . the first loaves of the morning, warm and round and crusty.

He learned to prepare parchment for drawing. From the leather tanner, pieces of skin from a very young calf were bought. These he washed, nailed to a wooden stretcher, and dried in the sunshine. Then, he picked up the chicken bones from under the dining table at night, where the apprentices threw them, and burned them in the fire until the ashes were white and soft. These ashes were ground on a smooth stone slab until they were even softer. Then, with a furry rabbit's foot, he dusted the powder back and forth, back and forth across the dried skin until it was velvet smooth and ready to take the lines made by charcoal, or if more delicate work was wanted, by a little piece of tarnished silver wire from the goldsmith's workshop.

And all the time he was learning these things, Giotto, in the little time he had left for himself, drew pictures . . . just as he had while he tended his father's sheep in the high hills.

Sometimes the other apprentices told him stories of the glory that came to a painter as skilled and admired as their master. Once Cimabue had received a commission to paint a picture of the Virgin Mary. She was to be surrounded by angels, and she would sit against a sky of gold. The picture would hang in a church in Florence in a spot where all would see it, including the visiting foreign kings and princes who came to Florence. It was springtime when Cimabue began the painting. One day the breezes blew so soft and pleasant, and the air smelled so sweetly of violets, that Cimabue moved his easel outdoors to his garden to paint. A neighbor, watching from a window, saw the picture and passed the word to a friend that it was more beautiful than anyone could possibly imagine. Word spread through the city, and next morning, when Cimabue came out to paint, many many people were already peeping over his garden wall to watch him while he worked. Even the king of France, who happened to be passing through Florence, joined the citizens as they stood and watched.

"How beautiful!" everyone said, as Cimabue painted in an apple-pink cheek.

"How glorious!" they said, as he burnished[4] the gold-leaf background with the smooth tooth of an ox, until the gold was dark and shining.

When the painting was done, the citizens nearly wept with joy at the sight of it; and they decided that a picture as special as this one needed as special a journey as possible to the church where it was to hang. And so on the day the painting made its journey from the workshop to the church, it was accompanied by a grand parade of fifers,[5] tambour drummers and trumpeters—and by everyone in the city, or so it seemed. Every apprentice hoped that such fame would one day come to him. Every young painter hoped that one day he would make pictures as fine as the pictures of Cimabue.

But for Giotto it was enough for now to draw and to hope that one day his master would say, "Here Giotto, paint in the face of this angel—the one in the far-left corner." Giotto worked, and he drew, and he lived the life of an apprentice.

At the time Giotto lived, in the city of Florence as in other cities, only the boys of the rich went to school. All other boys learned a trade. They were apprenticed to master craftsmen, who provided food, clothing and shelter, as well as learning. In return the boys worked for the master.

In Florence there was a strange custom that Giotto must have enjoyed. Each day when noontime came, all of the apprentices from all of the trades in the city left their workshops and ran to the marketplace for lunch. There they feasted on sausages and fresh figs, and drank cool sweet lemonade from the lemon vendor's stall faster than the poor man could squeeze it. But sometimes fights broke out between apprentices: the wooldyers fought

---

4. **burnished** (bur′ nisht) v. polished.
5. **fifers** (fī′ fərs) musicians playing small flutes.

with the painters; the carpenters fought with the apothe-caries;[6] the goldsmiths fought with the sculptors; for each trade thought its own the best. At times like that the market ran wild, and geese ran cackling shrilly underfoot; stall-keepers shouted vainly to the boys to stop while onions and lemons turned to weapons and went flying through the air. But suddenly the market bell would clang out loudly over the shouting and swearing, and the apprentices would return to work, always promising to finish the fight the next day. As they left, the unfortunate stall-keepers would sigh and swear and once more pile their goods neat and high.

Back at the workshop, Giotto and his fellow apprentices would dig into their work, having had their fling for the day. In Cimabue's workshop the apprentices were treated kindly. Although they worked hard, they ate well and slept in clean and comfortable beds.

But there were some painters who treated their apprentices badly and made them work too hard. One old painter, a stingy man, had but one apprentice, who was as lazy as his master was stingy. Each morning, in the cold darkness before dawn, the master woke the apprentice and set him hard at work grinding colors, preparing panels of wood and making brushes; then when day came the master could paint angels, although, to tell the truth, his angels were not beautiful. The lazy apprentice so hated waking up while it was still dark and shivery that he made up his mind to put a stop to it. Since he was not only lazy but an untidy housekeeper, in all corners of the workshop and under every piece of furniture, dust lay thick. Little creepy beetles lived in the dust. And one night while his master slept, the apprentice caught many, many of these little beetles. With a tiny dripping of wax, he fastened a very small candle to each beetle's back. Then, after lighting each candle, he set the beetle army loose in his master's bedroom and hid in the hall. As the beetles slowly proceeded across the floor, like a long, silent, flaming dragon, the old painter wakened and shouted and screamed in terror, while the apprentice sat outside giggling silently. When morning came, the painter, in a trembling voice, told the apprentice of the terrible thing that had happened in the night.

---

6. **apothecaries** (ə päth'ə ker ēz) *n.* pharmacists; druggists.

"I am sure," he said, "that those were demons come to get me. They are very angry because I have been painting so many angels, for angels are good and demons are bad! But the night belongs to strange monsters! Let us leave it to them; from now on we work no more until the sun, which chases away demons, is fully up in the morning."

And so it was that the lazy apprentice could sleep late in the morning. Indeed in all the workshops of Florence, everyone heard of the flaming demons and took heed; and from that time on, work was done only in daylight hours.

That did not stop apprentices from playing other tricks, however. Giotto, too, invented some. He was now allowed to paint small portions of the master's canvases himself. One day he painted a tiny fly on the nose of a figure on a panel. He giggled as his master tried unsuccessfully to brush it off, for he thought it was real. And although Cimabue would not admit it, the boy's joke also gave him pleasure, for it showed that the young shepherd from the hills was learning his trade remarkably well.

But there was much more to being a painter than painting a fly to fool the eye. Giotto had to make brushes, delicate brushes of ermine[7] tails for small and precise work, and hard strong bristle brushes made from the back hairs of a white pig for more general work. He learned to grind the priceless chunks of color that he had gotten from the apothecary shop. He would grind and grind until they seemed to be as fine as dust; but then, when he showed them to his master, they would still be too coarse.

"Grind them," the master would say, "until you are sure you have ground them enough, and then grind them some more."

And so he would grind them again, and then again. But at last they would be ready and he would place them in neat little pots. There were all of the colors. Some were made of ground-up stones or earth, and some were products of the mysterious arts of the alchemist.[8] Some behaved strangely when mixed with other colors and therefore had to be used pure. There were still others

---

7. **ermine** (ur′ min) *adj.* from the northern European weasel.
8. **alchemist** (al′ kə mist) *n.* someone who practiced alchemy, a medieval form of chemistry. Alchemists tried to turn common metals into gold.

that were highly poisonous. All of the rules for the use of all of the colors had to be learned before a painter could be sure that his pictures would not turn black in a short time.

Even worse, a painter who was careless of the way he handled some of the paint could develop symptoms of poisoning. He must not lick his brushes to make a point for delicate work. He must not inhale too much of the finely ground colored dust before it was mixed with water or oil or egg white to make it ready to spread on a picture.

The craft of a painter was filled with things that seemed magical and mysterious to those who had not learned the craft. And the images that grew on walls and panels, with blue made of precious ground lapis lazuli and reds of rare and rich cinnabar from Spain, and bright gold gleaming, seemed magical and mysterious to those who looked at them. But Giotto was now a part of those mysteries. He was becoming a painter.

The years passed, and the boy Giotto grew up. Wherever he went he looked at people and at the world around him. He noticed the way people stood and moved in the busy marketplace, and he noticed the way they looked when they laughed or cried. He watched the way the long drapery of their clothing fell in rich folds to the ground when they walked or gestured. And always he drew what he saw, as he had done up in the hills. But now it was different, for he had learned so many things that he could draw well whatever he wished. He had mastered all of the many skills he needed to be a painter with a workshop of his own. Indeed, there were many people who said that he surpassed his master, the most famous painter in the land.

Giotto was soon called upon by the neighboring town of Assisi to paint some pictures for them.

Nearly one hundred years earlier a man called Francis had been born in Assisi. He was the son of a rich merchant, but he gave up all of his money and fine clothes and called himself, "the Little Poor Man." As a beggar, he wandered throughout Italy doing good things. Not only did he love people, but he loved the sun and moon as if they were his brother and sister, and he loved all of the birds and creatures of the earth. He even seemed able to speak to wild animals in their own language. He wrote poems and songs in praise of the wild things of the earth. These were written in the language the people around him spoke every day, instead of the Latin of learned poets. He wanted to teach people to live together more happily, and at the same time he wanted to teach them to share the earth with the birds and flowers, wild wolves, and fire and water and cold winter wind. After he died he became known as Saint Francis, and his native town wished to honor him by building a church dedicated to him. Giotto was asked to decorate the church with murals, telling stories from the life of Saint Francis. And so Giotto journeyed to Assisi to begin the work.

First, carpenters constructed a strong wooden scaffolding where he could stand with his assistants to reach the high walls where they would make the paintings. Next the bare stone walls were covered with a rough coat of plaster. Upon this plaster Giotto drew with charcoal, carefully copying and enlarging a small picture he had drawn previously on paper. Then he went over the charcoal with a little brush and brown paint, until the whole picture could easily be seen on the plaster. When he was ready to begin the finished painting, he mixed a small amount of fine smooth plaster and covered with it just enough of the wall with the picture drawn on for one day's work. While the plaster was still wet, although set, he painted the parts of the picture that were in that area, using his dry colors mixed with water. The next day he again plastered a small area and painted it, generally the section adjoining the section he had finished the day before. Day after day he worked in this way. Many, many months passed, or perhaps longer, before the murals were done.

Then at last, there they stood, row after row of grand and bright paintings. Scenes from the life of Saint Francis covered the walls like pages from an enormous picture book for people to see, many of whom could neither read nor write.

These paintings were not like any that people had seen before. The pictures people of Giotto's time knew were stiff and unreal, painted in a way handed down from master to apprentice for hundreds of years. They looked more like other pictures than they looked like real life. But Giotto, like Saint Francis, had looked at the world around him and had seen that it was beautiful. He painted trees and animals, prickly plants and meadow flowers, strong boulders and tall city walls. But what was most unusual was the way he painted people. He filled many spaces with people, people who moved and smiled and cried and gestured as real people do, but who were larger than life. People loved what they saw in Giotto's pictures, but when they looked at him, they laughed, for they said he was as small and ugly as his pictures were large and beautiful.

From city to city Giotto went, climbing scaffoldings and covering wall after wall with pictures. One day after painting many pictures in many cities, he was walking down a narrow alley in Florence, chatting with a friend. He did not notice a runaway pig escaping from the butcher's stall in the marketplace. Squealing shrilly, the pig took one look at Giotto, headed straight toward him and darted between the painter's legs, tripping him up, head over heels. As he pulled himself up and brushed the dirt from his clothes, Giotto laughed and said, "That pig must have known I am the painter who has used so many of his brothers' back bristles for brushes. I have made a great deal of money with my pig-bristle brushes, but I have never given a pig even a bowl of leftovers. Now, at last, I have paid my debt to pigs!"

In the city of Padua[9] there had lived a man called Scrovegni. He was a wicked man who loaned money to people and then charged such high rates of interest that they could not pay, and sometimes had to forfeit land or goods instead. When he died, he was very rich, but he was hated, by all who had heard of him, for his greed and cruelty. His son decided to use his father's great wealth to build a fine church for the city, so that his father would be remembered for this instead of for his crimes. The son commissioned Giotto, who was by then more famous than Cimabue or any painter had ever been, to cover the walls of the new church with scenes from the life of Jesus. Some say that Giotto even helped the stonemasons plan the church, to make certain that he had plenty of wall space for his pictures. The son of the thief had planned well, for today people come from all over the world to look at Giotto's pictures, and the

---

9. **Padua** the oldest city in northern Italy.

Scrovegni family is still remembered for the beautiful paintings in the chapel that bears its name.

One day a messenger came to Giotto from faraway Avignon,[10] in France. This was the city where the the Pope lived at that time. The messenger had been sent to many artists in Italy, all of the best painters, to ask them to submit a painting for a contest. The prize would be a chance to do some well-paid work in Avignon. All of the artists the messenger approached worked very hard on their samples for the contest. But when the messenger asked Giotto for his picture, Giotto took a piece of charcoal and, resting his elbow on the table, with no compass to guide him, drew a perfect circle.

"Is this all I am to take?" cried the astonished messenger, when Giotto gave him the drawing of a circle.

And Giotto answered, smiling, that it was. But the Pope, looking at all of the pictures the artists had labored hard over, liked none of them. Not until he came to the perfect circle did he tell the messenger that he had, at last, found the man he wanted. The job went to Giotto. What it was, we shall never know, for the painting is gone today, but people still speak of something as being as simple as Giotto's "O."

Giotto went to Naples and painted for the king of that area. The king loved to watch the painter work and spent many hours doing just that. One hot day, as Giotto stood high on his scaffolding, without a breeze in the air, the king, who was resting below, eating cool and juicy fruits, called lazily up to him, "Ahhhhhh . . . Giotto . . . if I were you, I would not work on such a day as this!"

Giotto laughed and answered, "No, your majesty, I would not work either, if I were *you!*"

For it was hard work to be a painter. Besides the wonderful murals, which brought painters fame and wealth, there was other work for them to do. They painted coats of arms on shields, decorated bridal chests and floats for parades and festivals. And not only did they paint and design the floats, they even painted the faces of the ladies and children who rode on them, so that they might appear as pink-cheeked and rosy-lipped as angels.

---

10. **Avignon** city in southeastern France that served as the headquarters of the pope from 1309–1377.

As his father on the farm, long years before, had hoped, Giotto became very rich. He married and had eight children, each one, so it was said, as homely as himself. He trained many apprentices in his workshop, and one, named Taddeo Gaddi, he adopted as his own son.

The days passed, and slowly Giotto grew to be an old man. But still he painted. He was hard at work one day when some citizens of Florence came to him and asked him to design a bell tower for the city. Although Giotto was no architect, he felt this was a great honor, and he agreed to do it. He began work at once on plans and designs for the bell tower. On it he decided to put as many of the people he had seen in his long life as he could. There would be pictures of all the different trades men followed: farming and fishing, weaving and building, masonry, carpentry and wooldying. He did not forget the sheep, the sheep he had first looked at as he learned to draw. In a shepherd's tent a man sat, guarding three nibbling sheep. A wag-tailed dog stood nearby to help. To Giotto this represented the first herdsman in all the world. One panel, too, was for the painters. There a man stood patiently and intently at work upon a panel, his well-ground colors near him in a row of little pots.

The drawings Giotto made were copied in stone by sculptors to decorate the sides of the bell tower. Huge wooden scaffoldings were built, far stronger than any that were needed for a painter, and the work on the tall stone tower was begun. For three years Giotto worked on this and nothing else. He drew and planned and directed the stonemasons and carpenters. And the tower grew and grew.

But Giotto never saw it stand tall and proud and finished. In 1337, when he was seventy-one years old, he died, and the tower was not yet done. But today, when its bell rings out across the city and up into the hills where he wandered as a shepherd boy so long ago, people say,

"The bells are ringing on Giotto's tower."

Prologue
from The Merry Adventures of Robin Hood

Howard Pyle

Everyone has heard of Robin Hood and his merry men, who took from the rich and gave to the poor. Here is an account of how Robin Hood's adventures started.

In merry England in the time of old, when good King Henry the Second ruled the land, there lived within the green glades of Sherwood Forest, near Nottingham Town, a famous outlaw whose name was Robin Hood. No archer ever lived that could speed a gray goose shaft with such skill and cunning as his, nor were there ever such yeomen as the sevenscore[1] merry men that roamed with him through the greenwood shades. Right merrily they dwelt within the depths of Sherwood Forest, suffering neither care nor want, but passing the time in merry games of archery or bouts of cudgel play, living upon the King's venison, washed down with draughts of ale of October brewing.

Not only Robin himself but all the band were outlaws and dwelt apart from other men, yet they were beloved by the country people round about, for no one ever came to jolly Robin for help in time of need and went away again with an empty fist.

And now I will tell how it came about that Robin Hood fell afoul of the law.

When Robin was a youth of eighteen, stout of sinew and bold of heart, the Sheriff of Nottingham proclaimed a shooting-match and offered a prize of a butt of ale[2] to whomsoever should shoot the best shaft in Nottinghamshire. "Now," quoth Robin, "will I go too, for fain would I draw a string for the bright eyes of my lass, and a butt of good October brewing." So up he got and took his good stout yew bow and a score or more of broad clothyard arrows, and started off from Locksley Town through Sherwood Forest to Nottingham.

---

1. **score** *n.* an old word for the number twenty. So "seven score merry men" means a hundred and forty of them.
2. **butt of ale** a large cask of ale. It held about 130 gallons.

It was at the dawn of day in the merry May-time, when hedgerows are green and flowers bedeck the meadows; daisies pied and yellow cuckoo buds and fair primroses all along the briery hedges; when apple buds blossom and sweet birds sing, the lark at dawn of day, the throstle cock and cuckoo; when lads and lasses look upon each other with sweet thoughts; when busy housewives spread their linen to bleach upon the bright green grass. Sweet was the greenwood as he walked along its paths, and bright the green and rustling leaves, amid which the little birds sang with might and main: and blithely Robin whistled as he trudged along, thinking of Maid Marian and her bright eyes, for at such times a youth's thoughts are wont to turn pleasantly upon the lass that he loves the best.

As thus he walked along with a brisk step and a merry whistle, he came suddenly upon some foresters seated beneath a great oak tree. Fifteen there were in all, making themselves merry with feasting and drinking as they sat around a huge pasty, to which each man helped himself, thrusting his hands into the pie, and washing down that which they ate with great horns of ale which they drew all foaming from a barrel that stood nigh. Each man was clad in Lincoln green, and a fine show they made, seated upon the sward beneath that fair, spreading tree. Then one of them, with his mouth full, called out to Robin, "Hulloa, where goest thou, little lad, with thy one penny bow and thy farthing shafts?"

Then Robin grew angry, for no stripling likes to be taunted with his green years.

"Now," quoth he, "my bow and eke mine arrows are as good as thine; and moreover, I go to the shooting-match at Nottingham Town, which same has been proclaimed by our Sheriff of Nottinghamshire; there I will shoot with other stout yeomen, for a prize has been offered of a fine butt of ale."

Then one who held a horn of ale in his hand, said, "Ho! listen to the lad! Why, boy, thy mother's milk is yet scarce dry upon thy lips, and yet thou pratest of standing up with good stout men at Nottingham butts, thou who art scarce able to draw one string of a two stone bow."

"I'll hold the best of you twenty marks," quoth bold Robin, "that I hit the clout[3] at threescore rods, by the good help of Our Lady fair."

At this all laughed aloud, and one said, "Well boasted, thou fair infant, well boasted! and well thou knowest that no target is nigh to make good thy wager."

And another cried, "He will be taking ale with his milk next."

At this Robin grew right mad. "Hark ye," said he; "yonder, at the glade's end, I see a herd of deer, even more than three-score rods distant. I'll hold you twenty marks that, by leave of Our Lady, I cause the best hart among them to die."

"Now done!" cried he who had spoken first. "And here are twenty marks. I wager that thou causest no beast to die, with or without the aid of Our Lady."

Then Robin took his good yew bow in his hand, and placing the tip at his instep, he strung it right deftly; then he nocked a broad clothyard arrow, and, raising the bow, drew the gray goose-feather to his ear; the next moment the bow-string rang and the arrow sped down the glade as a sparrow-hawk skims in a northern wind. High leaped the noblest hart of all the herd, only to fall dead, reddening the green path with his heart's blood.

"Ha!" cried Robin, "how likest thou that shot, good fellow? I wot the wager were mine, an it were three hundred pounds."

Then all the foresters were filled with rage, and he who had spoken the first and had lost the wager was more angry than all.

"Nay," cried he, "the wager is none of thine, and get thee gone, straightway, or, by all the saints of heaven, I'll baste thy sides until thou wilt ne'er be able to walk again."

"Knowest thou not," said another, "that thou hast killed the King's deer, and, by the laws of our gracious lord and sovereign, King Harry,[4] thine ears should be shaven close to thy head?"

"Catch him!" cried a third.

---

3. **clout** *n.* the center of the target.
4. **laws of King Harry** There had been forest laws since Saxon times. All the deer in England belonged to the King. An Englishman who killed a deer might be tried by a special Forest Court, and hanged. Despite the terrible penalties, the people were so poor they sometimes hunted the King's deer and other game anyway.

"Nay," said a fourth, "let him e'en go because of his tender years."

Never a word said Robin Hood, but he looked at the foresters with a grim face; then, turning on his heel, strode away from them down the forest glade. But his heart was bitterly angry, for his blood was hot and youthful and prone to boil.

Now, well would it have been for him who had first spoken had he left Robin Hood alone; but his anger was hot, both because the youth had gotten the better of him and because of the deep draughts of ale that he had been quaffing. So, of a sudden, without any warning, he sprang to his feet, and seized upon his bow and fitted it to a shaft. "Ay," cried he, "and I'll hurry thee anon"; and he sent the arrow whistling after Robin.

It was well for Robin Hood that the same forester's head was spinning with ale, or else he would never have taken another step; as it was, the arrow whistled within three inches of his head. Then he turned around and quickly drew his own bow, and sent an arrow back in return.

"Ye said I was no archer," cried he aloud, "but say so now again!"

The shaft flew straight; the archer fell forward with a cry, and lay on his face upon the ground, his arrows rattling about him from out of his quiver, the gray goose shaft wet with his heart's blood. Then, before the others could gather their wits about them, Robin Hood was gone into the depths of the greenwood. Some started after him, but not with much heart, for each feared to suffer the death of his fellow; so presently they all came and lifted the dead man up and bore him away to Nottingham Town.

Meanwhile Robin Hood ran through the greenwood. Gone was all the joy and brightness from everything, for his heart was sick within him, and it was borne in upon his soul that he had slain a man.

"Alas!" cried he, "thou hast found me an archer that will make thy wife to wring! I would that thou hadst ne'er said one word to me, or that I had never passed thy way, or e'en that my right forefinger had been stricken off ere that this had happened! In haste I smote, but grieve I sore at leisure!" And then, even in his trouble, he remembered the old saw that "What is done is done; and the egg cracked cannot be cured."

And so he came to dwell in the greenwood that was to be his home for many a year to come, never again to see the happy days with the lads and lasses of sweet Locksley Town; for he was outlawed, not only because he had killed a man, but also because he had poached upon the King's deer, and two hundred pounds were set upon his head, as a reward for whoever would bring him to the court of the King.

Now the Sheriff of Nottingham swore that he himself would bring this knave, Robin Hood, to justice, and for two reasons: first, because he wanted the two hundred pounds, and next, because the forester that Robin Hood had killed was of kin to him.

But Robin Hood lay hidden in Sherwood Forest for one year, and in that time there gathered around him many others like himself, cast out from other folk for this cause and for that. Some had shot deer in hungry winter time, when they could get no other food, and had been seen in the act by the foresters, but had escaped, thus saving their ears; some had been turned out of their inheritance, that their farms might be added to the King's lands in Sherwood Forest; some had been despoiled by a great baron or a rich abbot or a powerful esquire,—all, for one cause or another, had come to Sherwood to escape wrong and oppression.

So, in all that year, fivescore or more good stout yeomen gathered about Robin Hood, and chose him to be their leader and chief. Then they vowed that even as they themselves had been despoiled they would despoil their oppressors, whether baron, abbot, knight, or squire, and that from each they would take that which had been wrung from the poor by unjust taxes, or land rents, or in wrongful fines; but to the poor folk they would give a helping hand in need and trouble, and would return to them that which had been unjustly taken from them. Beside this, they swore never to harm a child nor to wrong a woman, be she maid, wife, or widow; so that, after a while, when the people began to find that no harm was meant to them, but that money or food came in time of want to many a poor family, they came to praise Robin and his merry men, and to tell many tales of him and of his doings in Sherwood Forest, for they felt him to be one of themselves.

* * *

Up rose Robin Hood one merry morn when all the birds were singing blithely among the leaves, and up rose all his merry men, each fellow washing his head and hands in the cold brown brook that leaped laughing from stone to stone. Then said Robin: "For fourteen days have we seen no sport, so now I will go abroad to seek adventures forthwith. But tarry ye, my merry men all, here in the greenwood; only see that ye mind well my call. Three blasts upon the bugle-horn I will blow in my hour of need; then come quickly, for I shall want your aid."

So saying, he strode away through the leafy forest glades until he had come to the verge of Sherwood. There he wandered for a long time, through highway and byway, through dingly dell and forest skirts. Now he met a fair buxom lass in a shady lane, and each gave the other a merry word and passed their way; now he saw a fair lady upon an ambling pad, to whom he doffed his cap, and who bowed sedately in return to the fair youth; now he saw a fat monk on a pannier-laden ass; now a gallant knight, with spear and shield and armor that flashed brightly in the sunlight; now a page clad in crimson; and now a stout burgher from good Nottingham Town, pacing along with serious footsteps; all these sights he saw, but adventure found he none. At last he took a road by the forest skirts; a bypath that dipped toward a broad, pebbly stream spanned by a narrow bridge made of a log of wood. As he drew nigh this bridge he saw a tall stranger coming from the other side. Thereupon Robin quickened his pace, as did the stranger likewise; each thinking to cross first.

"Now stand thou back," quoth Robin, "and let the better man cross first."

"Nay," answered the stranger, "then stand back thine own self, for the better man, I wot, am I."

"That will we presently see," quoth Robin; "and meanwhile stand thou where thou art, or else, by the bright brow of Saint Ælfrida, I will show thee right good Nottingham play with a clothyard shaft betwixt thy ribs."

"Now," quoth the stranger, "I will tan thy hide till it be as many colors as a beggar's cloak, if thou darest so much as touch a string of that same bow that thou holdest in thy hands."

"Thou pratest like an ass," said Robin, "for I could send this shaft clean through thy proud heart before a curtal friar could say grace over a roast goose at Michaelmastide."

"And thou pratest like a coward," answered the stranger, "for thou standest there with a good yew bow to shoot at my heart, while I have nought in my hand but a plain blackthorn staff wherewith to meet thee."

"Now," quoth Robin, "by the faith of my heart, never have I had a coward's name in all my life before. I will lay by my trusty bow and eke my arrows, and if thou darest abide my coming, I will go and cut a cudgel to test thy manhood withal."

"Ay, marry, that will I abide thy coming, and joyously, too," quoth the stranger; whereupon he leaned sturdily upon his staff to await Robin.

Then Robin Hood stepped quickly to the coverside and cut a good staff of ground oak, straight, without flaw, and six feet in length, and came back trimming away the tender stems from it, while the stranger waited for him, leaning upon his staff, and whistling as he gazed round about. Robin observed him furtively as he trimmed his staff, measuring him from top to toe from out the corner of his eye, and thought that he had never seen a lustier or a stouter man. Tall was Robin, but taller was the stranger by a head and a neck, for he was seven feet in height. Broad was Robin across the shoulders, but broader was the stranger by twice the breadth of a palm, while he measured at least an ell[5] around the waist.

"Nevertheless," said Robin to himself, "I will baste thy hide right merrily, my good fellow"; then, aloud, "Lo, here is my good staff, lusty and tough. Now wait my coming, an thou darest, and meet me, an thou fearest not; then we will fight until one or the other of us tumble into the stream by dint of blows."

"Marry, that meeteth my whole heart!" cried the stranger, twirling his staff above his head, betwixt his fingers and thumb, until it whistled again.

Never did the Knights of Arthur's Round Table meet in a stouter fight than did these two. In a moment Robin stepped quickly upon the bridge where the stranger stood; first he made a feint, and then delivered a blow at the stranger's head that, had it met its mark, would have tumbled him speedily into the water; but the stranger turned the blow right deftly, and in return gave

---

5. ell This was an old way of measuring cloth. It was 45 inches—quite a bit, measured around a man's waist, but not too much when the man is seven feet tall.

one as stout, which Robin also turned as the stranger had done. So they stood, each in his place, neither moving a finger's breadth back, for one good hour, and many blows were given and received by each in that time, till here and there were sore bones and bumps, yet neither thought of crying "Enough," or seemed likely to fall from off the bridge. Now and then they stopped to rest, and each thought that he never had seen in all his life before such a hand at quarter-staff.[6] At last Robin gave the stranger a blow upon the ribs that made his jacket smoke like a damp straw thatch in the sun. So shrewd was the stroke that the stranger came within a hair's breadth of falling off the bridge; but he regained himself right quickly, and, by a dexterous blow, gave Robin a crack on the crown that caused the blood to flow. Then Robin grew mad with anger, and smote with all his might at the other; but the stranger warded the blow, and once again thwacked Robin, and this time so fairly that he fell heels over head into the water, as the queen pin falls in a game of bowls.

"And where art thou now, my good lad?" shouted the stranger, roaring with laughter.

"Oh, in the flood and floating adown with the tide," cried Robin; nor could he forbear laughing himself at his sorry plight. Then, gaining his feet, he waded to the bank, the little fish speeding hither and thither, all frightened at his splashing.

"Give me thy hand," cried he, when he had reached the bank. "I must needs own thou art a brave and sturdy soul, and, withal, a good stout stroke with the cudgels. By this and by that, my head hummeth like to a hive of bees on a hot June day."

Then he clapped his horn to his lips, and winded a blast that went echoing sweetly down the forest paths. "Ay, marry," quoth he again, "thou art a tall lad, and eke a brave one, for ne'er, I trow, is there a man betwixt here and Canterbury Town could do the like to me that thou hast done."

---

6. quarter-staff For many years, quarter-staff contests were popular, just as boxing or wrestling is now. The quarter-staff was usually six to nine feet of oak, tipped with iron. You held it with both hands, the right hand one quarter the distance from the lower end (that's how it got the name), and the left hand about at the middle.

"And thou," quoth the stranger, laughing, "takest thy cudgelling like a brave heart and a stout yeoman."

But now the distant twigs and branches rustled with the coming of men, and suddenly a score or two of good stout yeomen, all clad in Lincoln green, burst from out the covert, with merry Will Stutely at their head.

"Good master," cried Will, "how is this? Truly thou art all wet from head to foot, and that to the very skin."

"Why, marry," answered jolly Robin, "yon stout fellow hath tumbled me neck and crop into the water, and hath giving me a drubbing beside."

"Then shall he not go without a ducking and eke a drubbing himself!" cried Will Stutely. "Have at him, lads!"

Then Will and a score of yeomen leaped upon the stranger, but though they sprang quickly they found him ready and felt him strike right and left with his stout staff, so that, though he went down with press of numbers, some of them rubbed cracked crowns before he was overcome.

"Nay, forbear!" cried Robin, laughing until his sore sides ached again; "he is a right good man and true, and no harm shall befall him. Now hark ye, good youth, wilt thou stay with me and be one of my band? Three suits of Lincoln green shalt thou have each year, beside forty marks in fee,[7] and share with us whatsoever good shall befall us. Thou shalt eat sweet venison and quaff the stoutest ale, and mine own good right-hand man shalt thou be, for never did I see such a cudgel-player in all my life before. Speak! wilt thou be one of my good merry men?"

"That know I not," quoth the stranger, surlily, for he was angry at being so tumbled about. "If ye handle yew bow[8] and apple shaft no better than ye do oaken cudgel, I wot ye are not fit to be called yeomen in my country; but if there be any man here that can shoot a better shaft than I, then will I bethink me of joining with you."

"Now by my faith," said Robin, "thou art a right saucy varlet, sirrah; yet I will stoop to thee as I never stooped to man before. Good Stutely, cut thou a fair white piece of

---

7. forty marks in fee A mark was the same as 120 silver pennies. It was not an actual coin—it was just an easy way of counting pennies. The word "mark" meant eight ounces and 120 pennies weighed eight ounces.

8. yew bow Wood from the yew tree is hard, with an orange-red heart. It takes a fine polish, is close-grained, and elastic. Englishmen thought it was the best wood for the long bow.

bark four fingers in breadth, and set it fourscore yards distant on yonder oak. Now, stranger, hit that fairly with a gray goose shaft and call thyself an archer."

"Ay, marry, that will I," answered he. "Give me a good stout bow and a fair broad arrow, and if I hit it not strip me and beat me blue with bowstrings."

Then he chose the stoutest bow amongst them all, next to Robin's own, and a straight gray goose shaft, well-feathered and smooth, and stepping to the mark—while all the band, sitting or lying upon the greensward, watched to see him shoot—he drew the arrow to his cheek and loosed the shaft right deftly, sending it so straight down the path that it clove the mark in the very centre. "Aha!" cried he, "mend thou that if thou canst"; while even the yeomen clapped their hands at so fair a shot.

"That is a keen shot, indeed," quoth Robin, "mend it I cannot, but mar it I may, perhaps."

Then taking up his own good stout bow and nocking[9] an arrow with care he shot with his very greatest skill. Straight flew the arrow, and so true that it lit fairly upon the stranger's shaft and split it into splinters. Then all the yeomen leaped to their feet and shouted for joy that their master had shot so well.

"Now by the lusty yew bow of good Saint Withold," cried the stranger, "that is a shot indeed, and never saw I the like in all my life before! Now truly will I be thy man henceforth and for aye. Good Adam Bell[10] was a fair shot, but never shot he so!"

"Then have I gained a right good man this day," quoth jolly Robin. "What name goest thou by, good fellow?"

"Men call me John Little whence I came," answered the stranger.

Then Will Stutely, who loved a good jest, spoke up. "Nay, fair little stranger," said he, "I like not thy name and fain would I have it otherwise. Little art thou indeed, and small of bone and sinew, therefore shalt thou be christened Little John, and I will be thy godfather."

Then Robin Hood and all his band laughed aloud until the stranger began to grow angry.

---

9. nocking fitting an arrow to the bowstring.
10. Adam Bell, Clym o' the Clough, and William of Cloudesly three noted north-country bowmen whose names have been celebrated in many ballads.

"An thou make a jest of me," quoth he to Will Stutely, "Thou wilt have sore bones and little pay, and that in short season."

"Nay, good friend," said Robin Hood, "bottle thine anger, for the name fitteth thee well. Little John shall thou be called henceforth, and Little John shall it be. So come, my merry men, and we will go and prepare a christening feast for this fair infant."

So turning their backs upon the stream, they plunged into the forest once more, through which they traced their steps till they reached the spot where they dwelt in the depths of the woodland. There had they built huts of bark and branches of trees, and made couches of sweet rushes spread over with skins of fallow deer. Here stood a great oak tree with branches spreading broadly around, beneath which was a seat of green moss where Robin Hood was wont to sit at feast and at merrymaking with his stout men about him. Here they found the rest of the band, some of whom had come in with a brace of fat does. Then they all built great fires and after a time roasted the does and broached a barrel of humming ale. Then when the feast was ready they all sat down, but Robin placed Little John at his right hand, for he was henceforth to be the second in the band.

Then when the feast was done Will Stutely spoke up. "It is now time, I ween, to christen our bonny babe, is it not so, merry boys?" And "Aye! Aye!" cried all, laughing till the woods echoed with their mirth.

"Then seven sponsors shall we have," quoth Will Stutely; and hunting among all the band he chose the seven stoutest men of them all.

"Now by Saint Dunstan," cried Little John, springing to his feet, "more than one of you shall rue it an you lay finger upon me."

But without a word they all ran upon him at once, seizing him by his legs and arms and holding him tightly in spite of his struggles, and they bore him forth while all stood around to see the sport. Then one came forward who had been chosen to play the priest because he had a bald crown, and in his hand he carried a brimming pot of ale. "Now who bringeth this babe?" asked he right soberly.

"That do I," answered Will Stutely.

"And what name callest thou him?"

"Little John call I him."

"Now Little John," quoth the mock priest, "thou has not lived heretofore, but only got thee along through the world, but henceforth thou wilt live indeed. When thou livedst not thou wast called John Little, but now that thou dost live indeed, Little John shalt thou be called, so christen I thee." And at these last words he emptied the pot of ale upon Little John's head.

Then all shouted with laughter as they saw the good brown ale stream over Little John's beard and trickle from his nose and chin, while his eyes blinked with the smart of it. At first he was of a mind to be angry, but found he could not because the others were so merry; so he, too, laughed with the rest. Then Robin took this sweet, pretty babe, clothed him all anew from top to toe in Lincoln green, and gave him a good stout bow, and so made him a member of the merry band.

And thus it was that Robin Hood became outlawed; thus a band of merry companions gathered about him, and thus he gained his right-hand man, Little John; and so the prologue ends.

Haiku

Bashō

Translated by Harold G. Henderson (first 3) and Geoffrey Bownas (last 3)

Bashō is considered the greatest master of the haiku. The meaning of each haiku opens up to careful readers only after many readings.

The sun's way:
Hollyhocks turn toward it
Through all the rain of May.

Poverty's child—
He starts to grind the rice,
And gazes at the moon.

Clouds come from time to time—
And bring to men a chance to rest
From looking at the moon.

The cuckoo—
Its call stretching
Over the water.

Seven sights were veiled
In mist—then I heard
Mii Temple's bell.[1]

Summer grasses—
All that remains
Of soldiers' visions.

Translated by Daniel C. Buchanan

Precision and simplicity characterize this haiku, and its direct style reflects Bashō's Buddhist faith.

Falling upon earth,
Pure water spills from the cup
Of the camellia.

---

1. **Mii** (mē ē′) **Temple's bell** The bell at Mii Temple is known for its extremely beautiful sound. The temple is located near Otsu, a city in southern Japan.

The Renaissance
and the Reformation
in Europe

What Was the Renaissance?

from Leonardo and the Renaissance

Nathaniel Harris

The Renaissance changed the way people thought about themselves and the world. Here are some of the details of that exciting historical period.

A new outlook

The Renaissance is the name given to a new way of life that first appeared in Italy. It lasted from about the fourteenth to the sixteenth century, and during this period there was a great change in the way people thought about themselves and the world around them.

More than anything else, the Renaissance was based on the belief that human life was supremely interesting and valuable, and that "man can do all things." This self-confidence owed a great deal to the wealth of Italy, a land full of big bustling cities, industries and trades. Here there were wonderful new opportunities for adventurers, artists, scholars, architects and musicians. Splendid buildings and beautiful works of art were created. Men and women tried to develop all their talents to the full—that was why they had such an admiration for "universal men" like Leonardo [Da Vinci]. Trying to understand the past and improve themselves in the present, they opened up new subjects of study. And, thanks to the recent German invention of printing, their new ideas and new knowledge spread more widely and quickly than ever before.

"Renaissance" means "rebirth." Strangely enough, Italians did not think of themselves as doing something new: they believed they were reviving the glories of ancient Greece and Rome, whose history provided models of the kind of lives they themselves wanted to lead. But although they often imitated the ancients, Renaissance Italians nevertheless found themselves creating a new society.

The great cities

During the Renaissance, Italy was divided into many states of varying sizes. Most of these had grown up around a city that had gained territory by conquering its neighbors. So even when they were quite large, such states were named after the ruling city. When we talk about "Florence," for example, we sometimes mean the city, and sometimes the city-state stretching across the region of Tuscany. And Leonardo is always called a Florentine because the town of Vinci belonged to Florence.

Mantua, Urbino and other small cities made valuable contributions to the Renaissance. But the most important Renaissance centers were the four most populous and powerful cities. These were Florence, Venice, Milan and Rome.

The republic of Florence produced far more great writers, artists, financiers and men of action than any other city-state. These included the poet Dante, the sculptor Michelangelo and Leonardo himself. Venice, also a republic, was the greatest Italian naval and trading power in Italy. It had been built on the islands of a lagoon, and had canals instead of streets. Milan was a powerful dukedom. Rome was slightly different, since the pope, who ruled over most of central Italy, had his headquarters, the Vatican, in the city. All of these centers were transformed during the Renaissance, as proud rulers and citizens equipped their cities with magnificent public buildings, churches and palaces.

The wealth of Italy

The Renaissance was made possible by Italy's wealth. Elsewhere in Europe, most people lived and worked on the land. Money was used only by a few and the practice of art and learning was mainly confined to the Church or royal courts. But in Italy there were also merchants, bankers, traders, lawyers and many other city people who were willing and able to buy books, build fine houses and employ artists and musicians. They paid for Renaissance culture, which was largely shaped by their tastes.

Part of Italy's prosperity came from manufacturing. Florence was famous for woolen goods, and later for silks, which were exported all over Europe. The iron industry of Milan produced armaments, and the shipbuilding industries of Genoa and Venice were vital, since international trade was the lifeblood of the Italian city-states.

Italy was ideally placed by geography. In the eastern Mediterranean, Italian merchants could buy the spices and luxury goods that Europeans wanted. They then transported them through Italy to central Europe, or shipped them through the Straits of Gibraltar to northern Europe.

Through their international trade, Italians developed the financial skills they needed for their far-flung dealings: banking, credit, checks and insurance. The most famous bankers were the Medici family, who became rulers of Florence and great patrons of Renaissance culture.

Renaissance ideals

Renaissance men and women did not aim just to excel, but to achieve all-around excellence. They believed that men should, for example, be capable of fighting well, and also of talking intelligently and dancing gracefully; that the physical and mental sides of life should be in harmony. This was an ideal held by the ancient Greeks almost two thousand years earlier, and is one of the reasons why they were admired so much by the men and women of the Renaissance.

Like the Greek and Roman heroes, Renaissance men and women wanted to make the best of their lives, to be successful and, if possible, famous. To achieve these goals, they were prepared to study and learn, and others were prepared to teach. The Renaissance was the first great age of "do-it-yourself" books. Machiavelli's *The Prince* told its readers how to seize and keep power. Della Casa's *Galateo* taught them table manners. And Castiglione's *The Courtier* advised them on how to succeed at court—even how to tell good jokes!

Leonardo was not the only "universal man" who achieved excellence in many areas. Much earlier, Leon Battista Alberti shone as an architect, soldier, horseman, musician, writer and painter—and boasted that, with both feet together, he could jump over a man's shoulder!

from Leonardo da Vinci

Diane Stanley

Here is an account of the observations and inventions of one of the most important people of the Italian Renaissance.

All nature fascinated Leonardo. His notebooks are filled with descriptions of his extraordinary scientific studies. Based on this evidence, he has been called the first modern scientist. In those days people answered questions by looking them up in the Bible or in the writings of the ancient Greeks. Leonardo said that people who did that were using their memories, not their minds. Instead he followed what today we call the scientific method.

First he observed things carefully—the movement of water, the arrangement of leaves on a stem, the flight of birds. That led him to ask questions. Why does a pot lid jump up and down when water starts to boil? Water must expand when it turns to steam, he decided. In attempting to explain what he observed Leonardo was making a hypothesis. But then he had to prove it, and often he wasn't satisfied until he had also measured it. So he set up an experiment. He made a glass cylinder and put water and a piston inside. Then he measured how far the piston rose when the water was heated to boiling. Leonardo was so keen on measuring things that he invented all sorts of devices for that purpose—to measure humidity, altitude, distance traveled, angle of inclination, the speed of wind and water, and the intensity of light.

He often made astonishing mental leaps. When he threw a pebble into a pond, he noticed that circular waves formed around it, expanding steadily outward. From this it occurred to him that sound and light must also travel in waves through the air. What's more, he remembered that he always saw lightning before he heard thunder. He therefore concluded that light waves must travel faster than sound waves.

He trusted his own observations, even if others disagreed with him. For example, up in the mountains he saw fossils of shells, fish, and coral. How had they gotten there? The popular theory of the time was that they had floated up during the great biblical Flood. But Leonardo knew that shells were heavy and did not float. It seemed clear to him that the rock that now formed a mountain once lay at the bottom of the sea. Today we know that in this—as in so many other things—he was correct and far ahead of his time. . . .

As an inventor, Leonardo is probably most famous for having tried to build a flying machine. He was convinced that "the bird is an instrument functioning according to mathematical laws, and man has the power to reproduce an instrument like this with all its movements." So he analyzed the flight patterns of birds and bats, studied the anatomy of their wings, and observed air currents.

He sketched a variety of designs and finally, after years of preparation, built a model in a secret upstairs room at his workshop. On January 2, 1496, he wrote in his notebook, "Tomorrow morning, I shall make the strap and the attempt." Either he lost his nerve or it didn't work. At any rate, we have no record of it. But the next time he wrote of trying to fly, he was more cautious. "You will experiment with this machine over a lake," he wrote to himself, "and you will wear attached to your belt a long wineskin . . . so that if you fall in, you will not be drowned."

In 1503 he felt certain of success. Twice he wrote about it in his notebook, speculating grandly that the flight would dumbfound the universe and bring him eternal glory. Yet after years of work and study, Leonardo failed. We don't know any of the details, but much later the son of one of Leonardo's friends wrote these words about the attempt: "Vinci tried in vain."

At least he finally understood the problem. Birds are designed to fly—half the weight of their bodies is in the muscles of flight. Humans, on the other hand, with less than a quarter of their body weight in the arm and chest muscles, would never have the strength to fly like birds.

As a casual afterthought he designed a parachute as well as an airscrew, based on a toy, which some call the first helicopter. He also sketched the pattern of a leaf drifting to earth and under it showed a man on a winglike glider. If he had only worked along these lines instead of trying to imitate the flapping motion of birds, he might have been the first man to fly.

Art and Science

from Italian Renaissance

John D. Clare, Editor

Da Vinci would have been famous as a scientist and an inventor, but he was also a remarkable painter, as this selection shows.

Although he suffered numerous set-backs, Leonardo da Vinci was renowned in his own time and many artists were influenced by him. His sketches of churches, for example, formed the basis of Bramante's design for the new St. Peter's Church in Rome. Art historians date the period they call the High Renaissance from around 1495, when Leonardo began to paint *The Last Supper* for Ludovico Sforza, and some historians assert that Leonardo da Vinci changed the course not only of art but of the Renaissance.

Leonardo was responsible for several important developments in painting. First, his treatment of light was revolutionary. His knowledge of light allowed him to develop the techniques of *chiaroscuro* (light and shade) and *sfumato* (softening of the edges). Rather than using sharp lines, Leonardo used subtly blended colors and shading to define the outlines of his figures. This gave his paintings the sense of gentleness and mystery that fascinates people who see, for instance, the *Mona Lisa*, which was painted during his stay in Florence.

Leonardo also did detailed research for his paintings. He was not content to depict the outside of things; he wanted to see inside them, to understand why they worked as they did. "Art truly is a science," he explained. He dissected more than ten corpses in order to understand the anatomy of the human body. He filled his notebooks with thousands of pages of sketches and preliminary drawings.

Simple curiosity as well as research for his paintings led Leonardo to conduct what were in fact scientific investigations. His notebooks are packed with left-handed mirror writing describing his observations and discoveries in anatomy, mechanics, hydraulics, geology, and botany. He spent weeks experimenting with flies, trimming their wings or putting honey on them to study how this changed the sound of their buzzing. He made a particular study of the flight of birds. Later, he became obsessed with mathematics. In 1509, he illustrated a book by the mathematician Luca Pacioli (1445–1517) called *The Divine Proportion*. Pacioli had calculated that the perfect ratio was 1:1.6 and that a rectangle of these proportions was the shape most pleasing to the eye. This concept, which Leonardo renamed the golden section, is still studied by artists and mathematicians.

Leonardo rejected the medieval view of science, which held that nature was controlled by spiritual powers— that, for instance, it was the soul of a bird that allowed it to fly. "A bird is an instrument working according to mathematical law," he wrote. Leonardo insisted that observation and experiments were the only way to find out the truth about nature. In this, he can be said to be the founder of modern science.

As a young man, Leonardo wrote, "I wish to work miracles." In his old age, he seems to have felt that he had failed—throughout his notebooks he wrote comments such as "Tell me if anything at all was achieved." But Leonardo's obsession with experimental investigation, though it sometimes led to failure, also marked an important change in the direction of the Renaissance. Before Leonardo, artists and scholars had been content to imitate the Greeks and Romans; in the words of one modern historian, they had tried to "recover the past." After Leonardo da Vinci, during the High Renaissance, artists and scholars sought new knowledge about the unexplored possibilities of their fields.

Spain and the Power of Gold

from The Renaissance and the New World

Giovanni Caselli

As the country who backed the journey of Columbus, Spain was a leader in the European Renaissance, as this selection indicates.

Spain and Portugal were the first European countries to embark on a systematic policy of discovery. Their aim was to find sea routes to the famed trade lands of eastern Asia. In the late fifteenth century the rivalry between them was intense. Though all educated people by then believed that the earth was round, Queen Isabella of Castile, patron of Columbus, was the only ruler with sufficient vision to finance an expedition to try to reach the Asian lands by sailing west. Columbus, who landed in the continent of America in 1492, set out to reach the Far East, and all his life believed that he had landed in China. The Spaniard Balboa crossed the Isthmus of Panama in 1513 and was the first European to see the Pacific Ocean. Only then was the staggering truth apparent: Spain possessed a vast new continent. It proved to contain enough gold and silver to make Spain, for a while, the greatest power in Europe.

The leader of Europe

Spain's new wealth confirmed its sense of national dignity. It had driven the Muslim forces from its soil in 1400. Spanish armies were feared everywhere. Spanish fashions and manners were copied. Spain was a cultural leader; a new university, which became one of Europe's finest, was founded at Alcala' de Henares; Spanish writers and painters of this period, Lope de Vega, Cervantes, El Greco and later, Velazquez, are amongst the greatest of all time. Renaissance enthusiasm, coinciding with the influx of gold and silver from the New World, led to a burst of new building: new churches, hospitals, town halls and houses for the rich. Near his new capital, Madrid, Philip II built the magnificently sombre Escorial, a vast palace that was also a monastery and a royal tomb.

Living conditions in towns

The central feature of most Spanish towns was the Plaza Mayor, a large open square with colonnaded houses and public buildings. The roads opening from the square were often lined with small workshops and shops. In the south, in place of colonnades, awnings were hung from one building to the next to shade passers-by. Southern houses preserved the Arab plan, with a central patio on to which all the rooms opened. Further north, most houses had an entrance hall, a low room with an earth floor and light coming in from the doorway only. In richer houses this room was tiled and finely furnished. An upper floor contained living and reception rooms, and was little used except in cold weather; the hottest months were spent in the ground floor rooms, which were kept cool by sprinkling water on the flagstones.

The impoverished peasants

Most of the land belonged to the nobility or the church, neither of whom paid any taxes; these all fell on the common people. Success consisted in gaining a title and becoming a landowner. Unlike England, there was no middle class of merchants and professionals. Peasants rarely owned their own land. They were tenants of the great monasteries or of landowners in the towns. After paying tithes[1] to the church and dues to their landlord, and reserving enough grain for seed, only half the peasants' crop remained.

Spain's decline

Unfortunately, Spain did not use its great wealth to ensure its own future prosperity. A huge proportion of it was spent on the wars that Charles V and Philip II fought to preserve Catholicism in Europe. The rest, which should have been invested in Spain's own industry and agriculture, was spent on buying luxuries abroad. The aristocratic leaders of the Spanish people, and those who tried to copy them, disdained manual work, which they associated with the despised *Moriscos* (followers of Islam who had become Christian in order to be allowed to remain in Spain). Spanish raw materials—wool and silk— were sent abroad to be manufactured. The industries of

---

1. tithes *n.* a portion of income paid as a tax or a contribution.

other European countries benefited while Spain's dwindled. After the expulsion of the industrious Moriscos, which began in 1609, the situation grew worse. By spending treasure abroad, and producing little of value itself, Spain enriched its rivals at the country's own expense. When the flow of American gold and silver shrank to a trickle, Spain was helpless.

from A Man for All Seasons

Robert Bolt

In the following scene, Sir Thomas More, friend and colleague of King Henry VIII, is being forced to choose between his devotion to the Church and respect for its teaching, and his loyalty to his ruler. His strong religious principles prevent him from taking an oath of supremacy, an assertion that papal authority could not supersede the king's authority. This defiance cost him his life.

HENRY. I am a fool.

MORE. How so, Your Grace?

HENRY. [*A pause, during which the music fades to silence*] What else but a fool to live in a Court, in a licentious[1] mob—when I have friends, with gardens.

MORE. Your Grace—

HENRY. No courtship, no ceremony, Thomas. Be seated. You *are* my friend, are you not? [MORE *sits*]

MORE. Your Majesty.

HENRY. [*Eyes lighting on the chain on the table by* MORE] And thank God I have a friend for my Chancellor.[2] [*Laughingly, but implacably, he takes up the chain and lowers it over* MORE's *head*] Readier to be friends, I trust, than he was to be Chancellor.

MORE. My own knowledge of my poor abilities—

HENRY. I will judge of your abilities, Thomas . . . Did you know that Wolsey named you for Chancellor?

MORE. Wolsey!

HENRY. Aye, before he died. Wolsey named you and Wolsey was no fool.

MORE. He was a statesman of incomparable ability, Your Grace.

HENRY. Was he? Was he so? [*He rises*] Then why did he fail me? Be seated—it was villainy then! Yes, villainy. I was right to break him; he was all pride, Thomas; a proud

---

1. **licentious** (lī sen′ shəs) *adj.* disregarding accepted rules and standards.
2. **Chancellor** (chan′ sə lər) *n.* More's position as an important advisor to the king.

man; pride right through. And he failed me! [MORE *opens his mouth*] He failed me in the one thing that mattered! The one thing that matters, Thomas, then or now. And why? He wanted to be Pope! Yes, he wanted to be the Bishop of Rome. I'll tell you something, Thomas, and you can check this for yourself—it was never merry in England while we had Cardinals amongst us. [*He nods significantly at* MORE, *who lowers his eyes*] But look now— [*Walking away*]—I shall forget the feel of that . . . great tiller³ under my hands . . . I took her down to Dogget's Bank, went about and brought her up in Tilbury Roads. A man could sail clean round the world in that ship.

MORE. [*With affectionate admiration*] Some men could, Your Grace.

HENRY. [*Offhand*] Touching this matter of my divorce. Thomas; have you thought of it since we last talked?

MORE. Of little else.

HENRY. Then you see your way clear to me?

MORE. That you should put away Queen Catherine, Sire? Oh, alas [*He thumps the chair in distress*] as I think of it I see so clearly that I can *not* come with Your Grace that my endeavor is not to think of it at all.

HENRY. Then you have not thought enough! . . . [*With real appeal*] Great God, Thomas, why do you hold out against me in the desire of my heart—the very wick of my heart?

MORE. [*Draws up his sleeve, baring his arm*] There is my right arm. [*A practical proposition*] Take your dagger and saw it from my shoulder, and I will laugh and be thankful, if by that means I can come with Your Grace with a clear conscience.

HENRY. [*Uncomfortably pulls at the sleeve*] I know it, Thomas, I know . . .

MORE. [*Rises, formally*] I crave pardon if I offend.

HENRY. [*Suspiciously*] Speak then.

MORE. When I took the Great Seal your Majesty promised not to pursue me on this matter.

HENRY. Ha! So I break my word, Master More! No no, I'm joking . . . I joke roughly . . . [*He wanders away*] I often think I'm a rough fellow . . . Yes, a rough young fellow.

---

3. **tiller** (til' ər) *n.* bar or handle for turning a boat's rudder.

[*He shakes his head indulgently*] Be seated . . . That's a rosebay.[4] We have one like it at Hampton—not so red as that though. Ha—I'm in an excellent frame of mind. [*Glances at the rosebay*] Beautiful. [*Reasonable, pleasant*] You must consider, Thomas, that I stand in peril of my soul. It was no marriage; she was my brother's widow. Leviticus: "Thou shalt not uncover the nakedness of thy brother's wife." Leviticus, Chapter eighteen, Verse sixteen.[5]

MORE. Yes, Your Grace. But Deuteronomy—[6]

HENRY. [*Triumphant*] Deuteronomy's ambiguous!

MORE. [*Bursting out*] Your Grace, I'm not fit to meddle in these matters—to me it seems a matter for the Holy See—

HENRY. [*Reprovingly*] Thomas, Thomas, does a man need a Pope to tell him when he's sinned? It was a sin, Thomas; I admit it; I repent. And God has punished me; I have no son . . . Son after son she's borne me, Thomas, all dead at birth, or dead within the month; I never saw the hand of God so clear in anything . . . I have a daughter, she's a good child, a well-set child—But I have no son. [*He flares up*] It is my bounden *duty* to put away the Queen, and all the Popes back to St. Peter shall not come between me and my duty! How is it that you cannot see? Everyone else does.

MORE. [*Eagerly*] Then why does Your Grace need my poor support?

HENRY. Because you are honest. What's more to the purpose, you're known to be honest . . . There are those like Norfolk who follow me because I wear the crown, and there are those like Master Cromwell who follow me because they are jackals with sharp teeth and I am their lion, and there is a mass that follows me because it follows anything that moves—and there is you.

MORE. I am sick to think how much I must displease Your Grace.

---

4. rosebay (rōz' bā) *n.* any of the genus (rhododendron) of trees or shrubs with showy flowers of pink, white, or purple.
5. Leviticus (lə vit' i kəs), **Chapter eighteen, Verse sixteen** reference to the third book of the Pentateuch in the Bible, containing the laws relating to priests and their assistants, the Levites.
6. Deuteronomy (do͞ot ər än' ə mē) fifth book of the Pentateuch in the Bible, in which the laws of Moses are set down.

HENRY. No, Thomas, I respect your sincerity. Respect? Oh, man, it's water in the desert . . . How did you like our music? That air they played, it had a certain—well, tell me what you thought of it.

MORE. [*Relieved at this turn; smiling*] Could it have been Your Grace's own?

HENRY. [*Smiles back*] Discovered! Now I'll never know your true opinion. And that's irksome, Thomas, for we artists, though we love praise, yet we love truth better.

MORE. [*Mildly*] Then I will tell Your Grace truly what I thought of it.

HENRY. [*A little disconcerted*] Speak then.

MORE. To me it seemed—delightful.

HENRY. Thomas—I chose the right man for Chancellor.

MORE. I must in fairness add that my taste in music is reputedly deplorable.[7]

HENRY. Your taste in music is excellent. It exactly coincides with my own. Ah music! Music! Send them back without me, Thomas; I will live here in Chelsea and make music.

MORE. My house is at Your Grace's disposal.

HENRY. Thomas, you understand me; we will stay here together and make music.

MORE. Will Your Grace honor my roof after dinner?

HENRY. [*Walking away, blowing moodily on his whistle*] Mm? Yes, I expect I'll bellow for you . . .

MORE. My wife will be more—

HENRY. Yes, yes. [*He turns, his face set*] Touching this other business, mark you, Thomas, I'll have no opposition.

MORE. [*Sadly*] Your Grace?

HENRY. No opposition, I say! No opposition! Your conscience is your own affair; but you are my Chancellor! There, you have my word—I'll leave you out of it. But I don't take it kindly, Thomas, and I'll have no opposition! I see how it will be; the bishops will oppose me. The full-fed, hypocritical, "Princes of the *Church*"! Ha! As for the Pope! Am I to burn in Hell because the Bishop of Rome,

---

7. **deplorable** (dē plôr′ ə bəl) *adj.* regrettable or wretched.

with the King of Spain's knife to his throat, mouths me
Deuteronomy? Hypocrites! They're all hypocrites! Mind
they do not take you in, Thomas! Lie low if you will, but
I'll brook no opposition—no noise! No words, no signs, no
letters, no pamphlets—Mind that, Thomas—no writings
against me!

MORE. Your grace is unjust. I am Your Grace's loyal
minister. If I cannot serve Your Grace in this great matter
of the Queen—

HENRY. I have no Queen! Catherine is not my wife and no
priest can make her so, and they that say she is my wife
are not only liars . . . but traitors! Mind it, Thomas!

MORE. Am I a babbler, Your Grace? [*But his voice is
unsteady*]

HENRY. You are stubborn . . . [*Wooingly*] If you could
come with me, you are the man I would soonest raise—
yes, with my own hand.

MORE. [*Covers his face*] Oh, Your Grace overwhelms me!

Speech Before Her Troops

Queen Elizabeth I

Part of a leader's job is rallying support for the leader's causes, as Elizabeth does in this speech.

My loving people, we have been persuaded by some, that are careful of our safety, to take heed how we commit ourselves to armed multitudes, for fear of *treachery*; but I assure you, I do not desire to live to distrust my faithful and loving people. Let tyrants fear; I have always so behaved myself that, under God, I have placed my chiefest strength and safeguard in the loyal hearts and good will of my subjects. And therefore I am come amongst you at this time, not as for my recreation or sport, but being resolved, in the midst and heat of the battle, to live or die amongst you all; to lay down, for my God, and for my kingdom, and for my people, my honor and my blood, even the dust. I know I have but the body of a weak and feeble woman; but I have the heart of a king, and of a king of England, too; and think foul scorn that Parma or Spain, or any prince of Europe, should dare to invade the borders of my realms: to which, rather than any dishonor should grow by me, I myself will take up arms; I myself will be your general, judge, and rewarder of every one of your virtues in the field. I know already, by your forwardness, that you have deserved rewards and crowns; and we do assure you, on the word of a prince, they shall be duly paid you. In the mean my lieutenant general shall be in my stead, that whom never prince commanded a more noble and worthy subject; not doubting by your obedience to my general, by your concord in the camp, and by your valor in the field, we shall shortly have a famous victory over the enemies of my God, of my kingdom, and of my people.

Psalm 23

King James Version

Although the Book of Psalms contains 150 sacred poems, this one is undoubtedly the best known. It is recited at funerals, in times of trouble, and when people are in need of comfort.

1 The Lord is my shepherd; I shall not want.

2 He maketh me to lie down in green pastures: he leadeth me beside the still waters.

3 He restoreth my soul: he leadeth me in the paths of righteousness for his name's sake.

4 Yea, though I walk through the valley of the shadow of death, I will fear no evil: for thou art with me; thy rod and thy staff they comfort me.

5 Thou preparest a table before me in the presence of mine enemies; thou anointest my head with oil; my cup runneth over.

6 Surely goodness and mercy shall follow me all the days of my life: and I will dwell in the house of the Lord forever.

The Trial: Florence and Rome, 1632–1633

from Truth on Trial: The Story of Galileo Galilei

Vicki Cobb

In this account, a famous scientist is forced to publicly deny his own beliefs and his writings to save his life.

Galileo walked stiffly into the sunny courtyard of his villa just outside Florence. His arthritis was bothering him. Perhaps he would feel better in the early October sunshine. He sat down carefully, and lovingly caressed the thick, leather-bound book in his hands. It was his latest work, called *Dialogue Concerning the Two Chief World Systems*. At long last, the book he had dreamed of writing! Seventeen years had passed since Cardinal Bellarmine had warned him not to "hold or defend" the Copernican system of the universe. So much had happened since then. Galileo had overcome many obstacles to make the book a reality.

In 1616 he had returned to Florence from Rome with all hopes for writing the book destroyed. For eight years he was silent, obeying the command delivered by Cardinal Bellarmine. He turned his attention to other problems in science involving motion and navigation. He had improved his telescope and had developed a simple microscope. Then in August 1623 came good news. His old friend Maffeo Barberini had become Pope Urban VIII. Galileo's spirits rose. Surely this ruler would be in favor of new ideas! With high hopes he went to Rome to seek permission to write his book.

Pope Urban welcomed him and spent many hours in conversation with his old friend. Finally, he gave Galileo the permission he wanted, but with reservations. First, Galileo must present the Copernican system as only an idea, not as a fact in reality. Second, Galileo must get Church approval of the manuscript before publishing the book. Galileo agreed happily to these conditions. Cardinal Bellarmine's old warning did not come up much in their conversations, since the new Pope wanted to establish his own authority. He also wanted his reign to be known for great works, and Galileo's book would show the world that the modern Church was not threatened by new ideas.

The writing turned out to be very slow work. Galileo wanted to be careful and thorough. He wrote the book as a conversation among three men. One character spoke for Galileo (and Copernicus). Another spoke for the traditional Ptolemaic view. His name was Simplicio, which meant "simple-minded." The third character was named Sagredo, after his old friend, who had died a few years earlier. In the book, Sagredo was an intelligent person with an open mind, as the real Sagredo had been. The purpose of the dialogue was to let Sagredo decide which system of the universe was correct. All the arguments for and against each system were presented. Though Galileo was fair in presenting both sides, no intelligent reader could have any doubt which side was correct. There was no denying that the Copernican system was simpler and more useful than the Ptolemaic for predicting the positions of the planets.

Galileo wrote the book in everyday Italian, rather than in Latin, the language of churchmen and scholars. Thus the book would be available to intelligent people in the public who were not connected with the Church or the universities. Still, Galileo did appear to follow the Pope's orders. At the end of the book, Simplicio (the character who spoke for Ptolemy) says that the Copernican system is simply an idea, one of many possibilities. But the arguments in favor of the Copernican system had been presented so powerfully that this small disclaimer was like closing the barn door after the horses had escaped.

After the writing, which took five years, came the problem of getting approval from the Church. Some of the official readers raised their eyebrows. They felt Galileo had only gone through the motions of obeying the Pope. Finally, however, approval for publication was granted. It was done. The first publication was in Florence, where Galileo had presented his patron, the Grand Duke, with a finished copy of the book seven months before. Then the book was published in Rome in June. It was an unexpected instant success. Copies disappeared from bookstores faster than they could be replaced.

Suddenly, without warning, trouble started. In August, Church officials removed all copies of the *Dialogue* from bookstores, and soon afterward the book was put on the Church list of banned books, so that reading or owning the book was a crime against the Church. Galileo was completely bewildered by this turn of events, but he did not know yet that Pope Urban had become his personal enemy. Apparently someone had convinced him that Galileo had used him as the model for Simplicio, the "simple-minded."

Galileo tenderly opened the book in his lap and leafed through the pages in the early autumn sunlight. So much pain and joy had gone into its creation! It was like a child to him, a child in trouble.

Suddenly his peace was disturbed by a servant.

"Signore Galileo, the Inquisitor of Florence is here to see you."

With a sinking feeling in the pit of his stomach Galileo said, "Show him in."

Galileo's old friend Father Stefani entered the courtyard. "It is with great regret, Galileo, that I perform my duty. On this day of October 1, 1632, I serve this official summons by the Inquisition in Rome. You have thirty days to journey to Rome to answer charges against you by the Inquisition."

The summons was more than Galileo could stand. It was so unjust! He was innocent! This he knew in the depths of his soul. He truly believed he had only told the truth in his book *with the Pope's approval.* The news was too much for him. He collapsed and had to be put to bed.

Friends wrote the Pope and anyone else who might have some influence. They explained that Galileo was almost seventy years old and very ill. They feared the 200-mile journey would kill him. But Pope Urban insisted. The Holy Father felt that Galileo had made a fool of him. After a few months' delay the Holy Office ordered Galileo to make the trip or else be brought to Rome in chains. In January 1633, Galileo slowly and painfully set off for Rome. To give him as much comfort as possible, the Grand Duke had loaned him his own coach for the trip.

In Rome, Galileo stayed at the home of the Tuscan ambassador, where he was treated with every kindness. Strangely, the Church didn't seem to be in a hurry to bring him to trial now that he was in Rome. Weeks went by. Galileo slowly regained his health and his fighting spirit. For the life of him he couldn't figure out why the

Pope had turned against him. Deep in his heart he believed that he could still convince his old friend that his views were correct and that he had not committed a crime against the Church.

But Pope Urban VIII was very different from the Cardinal Barberini he had once been. His reign had truly changed him. He saw enemies everywhere. He even lived in a palace outside Rome with guards stationed along the road, because he feared he would be poisoned. It was hard for a reasonable person like Galileo to understand such unreasonable behavior in another.

In March, the Tuscan ambassador heard from the Pope that Galileo would soon be called to trial. Galileo was ready. He listened carefully as the ambassador reported to him about his visit with the Holy Father.

"The Pope told me that you had been his friend and that he was sorry that you had to suffer these troubles. But it is a matter of faith and religion. He said that it is not our job to decide how God does His work." Galileo leaned forward and stroked his beard.

"I thought you would be willing to say that you don't believe in the motion of the earth," the ambassador continued, "but that you would maintain, since God was all-powerful and could make the universe in a thousand different ways, that He could have made it his way, too, with the sun at its center. The Pope became furious at this statement, so I stopped saying anything that could hurt you. I feel it is very important that you obey him and do whatever he asks in the interest of religion."

Galileo nodded his agreement. But his eyes were sad.

Finally, in the middle of April, Galileo was transferred to the Inquisition headquarters and kept as a prisoner. He began a series of appearances before the ten judges of the Inquisition, where many questions were asked of him. Things began to close in when they brought up the subject of that meeting long ago with Cardinal Bellarmine:

"What did Cardinal Bellarmine tell you in February 1616?"

"He told me I was not to hold or defend the Copernican system."

Galileo produced a letter that Cardinal Bellarmine had written him after the spoken warning. It confirmed that Galileo was telling the truth.

"Who was present during this meeting?"

Suddenly Galileo was afraid.

"Some Dominican fathers. But I do not know their names and I haven't seen them since."

Galileo saw the danger. Cardinal Bellarmine was dead. He had no witnesses to that long ago confrontation.

Then came the cruelest blow of all. The Inquisitors produced a document dated at the time of that meeting. It was a formal warning from Bellarmine to Galileo. The language was much stronger than any Galileo remembered:

"Your opinion of the universe is wrong. You must forget it. You must not teach or defend it in any way whatsoever. If you do, you will have to answer to the Inquisition of the Holy Office."

Galileo was dumbfounded. Bellarmine had never told him he could not "teach" the Copernican system "in any way whatsoever." Clearly his book would be in violation of this order. The book did not violate Bellarmine's instructions as Galileo had understood them. In it he had only presented the Copernican view. But he personally had not "held" or "defended" it. There was no way he could now convince the Inquisition that he had not gone against the Pope's orders. Just to mention the Copernican system went against the order not to teach it "in any way whatsoever."

Where had this document come from? Galileo had never set eyes on it before. It was entirely possible that it was a forgery made by some of the present authorities who wanted to make sure of the case against him. If so, their trick had worked. Obviously the Pope was convinced that Galileo had committed a crime against the Church. Galileo had no proof on his side.

Galileo was defeated. The Inquisition found him guilty. Now came the painful wait for sentencing. They could do with him what they wished.

The Tuscan ambassador had some hope about the sentence. After all, Galileo was an old man and well respected. But the methods of the Inquisition were well known. If there were any resistance, if a prisoner clung to his forbidden beliefs, they simply used torture. The most common instrument of torture was the rack. They strapped a man to it and stretched him until his spine cracked and his muscles were torn apart. A younger man might survive it, but it would kill Galileo. Again the ambassador advised him to be quiet and obedient.

It was now the middle of June. For two months Galileo had been a prisoner. Although he had been treated well and allowed three rooms and a servant, the strain of being under lock and key showed.

On the morning of June 22 he was dressed in a coarse white robe and brought before the full court of the Inquisition. He now had little hope of being treated with mercy. The day before, the judges had asked:

"Do you or do you not believe in Copernicus?"

"No," answered Galileo, "not since before the warning in 1616."

"Doesn't your book, the *Dialogue*, support Copernicus?"

"No," answered Galileo. "I tried to show that neither Copernicus or Ptolemy are certain."

"Do you believe the earth moves?"

"No," answered Galileo. The judges had to lean forward to hear his answer. The old man in the rough clothing of a Church prisoner seemed to shrink before them. They did not see the tears in his eyes. They could not begin to understand the depths of his anguish.

"I am here to do whatever you want of me," the old man murmured.

And today he would find out what that was. He felt his public life to be over. There was no hope of convincing the Pope or the Church. His book was banned. He could not sink any lower in his own eyes. Now what? He knelt before his judges while they read the charges and the sentence.

Life imprisonment! But first he had to swear before the world that the truth—as he knew it—was false. He had to make a public denial, undoing all his work. His denial of the earth's movement in court the day before was not enough.

This was his greatest humiliation!

With a shaking hand Galileo wrote the document:

"I, Galileo, son of the late Vincenzo Galilei, aged seventy years . . . do swear that I have always believed . . . all that is taught and preached by the Holy Catholic Church. I wholly give up the false opinion that the sun is the center of the universe and does not move and the earth is not the center of the universe and moves. . . . I have abjured, sworn, and promised the truth of this document. . . ."

His life imprisonment turned out to be not such a heavy burden. He was allowed to return home to Florence, where his home was his prison. He wasn't allowed to leave. He spent the remaining eight years of his life writing a book on two new sciences, which became the beginning of modern physics. He played his lute and cultivated his olive trees. Always there was a steady stream of visitors.

There are some who feel that Galileo betrayed his beliefs, that he should have held fast and been burned at the stake. But Galileo was an intelligent man who saw through the men of the Church. He came to realize that the authorities were not interested in truth, only in their own power. By submitting he saved his own life. He knew that he had work of great value still to do.

And it was no secret to his many friends that Galileo believed to his dying day that the earth does in fact move around the sun and that it spins to create night and day. Galileo had absolute faith that, in the end, truth would be victorious.

Exploration
to the Enlightenment
in the Western World

Vasco Núñez de Balboa

from Around the World in a Hundred Years

Jean Fritz

This biography of the famous explorer brings his spirit and his sense of adventure to life.

After Columbus had returned from his third voyage and reported seeing pearls and gold in what he thought was the Garden of Eden, explorers rushed to the site. Indeed, how could an adventurous man resist? Among the first to go was a twenty-five-year-old fencing master, a blond, good-looking man named Vasco Núñez de Balboa. He left Spain in 1500 with an expedition headed by Rodrigo de Bastidas, who had seen Columbus's chart of 1498 and knew how to get to the Gulf of Darién, where the Isthmus of Panama joins the South American mainland. This is where the pearls and gold were. Bastidas loaded up, explored the coast of what is now Colombia, and headed home. On his way his two ships crashed into rocks at the extreme western tip of Hispaniola. Bastidas and his men got to shore safely, but captive slaves on board, with their legs in chains, were left to go down with the ships. But not the pearls and the gold. The men managed to save them. They carried those heavy treasure chests all the way across the island to the new capital, Santo Domingo.

If he had to be shipwrecked, Balboa had found a convenient place. As unruly as the island was, a new system had recently been introduced in which each settler was given a plot of cultivated land, complete with ten thousand cassava[1] plants and all the Tainos who lived on it. The owner could use those Tainos as he pleased. Since Balboa was not ready to leave the New World, he decided to become a settler. He moved in with his cassava plants and his slaves, making friends, running his farm, and hoping somehow to go exploring again. Balboa was a hard worker, yet for some reason he kept running into debt. And the rule was: No one who was in debt was allowed to leave the island. Balboa watched people come and go from Santo Domingo while he stayed and stayed.

---

1. **cassava** (kə sä′ və) *n.* a tropical American plant with edible roots.

For seven years he stayed. Even his friend Ponce de León left to conquer Puerto Rico. Before leaving he gave Balboa one of Bercerillo's pups. Balboa named him Leoncico after his friend, and together they stayed, trapped with ten thousand cassava plants and those stubborn debts.

In 1509 Alonso de Ojeda suddenly turned up in Santo Domingo, looking for recruits for a new colony. Everyone knew Ojeda, at least by reputation. He had proved himself a fierce and cruel fighter on Columbus's second voyage, had been in Santo Domingo in 1499 with Amerigo Vespucci, and was there again in 1502 when his captains had mutinied and brought him in shackles to be jailed. And now here he was, back with an appointment as governor of a new colony to be established in the area around the Gulf of Darién near where Balboa had been.

Ojeda was to share the governorship with Diego de Nicuesa, another unsavory character, who was already at Santo Domingo, but when the two men met, they couldn't stand each other, so they decided to divide their territory between them. Ojeda would rule the eastern side of the gulf, and Nicuesa would rule the western side. They invited Martín de Enciso to join them as a third partner to follow later with more recruits and supplies.

If it hadn't been for his debts, Balboa would have jumped at the chance to sign up as a recruit, no matter how unpleasant the leaders were. Anything would be better than rotting here forever with his cassava plants, but the only way he could leave the island would be to sneak away. He'd have to become a stowaway. He enlisted the help of a friend who agreed to smuggle his two most precious possessions on board Enciso's ship—his sword and Leoncico. And Balboa hid himself in a barrel. When the other barrels filled with supplies were rolled on deck, so was the barrel filled with Balboa. He stayed scrunched up in his hiding place until he felt the ship sail and was sure that Enciso had gone too far to be willing to turn back. Then he let himself out.

Enciso was furious. If there was one thing he didn't want, it was a man who would argue with him. Yet that is exactly what he got. Balboa told Enciso to settle on the west side of the gulf because on his previous trip he'd heard that the people there did not use poisoned arrows. Those on the east side did. Enciso didn't like the idea of poisoned arrows, so he took the suggestion. They named their settlement Santa María de l'Antigua del Darién, or simply Antigua for short.

Then there was the question of government. Enciso said he was in charge and all the gold and pearls found would belong to him. Balboa argued. Since neither Ojeda nor Nicuesa was there, he said, the place belonged to no one. The settlers should elect their leader. And they did. They elected Balboa.

Not surprisingly, the three original leaders of the expedition not only caused trouble, they got into it. Enciso made so much trouble that Balboa's men expelled him and he headed back to Spain. And Ojeda, the famous Indian fighter, had to run for his life from men on the east side who had poisoned arrows. As for Nicuesa, he was doing so poorly in his settlement down the coast that he moved to Balboa's colony, but the colonists didn't want him. They told him to get out, and when he didn't, they chased him down the beach, forced him into a leaky boat, and pushed him out to sea. He was never heard from again.

On December 23, 1511, King Ferdinand of Spain appointed Balboa acting governor of Darién. Compared to other Spanish governors, Balboa was a good one and well liked. Most Spaniards took for granted that natives should be fought and turned into slaves. What else were they good for? Although Balboa was not afraid to fight if necessary, he preferred to make friends with local people and avoid violence if possible. He was a firm man but a kind one, and within a short time he was on such good terms with Careta, a nearby chief, that he became his blood brother. When he married the chief's beautiful daughter, Caretita, he treated her as a true wife. For her part, she was loyal and counseled him well on how to deal with her people. Both father and daughter were given Christian baptism, and while Careta agreed to supply the Spaniards with food, Balboa agreed to help Careta fight his enemies.

It was, however, when Balboa was visiting the palace of a distant chief, Comagre, that his career as an explorer took its most promising turn. Comagre and his seven sons were so friendly that they distributed gold to Balboa's men, but at the sight of gold the Spaniards became as quarrelsome and greedy as spoiled children. Who had the most gold? Were the shares equally divided? Could they have more? Comagre's oldest son was disgusted. "If you love gold so much," he said, "I'll show you more." He offered to take them to another sea. The people there were very rich and had gold mines, he said.

Another sea! A gold mine! Balboa was so excited that he ordered Comagre and all his sons to be baptized immediately. He gave Comagre the Christian name of Carlos. It would be a difficult trip, Carlos explained—across mountains, through swamps, in forests too thick to let in sunshine. And since there were cannibals on the way, Balboa would need to take a thousand soldiers with him. Balboa rushed back to Antigua and wrote to the king of Spain, telling him the good news and asking for one thousand men to make the trip across that narrow neck of land that we now call Panama. As the people waited for the king's reply, all they talked about was the gold, the pearls, the spices that awaited them.

The king was delighted with Balboa's news, but by this time Enciso had arrived in Spain and charged Balboa with crimes he had never committed. The king believed him. Obviously, the king was not pleased, and rumors of his displeasure reached Balboa. There was even talk that the king would send another governor to take his place. Balboa was not going to let another governor find *his* sea. He'd go now, he decided. Even if he didn't have a thousand men, he'd go. Gathering 180 Spaniards and 800 natives, he set out in September 1513. As usual Leoncico, who received a captain's pay on every expedition, led the pack of attack dogs.

The trip was even harder and the going rougher than the Spaniards had expected. When they tried to wade through swamps, they found the mud so deep, they had to take off their clothes, pile them on their shields, and carry them on their heads. When they came to a river, they had to stop and build rafts. When they came to cannibals, they let loose their dogs and fired their guns, killing the chief and six hundred warriors. The rest fled for their lives. So there was nothing else to fear, Balboa figured. If only the natives were telling the truth about that other sea.

On Sunday, September 25, the native guides pointed to a mountain ahead. From the top of that mountain, they said, the sea could be seen. Everyone scrambled up the mountain, but when they neared the top, Balboa told them to wait. What if there was no sea? He took Leoncico with him and went the rest of the way alone.

Yes! The sea was there. Blue as any sea he'd ever seen. Calling for the others to join him, he fell to his knees, praising God. Together they all sang and celebrated while the natives looked on in amazement. All this fuss about nothing more than a sea?

Four days later Balboa reached the shore, waded into the water up to his knees, and with his sword drawn, took possession of the sea (later to be called the Pacific) and all lands touching it, including, of course, China and Japan. Then he scooped up a handful of water to taste it. Yes, it was salty, but neither Balboa nor anyone else knew for sure if this was a new sea or an extension of the old one. In any case, Balboa called it the South Sea and began exploring nearby islands for pearls.

On January 19, 1514, he returned to Antigua, loaded down with large pearls and six thousand pesos' worth of gold. The settlers, wild with excitement, followed Balboa and his party in a triumphal procession. The pearls and gold were divided up: one-fifth to the king and the rest of the settlers according to their rank, some even going to Leoncico. Balboa could also be proud of the fact that he'd made friends along his route and not a single Spaniard had been lost. It was no wonder that the settlers called him a hero.

There was one outsider in town who stood by, watching the celebration. Pedro de Arbolancha had just arrived, an agent of the king sent to find out how the colony was doing and to prepare the way for a new governor. Of course Arbolancha could see that Balboa was well liked and that the colony was doing well under him. But in case the king didn't believe it, the settlers wrote a petition, asking that Balboa be kept as their governor. If Arbolancha had hurried back to Spain with this petition, history might have been changed—at least Balboa's history. But Arbolancha hung around Antigua for three months. Perhaps he was having a good time; perhaps the weather was bad. In any case, he didn't sail for Spain until March, and by that time the new governor was already on his way to Antigua. His name was Pedrarias de Avila, but in Antigua his nickname became the Wrath of God. He arrived on June 29, 1514, with two thousand new settlers, fifty horses, one hundred cattle, eleven bells for a new church, and his brother, who became know as Count Fist-in-the Face. Worst of all, he brought back Enciso.

One of the first things de Avila did was to charge Balboa with all the offenses that he could think of. Balboa was fined and his house taken from him, but de Avila did not send him back to Spain for trial, nor did he put him in jail. Perhaps he was afraid to lock up a man who had so many friends. Perhaps he simply wanted to make use of Balboa for a while. Soon, however, it would be too late to punish him. When word reached Europe that a new sea had been discovered, Balboa became an instant hero, as popular as Columbus had been. King Ferdinand ordered de Avila "to favor and deal well with Balboa." He wrote to Balboa, praising him, calling him "Adelantado" (leader), and asking him to give advice to de Avila. But Balboa not only didn't want to give de Avila advice, de Avila didn't want to take it. Balboa complained to the king that de Avila treated the natives harshly. "Where the Indians were as sheep," he said, "they have become as fierce lions." And de Avila complained that Balboa was covetous, ungrateful, and ambitious.

But de Avila did make use of Balboa. He assigned him the job of building a road from one sea to the other with a town at each end. He was also to build ships and explore the coast that led south into the area we now call Peru. According to the natives, this was a fabulous place with so much gold, it sounded like Japan. Balboa had his heart set on this expedition, but the work proceeded so slowly that de Avila became suspicious. How could he trust Balboa? Was he already setting himself up as ruler of this new land? So de Avila sent soldiers to bring Balboa back.

On his return, Balboa was accused of treason, tried, and convicted. And in January 1519 he was beheaded. Like so many explorers, he came to a violent end. Indeed, it was said in Europe that people who thought they were going to the "new world" were more often going to the "next world." As it turned out, Francisco Pizarro, the soldier who arrested Balboa, was the one who eventually conquered Peru.

Still, the new sea was Balboa's, and hope revived that China and Japan lay only a short distance over *that* horizon.

A Strange, Funny-Looking Vegetable

from The Amazing Potato

Milton Meltzer

What is so amazing about the potato? This common vegetable has a fascinating history, as this selection shows.

One day in the 1530s a scouting party of Spaniards entered an Inca village, high in the Andes in what we now call Peru. Reports of cruel and greedy white invaders had already spread throughout the mountains, and the villagers had fled at word of their coming. The Spaniards went from empty house to empty house, hunting for loot. They found only maize (corn), beans, and a strange vegetable that was like nothing they had ever seen.

The vegetable came in many sizes, tiny as a nut to big as an apple. Its shape ranged from an irregular ball to a twisted oblong. Its skin was white, yellow, blue, purple, red, brown. Inside, its color could be white, yellow, purple, pink. The Spaniards were not impressed. They had come to the Andes searching for gold, silver, and precious stones. What good was this funny-looking vegetable?

Gradually they found out. First of all, it was the staple food of these mountain people. And secondly, the vegetable was believed to have healing powers. Raw slices were fixed to broken bones, pressed against the head to cure aching, eaten with other food to end a bellyache. The Incas also rubbed it on their bodies to cure skin diseases and carried slices to prevent rheumatism.

The Inca name for the vegetable was *papa*. It means tuber, a short, fleshy underground stem or root. The Inca gave other names to the many kinds of *papas* they grew. Those with red flesh they called "weep blood for the Inca." An especially hard kind was "knife breaker," and still others were "human-head" and "red mother." When the Spaniards tasted the potato, they found it delicious— "a dainty dish even for Spaniards," one conquistador admitted.

The diet of the common people of Peru was mainly vegetarian. True, some people fished along the coast or in the mountain waters of Lake Titicaca. Others occasionally hunted in groups, chasing down deer, wild llamas, bears, pumas, and foxes. Still others raised guinea pigs and ducks. But those were luxury foods. The main diet was maize and other vegetables in the lowlands. But in the highlands, where maize would not grow, it was the potato above all that people depended on. We now know that the native people living along the western coast of South America were growing and eating potatoes two thousand years before Columbus set sail.

They knew not only how to grow the potato but how to preserve it. After harvesting the crop, they spread the potatoes on the ground and left them overnight to freeze in the biting air of the high mountains. The next day the men, women, and children assembled to stamp out the potatoes' moisture with their bare feet. They repeated this process for four or five days, until all the moisture was gone. What was left was a white potato flour that could be stored for years. The Inca name for what was probably the world's first freeze-dried food was *chuno*.

Scientists exploring the ancient tombs of the Inca have found evidence that *chuno* was bartered for other products. It was carried on the backs of llamas to the lower valleys and coastal towns, where it was exchanged for maize and manioc (another root food), clay pottery, and woven cloth.

When the Spaniards discovered the rich silver mines of Potosí (now in Bolivia) in 1545, they were quick to see the use of the potato, fresh or freeze dried, as food for the Inca they forced to work for them. It didn't take long for speculators in Spain to see a new way to get rich. They sailed across the Atlantic, bought up potatoes cheaply from the Inca farmers, and sold them at high prices to the native workers in the mines.

Here is a strange twist of history: The annual $100-billion value of the potato crop is three times greater than the value of all the gold and silver the Spanish lugged away from the Americas. The potatoes they took so lightly turned out to be worth far more than the gold and silver they killed for.

In which I confess

from I, Juan de Pareja

Elizabeth Borton de Treviño

Imagine the injustice of being forbidden to do what you love. In this selection, one artist finds the support he needs in the friendship of another.

Our apprentices[1] came and went. Master never sought them, but often he felt obliged to take in some stripling whose father, some courtier, or a friend, asked it.

In those later years, after Paquita was married, the studio was a quiet, even a somber place, for Master took no apprentices at all for two or three years. Such apprentices as he felt obliged to consider, he sent over to Juan Bautista, Paquita's husband, no doubt thinking that the young people could use the money, such as it was, that apprentices brought in from the fees they paid for learning, or by sales of copies they made of pictures done by their Master. Also he felt that Paquita, with her new baby girl, should have the help and the companionship of young people around her. She had had a hard birth and had not been well since, and was much inclined to tears and despondency.

Then one day a young man came riding into our courtyard on a heavily laden mule. He was dressed simply in a white shirt and woolen knee-trousers, and he wore cheap cloth shoes on his feet, laced on around the ankles. Lashed onto the mule's back was a bundle of clothes, a rug, a guitar, and painting gear.

"Hola!" he called up to where I looked down on him from our second-story windows. "I have come to pay my respects to Maestro Velázquez!"

I hurried down the stairs to ask him his business, and by the time I arrived in the patio he had begun to unload his mule, singing a merry song meanwhile. I stopped in my tracks. It was wonderful to hear that lighthearted caroling, and I realized how sad and silent our household had become, with Paquita gone, and Mistress spending

---

1. apprentice (ə pren′ tis) *n.* someone learning a trade under a master craftsman.

half her time in her daughter's house, trying to build her up and lift her spirits.

"I am Juan de Pareja, Master's servant," I told him. "Before you unload, we had better find out if you can stay."

"Oh, I'll stay!" cried the young man confidently. "I have letters from old friends of his in Seville. And besides, even if I am turned away, you must let me rest my animal. Poor old Rata!" He petted the dejected mule's nose. "He has come a long way and he is tired!"

I could hardly resist his kindness to the animal; that was always a way into my soft heart.

"I will go and ask if Master can speak to you," I told him. "Who is calling on him?"

"Bartolomé Esteban Murillo. From Seville. And I have come to be his apprentice and to learn from him because he is the best in the world!"

He was stocky and broad, with a round dark face and undistinguished features save for the fine brown eyes. They were full and lively, and sparkling with kindness and good humor. His hair, roughened by the autumn breeze, was a dark chestnut brown, curly and worn rather long, though not as an affectation, I am sure, but only because he had no money to cut it. On his brown chest, showing in the open throat of his travel-stained shirt, lay a crucifix, suspended from a black leather cord.

"Lead on, Señor Pareja," said the young man. "I want to feast these eyes on the finest painter who ever lived!"

Now I had never been called Señor Pareja in my life. Slaves are not addressed in this way. It showed the young man's ignorance, or perhaps merely his preoccupation. I did not say anything; he would soon learn. Everyone called me Juanico.

"If you have letters, Master will want to see you at once," I told him. "Follow me."

The young man patted his bulging sash, to make sure his letters were still safe, and came trotting along behind me. But he turned and said, "First, could I get some water for my mule? Poor fellow, he's thirsty."

I went to draw a bucketful myself. It gave me time to think over young Sr. Murillo from Seville. I began to hope that Master would accept this simple young man, for I liked him well.

After old Rata had sunk his nose in the bucket of water and I had found him some fodder, Bartolomé tethered him in the shade. Then he laid a light blanket over him. Only after all this had been done, did he turn, ready to follow me into Master's studio.

That day Master had begun to work out an idea for painting several people in the same room by reflecting them in mirrors. He was busy placing mirrors here and there, checking their positions, going to his easel to observe the proportions of the images reflected and sketching a few lines. He was not satisfied and had begun to rub out some of his charcoal lines with a clean white rag when we reached the door.

Bartolomé ran forward, dropped on one knee, seized Master's hand still holding the paint rag, and pressed it to his lips.

"Bartolomé Esteban Murillo," he announced himself. I saw that his dark eyes were glittering with tears of emotion. Master looked at the kneeling young man without expression; I had no clue as to what he was thinking.

"You have got charcoal dust on your face," he said then. "Get up, young fellow. One should kneel and kiss hands only to the King. What brings you here?"

Wordless, Bartolomé got to his feet and took two letters from his sash, which he gave to Master. Master carefully wiped his hands clean and then went to sit in his big chair near the window. He opened and read his letters.

"It is good to have news of old friends," he said, turning. "So you are a painter, Murillo?"

Bartolomé crossed himself in the most natural manner and answered, "With the grace of God, I sometimes do pretty well. But I have much to learn, and I want to work in your studio."

"Did you bring some of your work to show me?"

"I did!" And without another word, Bartolomé flew down the stairs to where he had left the load of luggage beside his mule. In a couple of minutes he was back again with several rolls of canvas. Instinctively choosing the right place to stand so as to show his painting in a good light, he unrolled his canvases, one by one.

Master studied each one in silence.

"You paint saints and angels," he said, in his customary, dry, serious tone. "But you paint from live models."

Bartolomé stepped forward smiling, eager to explain. "Christ is in each one of us," he explained. "When I need to paint a saint, I find holiness in the face of anyone available. It is always there. As for angels, I use little children! There is so little difference between an angel and a child!"

Master studied his face, and then I saw one of his rare, slow smiles move his lips slightly and light up his deep-set eyes.

"Juanico, help Murillo bring up his things and give him the small room next to yours."

"Maestro!" Bartolomé stepped forward impetuously, as if about to seize Master's hand again, but Master quickly put it behind his back and laughed out loud.

"Control yourself, Murillo! I am not used to such open adulation.[2] You will turn my head!"

"Oh, forgive me. It is only that I am so happy!"

And so he came to live with us and to bring laughter and singing and joy back into our quiet studio.

Murillo's jokes all day and his songs to the guitar after supper brought Mistress much joy, and when he was in the studio he was an indefatigable[3] painter. At first Master set him to copying some of his own religious works, for there were always orders coming in from churches and convents and he could never keep up with them. Then, little by little, he simply let Bartolomé paint along at his side, Master suggesting and correcting, and Bartolomé listening and learning. Master began bringing in models once more, especially street children (that Mistress fed and coddled in the kitchen) and old men, to whom Mistress gave warm cloaks and odds and ends of clothing. Master painted the men in the guise of great personages of the past or dressed as saints and holy people. Murillo saw the Christ-light in each one, but Master's interest was in what these people represented individually, in what made them different from everyone else. In that way, he found his truth.

Now I must confess that in that happy, tranquil time, with Mistress presiding over dinner and supper, Master working all day by the side of Bartolomé, and Paquita coming often to visit, with her little plump dark-eyed

---

2. **adulation** (a jōō la′ shən) *n.* intense praise.
3. **indefatigable** (in di fat′ i gə bəl) *adj.* untiring.

daughter, in that time I returned with passion to my secret vice, painting. I used the ducats the King had given me to buy canvases and brushes and, God help me, I stole colors constantly. I kept on because it seemed to me that at last I was beginning to progress in that difficult, demanding art. Why should I not? I also worked by the side of the greatest Master in the world, though my work was invisible to him. And Murillo, too, though he painted in another way from Master, being softer and more sentimental generally, was worth learning from. I copied them carefully and began to make my own direct studies of color, and of light and shade, and perspective. Everyone in that household was busy and happy, and therefore they were not alert to suspicion. I had many hours to myself. This is what gnawed at my conscience and made me unhappy all the while—that Master trusted me.

Especially did I feel sick with repentance when I went with Murillo to early Mass. He was a daily communicant, and I often marveled, as I watched him lift that round, earthy, commonplace face with closed eyes to receive the Host, how God laid a light of sanctity around his ordinary features at that time. And I? Unable to promise that I would stop deceiving Master, stealing his colors, and painting by myself . . . I could not confess and be absolved. Shamed, guilty, I knelt, but I could not receive the grace, and therefore Murillo, good soul, began to worry about me.

"Juan, my friend," he used to say, "go to confession! Cleanse your soul so that you may receive the Eucharist once more! There is no earthly joy to compare with it!"

He never called me Juanico, as everyone else did. On Master's lips, and Mistress's, and even Paquita's, "Juanico" sounded good to me, sounded affectionate and intimate and kind. But I hated it when other men addressed me so, for they were giving me careless treatment, as they might a dog. And yet, being a slave, I could not expect to be called "Señor Pareja." I braced myself each time some stranger snapped his fingers at me and called me "Juanico," and the years never softened my resentment. As often as I could, I pretended not to hear. I loved Bartolomé for finding, in his kindness, the right way to address me. "Juan, my friend."

"Juan *amigo*," he said, "if I can help you, let me."

"I will think things over," I promised him.

And I thought. I wrestled with my problem. But I could not bring myself to speak of it to him, nor yet to confess. And this was a torture, for at any time I might be taken ill, or have some accident, and if I died I would have to appear before the Judgment Seat with all my sins on my head, unconfessed, unrepentant, and unpurged.

I was then trying, hidden in my room, to paint a Virgin. Such temerity had I. But I felt an overpowering need to represent on canvas the tender, youthful face of Our Lady at the moment when the angel appeared to her and said, "Hail, full of grace! Blessed art Thou amongst women!" and told her that she was to be the mother of God.

I had stretched a good piece of Holland linen, which had cost me dear, and I had drawn in the figure, full length, with folded hands. The eyes were downcast and the face was gravely serious, as would become a maiden being told such transcendental news. All the proportions were true. All was ready for the laying on of the color. I had labored over that drawing for many hours.

At last I was ready to begin stroking on the color. I had ready two brushes, one delicate and fine, made of squirrel hair, and another coarser, heavier, for strong strokes.

I began. I had been careful in sketching the garments—the way the skirt molded itself around the young limbs, the folds in the long sleeves, the way the cloak clung around the hair and opened softly over the high-necked bodice of the dress. I worked happily, and it seemed to me that I had caught at last Master's way of laying on a tiny sparkle of light where the material folded, and a soft depth of shadow where it fell away.

A few days later I began to paint the face. First I stroked on the undercolor, in deep earthy rose, as Master always did, then bringing up the colors, layer on layer, until the flesh tones were perfect, reflecting the life and light, suggesting the fullness of flesh and veins and beating blood beneath the warm skin. As I painted, working up the colors on the bit of broken porcelain I used for a palette, some changes began to take place. My hand made those changes while my eyes watched in wonder, as if I had no control over myself at all. The face of the Virgin I was painting became subtly darker, the features softer and more round. The face was becoming that of a girl of my own race, the eyes enormous, velvety black, faintly showing the sparkling white around them, the nose broad with sensitive, flaring nostrils, the lips fleshy, with deep corners. The hair, where it showed beneath the hood of her cloak, was black, tightly curling. I had painted a Negro madonna.

At first I was satisfied, even happy with my painting. Then I felt sorrow, for it seemed as if some devil had guided my hand and that I had painted Our Lady as a Negro maid in order to exalt myself and to protest that my race was the chosen one. I put my head into my hands and wept.

Then I thought, Could it be that an angel had guided me to paint in this manner so as to make me realize fully how wrong it was to try secretly to put myself on the same plane as Master, to show him that I could be as good as he was, could paint as well, could reveal my race in beauty, just as he showed the dignity, the pride of the Spaniard? I was all confused and I did not know what to do, and so I wept and suffered great torment of soul.

Until I remembered the kindness of Bartolomé and that he always called me Friend.

One day, not long after I had finished my painting and before it was yet dry, Master came down with one of his crippling headaches. I did all I could for him with massages, cold cloths on his neck, and teas to induce sleep, and when at last he was dozing fitfully and would be better, I knew, I darkened his room and crept out. Mistress came to sit beside Master, and I was quite free for a few hours. The decision, sudden and final, came into my mind to ask Bartolomé's help. I went to find him in the studio, where he was working on a very large canvas covered with angels and clouds.

"Bartolomé, I need you. Come with me," I begged him simply, and he at once put down his palette, cleaned his hands, and prepared to follow me. I led him to my little room and closed the door behind us. As soon as his eyes had become accustomed to the semi-dark, he saw my painting.

He cautiously stole over to open the door slightly so that he could get good light on my picture, and so he studied it for a good twenty minutes. Then he turned it gently against the wall, and shut the door.

"Let us go out where we can talk freely," he said, and telling the cook that we would be back in about an hour, in case Master wakened and asked for either one of us, we left. Outside, as if in perfect accord, we took the street that led to a little church where we often attended Mass together.

Looking around to make sure that no one would over-hear us, Bartolomé then clasped my hand and said, "It is a fine painting, *amigo*. I congratulate you! You handled the figure, the draperies, the light with all the skill of a pupil of Maestro Velázquez! But what troubles you so?"

"It is unlawful for me, a slave, to paint," I told him.

At this news his jaw dropped and he looked upset and bewildered. "But how can that be?" he protested.

"It is the law in Spain. Slaves may be artisans or craftsmen, but they may not practice any of the arts. That is why I have been painting in secret. I have been copying Master's work for years, and practicing drawing. Alone."

"I am a stupid fellow," said Bartolomé, "and never see beyond the end of my nose. I may have heard of this law, but I cannot remember. I am poor; my family never had slaves. But, Juan, if you have never offered any competi-tion to free men, how can it be thought that you have broken the law?"

In his simplicity, he saw intent as the very essence of the law and could not accept the idea that I had been at fault.

"And you have studied well," he went on. "I myself would be proud to sign the canvas you have just shown me."

"You are always kind. But, you see, that is why I can-not confess. The priest would ask me to give it up, and I cannot! I cannot!"

"Now wait," said Bartolomé. "Wait a moment. Let us think this matter over quietly. Is it a *sin*, then, to paint? I have never heard so."

"But I am a slave!"

"Is it a sin, then, to be a slave?"

"No. It is an injustice. But I am a religious man. I do not expect justice here on earth, but only in heaven. And I am not a rebellious slave. I love Master and Mistress."

"You are a good man. And I cannot see that you have done any wrong. When you confess, does the priest ask you your status? Does he say, 'Are you a slave?' or 'Are you a sinner?'"

"He never asks. I only say that I am a sinner. That I have sinned." I saw what he was driving at and I began to feel the most exquisite pang of hope.

"I cannot see that you are obliged to confess your painting, my friend," said Bartolomé, "and mind you, I am very scrupulous. Painting is no sin and it has nothing to do with your receiving the Host."

"But I have stolen colors."

"Well then, you must confess that and promise to do it no more. You won't have to, for I will give them to you. Now where is the problem? Let us go and find a confessor this very moment."

We went quickly toward the little church and took our places in the line of folk who had gone to confess. Bartolomé, as was his custom, fell almost at once into ecstatic prayer. As for me, I confided in him absolutely. Because I wanted to believe what he told me, of course. That was part of it, I know now. But also because it had been made clear to me in my mind that he was right.

At last my turn came, and I confessed. I told of angers I had felt, of times when I had been slothful, of having stolen little mounds of color. I told of the worst sin, that I had despaired of the love of God, and that I had, in my pride, supposed that God's mercy and forgiveness, which are boundless, would be withheld from me.

The priest gave me a stern penance and I rose from my knees and went to kneel once more beside Bartolomé. He could not know, ever, what a gift he had made me, by making me see that I could be shriven[4] and could once again receive Our Lord. I vowed in my heart that I would serve him as faithfully as I served Master in whatever time I had free.

As we strolled home he said in his simple way, his countenance all radiant with joy, "Now you can be a communicant again, Juan my friend! I rejoice for you!"

"I wish I could show my painting to Master!" I cried then. I had a great longing for his eyes to rest on my work.

Bartolomé's face changed swiftly, and peasant prudence showed in it.

"If you wish my advice, do not show it. Not just yet. The time will come. . . . You will realize when the hour

---

4. shriven (shriv′ ən) v. absolved; forgiven.

has struck that you should show it, and let him know what you have been doing. Not yet. . . ."

"Do you think it was a mistake to paint Our Lady as a Negro girl?" I asked, humbly.

"How so?" asked Bartolomé. "Our Lord appears in many forms to loving Christian souls. As a child, as an old man, sometimes even as a leper. And Our Lady can reveal herself within the body of a child, of an Italian girl, a Spanish maid, or a young woman of the black race. Her tenderness, her gentleness, her sanctity can shine through whatever vessel she chooses to house her spirit for a time. And," he turned to me and laid his hand on my arm in affection, "and the gentle women of your race, Juan, have a beauty Our Lady would never scorn."

So we returned, and my life from that moment grew broader and happier and I became a better person, I think, for Bartolomé had turned my mind away from small preoccupations, and led it into paths of Truth. I stole no more colors. He gave them to me, and he gave me brushes and canvas also.

I served Master and Mistress and Bartolomé and I painted. I felt that life could offer me no further joys.

The Battle of Gainsborough

from Cromwell's Boy

Erik Christian Haugaard

A young messenger has a life-changing experience in the heat of battle in this selection of historical fiction.

"Oliver!" Colonel Cromwell called. I touched the flanks of my horse and rode quickly to his side.

"Go to the rear and see how the supply wagons are faring."

I turned my mare. To ride against an army on the march is as difficult as swimming against the current of a swift river. It took all my skill as a horseman and I received little thanks from those in whose way I got.

"Two of the wagons broke down. One was beyond re-repair," said the lieutenant in charge of the train of supplies. He looked harassed. His was not an enviable lot: If he did his work well he would receive no glory; but if the shaft of one of the wagons broke, he would be held responsible as if he had split it himself.

"I had the supplies reloaded onto a couple of carts," he grumbled.

I nodded and he looked away. I did not ask where the carts had come from. Somewhere behind us there was one farmer, if not more, who would now curse the army of Parliament.

As I rode away, I thought, "If anyone complains about the theft of a cart, the lieutenant will be blamed; and yet if the supplies had been lost he would have been in an even worse position." I was thankful I was only a messenger.

"That is well," Colonel Cromwell said when I reported to him that the supplies were following as quickly as could be expected. With a slight wave of his hand he indicated that I should fall back.

We were some twelve miles from Gainsborough, at a small village called North Scarle, when the troops of Lord Willoughby joined ours. Now it seemed to me that we were so many regiments of foot and horse that we could conquer all of England. It was a gay and splendid scene, and I thought that no life could be finer than that of a soldier.

It was my ignorance that made me believe our army was invincible. I saw soldiers where, in truth, there were only armed farmers, artisans, and runaway apprentices. Nor were they well armed. Many of the mounted men did not even carry pistols; and those who did, as often as not, had weapons with poorly made flintlocks that could not be depended upon to fire. Most of their swords were the work of a village blacksmith, and had neither strength nor sharp edges. As for their armor, only some of the men had breastplates or iron headpieces; more wore only caps, and there were those who did not even have a proper heavy leather coat.

As we neared the besieged town of Gainsborough, we encountered a small contingent of the King's dragoons. They were easily routed; but they made Colonel Cromwell wary, and he ordered the army to spread out in order to offer room for quick movement.

His caution proved wise. On approaching a hill that commanded the road over which our supplies would have to pass, we found that it was held by Royal forces. The more permanent proprietors of the heights were rabbits, and the holes they had burrowed were just perfect for breaking the leg of a horse.

The foot soldiers of Lord Willoughby, who were Lincolnshire men, were in the vanguard. They rushed up the hill to give battle, while we on horseback looked for a trail, free of rabbit holes, by which to gain the crest.

I should have stayed below, for I was unarmed, carrying only a dagger in my belt. What I did was against the Colonel's orders, for he had told me that in case of battle I was to retire to the wagons.

To ride with the rest up that hill was not bravery but foolishness; yet I did it. Was it that fever which comes to a soldier as he goes into battle that had overcome me? All I shall ever know for certain is that I followed the man in front of me, as a sheep follows its leader.

The men of Lincolnshire were in the center, with a regiment of horse on either side. We were well spread out. As we came near the top of the hill, the Royal forces charged. Now we had only the choice between fleeing and attacking.

The ground was not the best, for we would be fighting uphill. Yet none hesitated. With drawn swords and at a gallop, the opposing troops met each other.

There were but few shouts. It was bloody work: sword against sword, horse against horse.

"What brings you here, boy?" a giant of a man whom I knew by sight was shouting at me.

His words brought me to my senses. What, indeed, was I doing there, weaponless as I was? And I reined in my horse.

"Get back!" With a string of curses the soldier passed me, and I turned my mare.

Once free of the tumult, I stopped and looked back. The Royal troops were fleeing and our men were pursuing them.

But the battle was not over. The enemy held in reserve a regiment of horse and some troops of foot soldiers commanded by Colonel Cavendish.

Not far from me, next to a Royal soldier who would never ride again, lay a sword. I leapt from my horse and picked it up. I swung it in the air. It was light and finely made. Its edges were so sharp that had I been able to grow a beard, I could have shaved with it. It was a precious weapon, but it had not saved the life of the man who had owned it. I recalled a youngster whom I had been with at the Battle of Edgehill. He had longed for just such a sword, because he thought it the emblem of manhood.

I almost let the weapon fall to the ground, for it had occurred to me that this gift was of the devil, and once I called the sword mine, I should never be able to get rid of it again. Yet I kept it.

No sooner had I remounted, than the second part of the battle began. Colonel Cavendish advanced, routing what was left of the Lincolnshire troops. All around me they were falling back; and suddenly I was in the midst of the fighting.

Had Colonel Cromwell not succeeded in halting the Parliamentary cavalry, who were still pursuing the fleeing cavaliers, we might have duplicated the folly of Prince Rupert's men at Edgehill: of being more eager than wise. But unlike the Royal troops, our men responded to orders and returned to the field. Colonel Cavendish had to abandon his attack on the exhausted men of Lincolnshire and face about to defend himself.

All battles are a mass of confusion to those who take part in them. Most of the time you are fighting not to win but to survive, guarding your own little precious life.

I kept my sword ready to parry any blow aimed at me, rather than to strike myself. A young cavalier sought me out, probably because he believed I would be an easy conquest. His first attack I repulsed, my sword deflecting his.

He turned his horse and advanced towards me once more, his weapon lifted for what I feared would be my death blow. I held my sword out in front of me and dug my heels into the sides of my mare. Startled, the poor beast leapt forward and my sword pierced the chest of the cavalier!

He cried out, as his weapon dropped from his hand. Wildly he tried to grasp the blade of my sword, which was now red with his blood. His horse swerved and the cavalier fell from his saddle.

What breadth of time did all this take? How many ticks of the clock? Stupefied, I looked down at the young man, who with sightless eyes stared back at me.

I heard the calling of words of command nearby. It was Colonel Cromwell's voice. Around me the enemy were fleeing, their only thought now being to escape. Down the hill they went, with our troops chasing them, shouting as they swung their swords.

"Oliver!" The Colonel had seen me and I trotted dutifully towards him. He and some of his officers had reined in their horses and were contemplating the scene.

"What are you doing here?" the Colonel demanded sternly.

I did not answer but looked unhappily down at my sword.

His eyes followed mine. "You are pale," he said. "Are you wounded?"

"No, sir," I whispered and shook my head.

"Go to the rear and tell the lieutenant in charge of supplies that the road to Gainsborough is clear." Though his manner was still severe, there was a tone of kindness in his voice.

I was grateful to have once more a duty to perform. Carefully, remembering the rabbit holes, I started down the hill.

"You have killed a man," I thought, as I wiped my sword on the coat of my horse. "What did he look like?" I asked myself. I could not remember! And the tears ran down my cheek. Whether it was for the young cavalier or myself that I was crying I do not know.

Biographical Notes

Matsuo Bashō (1644–1694) Generally regarded as the greatest writer of Japanese haiku, Bashō lived the life of a hermit, supporting himself by teaching and judging poetry contests. Carrying only the barest essentials, he traveled through central and northern Japan recording his observations and insights in poems and in thoughtful travel diaries.

Robert Bolt (1924–1995) Born in Manchester, England, and educated at Manchester University, Bolt served three years in the Army and Air Force before trying his hand as a playwright. He was teaching when his first play, *Flowering Cherry*, was produced in London. Its great success led Bolt to leave the classroom for the stage. Bolt wrote the screenplays for several successful movies, including *A Man for All Seasons, Dr. Zhivago, Lawrence of Arabia,* and *Ryan's Daughter.*

Joseph Bruchac (b. 1942) When he was growing up, Joseph Bruchac was strongly influenced by his grandfather, a member of the Abenaki people. That influence led Bruchac to devote much of his time to writing about Native Americans. He has written more than sixty books about Native American culture. He and his wife founded Greenfield Review Press, a publishing company that specializes in multicultural works.

Alvar Nuñez Cabeza de Vaca (1490?–1557?) In 1528, Pánfilo de Narváez and 400 Spanish soldiers landed near Tampa Bay and set out to explore Florida's west coast. Cabeza de Vaca was second in command. Beset by illness and the prospect of starvation, Narváez and his men set sail for Mexico in five flimsy boats. He and most of the men drowned. Cabeza de Vaca and a party of about sixty reached the Texas shore. Cabeza de Vaca's adventures and his reports on the richness of Texas sparked exploration of the region.

Giovanni Caselli (b. 1939) Born in Italy, Caselli now lives in England. He is an internationally known author and illustrator.

Vicki Cobb (b. 1938) Cobb has written more than eighty books for young people, including *Science Experiments You Can Eat* and *How the Doctor Knows You're Fine*. She has a degree in biology from Barnard College and a master's degree from Columbia University Teachers College.

Harold Courlander (1908–1996) The fact that Courlander's father was a primitive painter helped to interest him in the art of other cultures. Through his writing, he worked hard to bring the legends and folk tales of different peoples to the rest of the world.

N. J. Dawood (b. 1927) Born in Baghdad, Nessim Joseph Dawood won a scholarship to attend the University of London and, after completing his studies, remained in England as a publishing executive and Middle East consultant. His translation of *The Thousand and One Nights* first appeared in 1954.

Mbella Sonne Dipoko (b. 1936) Dipoko, who was born in Cameroon, was educated in Cameroon and in Nigeria. He has written stories and poetry published in journals as well as two novels, and he has worked for the Nigerian Broadcasting Company in Lagos as a reporter.

Michael Dorris (1945–1997) Dorris knew a great deal about Native American cultures, past and present. He himself was of Modoc heritage and did much research in the field of cultural anthropology, the study of the many social customs and relationships as well as physical characteristics of different cultures. At the age of twelve, Dorris worked through the International Friendship League to establish a list of more than thirty pen pals from all over the world. He kept in touch with many of these pen pals throughout his life.

Elizabeth I (1533–1603) The only child of Henry VIII and Anne Boleyn, Elizabeth Tudor had a childhood filled with sadness and danger. Her mother was executed by her father when Elizabeth was not yet three years old. Then, Elizabeth was proclaimed illegitimate by Parliament when Henry's son by Jane Seymour was born. Finally, in 1558, after the death of her half sister, Mary, Elizabeth was crowned queen of England and Ireland.

Jean Fritz (b. 1915) An only child, Fritz lived in China until she was thirteen. She sees the research she does for her books as a kind of detective work. As a writer of biographies, she brings historical figures to life for young people.

Roy A. Gallant (b. 1924) Gallant was born in Portland, Maine, and wrote poetry in high school. He studied at Bowdoin College and at Columbia University, where he also taught writing. He has been a writer, an editor, an instructor, and the director of a planetarium.

Moses Hadas (1900–1966) The Jay Professor of Greek at Columbia University and the former chair of its Department of Greek and Latin, Hadas was a well-known authority on the ancient world.

Erik Christian Haugaard (b. 1923) An internationally known playwright, poet, translator, and author, especially of books for young people, Haugaard was born in Denmark and now lives in Ireland.

Priest Jakuren (c. 1139–1202) A Buddhist priest, Jakuren was a prominent tanka poet whose poems are filled with beautiful yet melancholy imagery. After entering the priesthood at the age of twenty-three, he spent his time traveling the countryside, writing poetry, and seeking spiritual fulfillment.

Wolf Leslau (b. 1906) Leslau has studied languages that were unknown in much of the world. Once, after months of research in Africa, he discovered a group of four people who were the last people in the world who still spoke their language. His research has helped to preserve the history that can be found in the languages of many cultures.

Li Po (c. 701–c. 762) He is considered one of the greatest poets of the T'ang period along with Wang Wei and Tu Fu.

Mary MacLeod (?–1914) MacLeod made legendary heroes come alive for young people by rewriting Shakespeare's plays and the classic tales of Robin Hood and King Arthur. She based her tales of King Arthur on the stories of Sir Thomas Malory, author of *Morte d'Arthur*.

Milton Meltzer (b. 1915) Meltzer has written more than seventy books on history, biography, and social reform. Born in Worcester, Massachusetts, he went to Columbia University. He lives in New York City.

John Minford (b. 1946) Minford is an Englishman who has written about Chinese artists and scholars and has translated Chinese folk tales.

D. T. Niane (b. 1932) After listening to the stories told by Mamadou Kouyate, a griot (or storyteller) of the Keita clan, Djibril Tamsir Niane wrote *Sundiata: An Epic of Old Mali* in his Malinke language. Naine's own ancestors were griots; in his translations of their ancient oral histories, he affirms their value. A noted historian, his specific area of interest is medieval African empires.

Po Chü-i (772–846) A Chinese poet of the T'ang dynasty, Po Chü-i began writing poetry at the age of five. He believed that poetry should have a social purpose, and he used his poetry as a form of protest.

Howard Pyle (1853–1911) Pyle, who taught at Drexel Institute in Philadelphia and lectured at the Art Students League in New York, wrote and illustrated a number of books. He was convinced that his students should look for their training and their inspiration in America rather than in Europe.

John Roberson (b. 1930) Roberson was born in Roanoke, Virginia, and educated at the University of Virginia, the University of Grenoble (France), the City University of New York, and the Army Language School, where he studied Mandarin Chinese. He lives in Connecticut and worked for many years as an editor at Reader's Digest Condensed Books.

Gail Robinson (b. 1935) and **Douglas Hill** (b. 1935) Gail Robinson and Douglas Hill are Canadian. They lived among Native Americans for many years and heard the stories of the Crow people firsthand.

Anne Rockwell (b. 1934) Rockwell, who was born in Memphis, Tennessee, grew up in many places. She once lived in New Mexico, where she developed a great admiration for the Pueblo people. She is both a writer and an artist; it is her interest in art that inspired her to write "The Boy Who Drew Sheep."

Sir Walter Scott (1771–1832) Born into an old and wealthy Scottish family, Scott grew to love his country's history while listening to elderly relatives' stories and accounts. "Lochinvar," like many of Scott's works, reflects his love for the Scottish border ballads, or storytelling songs. His keen ear for the way people speak and his knowledge of history helped him make the past come alive with romance, heroism, and adventure.

Ian Serraillier (1912–1994) Born in London, Serraillier wrote mainly for young people. He wrote novels, poetry, and educational and local history books as well as retellings in poetry and prose.

Sei Shōnagon (c. tenth century A.D.) A lady-in-waiting in the imperial Japanese court, Sei Shōnagon wrote her *Pillow Book* during her ten years of court service. It is a collection of character sketches, descriptions, anecdotes, lists, and witty insights that provides detailed portraits of upper-class life in tenth-century Japan.

Alexander McCall Smith Smith was born and raised in Zimbabwe, a country in south-central Africa. He has traveled widely throughout that country gathering its folklore.

Diane Stanley Stanley was born in Abilene, Texas, where she lived with an aunt and uncle for several years while her mother was ill. At Trinity University in San Antonio, she became interested in illustration; eventually she became a writer and illustrator of children's books about history. She and her mother, a writer of mysteries, published a book called *The Last Princess* together.

Elizabeth Borton de Treviño (b. 1904) De Treviño was born in Bakersfield, California, and graduated from Stanford University. She has been a reporter, an interviewer, and a violinist as well as a writer. In 1966, *I, Juan de Pareja* won the Newbery Medal.

Ki no Tsurayuki (872–945) The chief aide to Emperor Daigo and one of the leading poets, critics, and diarists of his time, Tsurayuki helped assemble a major anthology of Japanese poetry from the previous eleven hundred years.

Louis Untermeyer (1885–1977) Born in New York City, Untermeyer was a poet, a critic, and a biographer, but he is best known for his many anthologies. He published more than eighty books.

Dr. Fred Warren In 1968, Dr. Warren went to Africa to collect materials on African culture, a trip made possible by a U.S. State Department grant. He and his wife, Lee Warren, with whom he wrote *The Music of Africa,* also attended the first Pan-African Cultural Festival in 1969. Dr. Warren has written many articles on African music.

Ralph Whitlock (1914–1995) Whitlock, a writer and a broadcaster, explored many of the Mayan ruins himself and knew their territory well.

Acknowledgments continued from copyright page

Daniel C. Buchanan. Copyright ©
1973 by Japan Publications
**Barbara S. Kouts for Joseph
Bruchac** "Loo-Wit, the Fire-Keeper,"
from *Keepers of the Earth: Native
American Stories and Environmental
Activities for Children* by Michael J.
Caduto and Joseph Bruchac.
Copyright © 1988 by Joseph Bruchac.
**The Millbrook Press and Editions
Nathan, Paris** "Sharing Knowledge"
from *The Arabs in the Golden Age* by
Mokhtar Moktefi. Copyright © 1992
Editions Nathan, translation copyright
© 1993 by The Millbrook Press.
Reprinted by permission of The
Millbrook Press. All rights reserved.
**William Morrow & Company, a
division of HarperCollins Publishers,
Inc.** From *Leonardo da Vinci* by Diane
Stanley. Copyright © 1996 by Diane
Stanley.
New World Press, Beijing, China
"Hailibu the Hunter" from *Favourite
Folktales of China,* translated by John
Minford.
Oxford University Press UK "In
Spring It Is the Dawn" and "The Cat
Who Lived in the Palace" from *The
Pillow Book* by Sei Shōnagon,
translated and edited by Ivan Morris.
Penguin Books Ltd. "One cannot ask
loneliness" by Priest Jakuren and
"When I went to visit" by Ki no
Tsurayuki from *The Penguin Book of
Japanese Verse,* edited and translated
by Geoffrey Bownas and Anthony
Thwaite (Penguin Books, 1964).
Translation copyright © Geoffrey
Bowans and Anthony Thwaite, 1964.
"The Fisherman and the Jinnee" from
*Tales from The Thousand and One
Nights* (pp. 79–92) translated by N. J.
Dawood (Penguin Classics 1954,
Revised edition 1973).
Prentice-Hall, Inc. "African Musical
Instruments" from *The Music of Africa*
by Dr. Fred Warren with Lee Warren.
Copyright © 1970 by Dr. Fred Warren
and Lee Warren.
**G.P. Putnam's Sons, a division of
Penguin Putnam, Inc.** "Vasco Núñez
de Balboa" from *Around the World in a
Hundred Years: From Henry the
Navigator to Magellan* by Jean Fritz.
Text copyright © 1994 by Jean Fritz.
"The Historical Background" from
Everyday Life of the Maya by Ralph
Whitlock. Text © Ralph Whitlock,
1976.

**Random House, Inc., and Methuen
Publishing Ltd.** From *A Man for All
Seasons* by Robert Bolt. Copyright ©
1960, 1962 by Robert Bolt. Copyright
renewed 1988, 1990 by Robert Bolt.
John Roberson "Barbarians from the
West" from *China: From Manchu to
Mao (1699–1976)* by John R.
Roberson. Copyright © 1980 by John
R. Roberson.
Ian Serraillier "Grendel" from
Beowulf, the Warrior, retold by Ian
Serraillier. Copyright © 1961 by Henry
Z. Walck, Inc.
Silver Burdett Company "Who Are
the Muslims?" from *The Muslim World*
by Richard Tames. © Macdonald & Co.
1982.
**La Société Nouvelle Présence
Africaine** "Childhood" and "The Lion's
Awakening" from *Sundiata: An Epic of
Old Mali* by D. T. Niane, translated by
G. D. Pickett. Copyright © Présence
Africaine, 1960 (original French
version: *Soundjata, ou L'Epopée
Mandingue*). © Longman Group Ltd.
(English).
Time, Inc. From "The Pax Romana"
from *Imperial Rome* by Moses Hadas.
Copyright © 1965 by Time, Inc.
**Lawrence Starr Untermeyer for the
Estate of Louis Untermeyer** "The
Dog of Pompeii" from *Donkey of God*
by Louis Untermeyer. Copyright 1932
by Harcourt, Inc. renewed 1960 by
Louis Untermeyer.
**Watson, Little Limited, Authors'
Agents** "How Coyote Stole Fire" by
Gail Robinson and Douglas Hill from
*Coyote the Trickster: Legends of North
American Indians.* Copyright © Gail
Robinson and Douglas Hill, 1975.
Henry Z. Walck, Inc. "The Old Man
Who Made the Trees Bloom" from
Japanese Tales and Legends, retold by
Helen and William McAlpine.
Copyright © Helen and William
McAlpine.
Wayland (Publishers) Ltd. "What Was
the Renaissance?" from *Leonardo and
the Renaissance* by Nathaniel Harris.
Copyright © 1986 by Wayland
(Publishers) Ltd.

**Note: Every effort has been made
to locate the copyright owner of
material reprinted in this book.
Omissions brought to our attention
will be corrected in subsequent
printings.**